Minor Characters

Minor Characters

Joyce Johnson

HOUGHTON MIFFLIN COMPANY
BOSTON 1983

The names of some people —
not the principals —
in *Minor Characters* have been changed.

Library of Congress Cataloging in Publication Data

Johnson, Joyce, 1935–
Minor characters.

1. Johnson, Joyce, 1935–   — Biography.   2. Kerouac,
Jack, 1922–1969 — Biography.   3. Authors, American — 20th
century — Biography.   4. Bohemianism — United States —
Biography.   I. Title.
PS3560.03795Z47   1983   818′.5403 [B]   82–12185
ISBN 0–395–32513–7

Printed in the United States of America

S 10 9 8 7 6 5 4 3 2 1

For my son and friend,
Daniel Pinchbeck

HURRY UP PLEASE ITS TIME
— *T. S. Eliot*

Momma may have
Poppa may have
But God bless the child
That's got his own.
— *Billie Holiday*

Acknowledgments

The following people have been important to the writing of this book:

I am particularly grateful to Berenice Hoffman, who had an uncanny sense of what I was trying to get at before I even had the words for it myself.

Nan A. Talese has been the most responsive and persistently supportive editor any writer could wish for.

Hettie Jones and Anita Feldman have always been willing to share with me their own versions of our common history.

John Diamond and Alan Hruska have given me helpful — and clarifying — legal advice.

And finally, I must thank Juris Jurjevics for his tough listening.

Minor Characters

1

THE SNAPSHOT IS in a book now. Four young men on the Columbia campus on a day in 1945. Early spring, maybe, because the coats of three of them are open at the collar and the tree in the background is bare. They're boys, really.

As I've grown older, the figures in the photo have grown younger. They're dressed with that startling formality of the period that seems peculiarly innocent now. Short hair, long overcoats. Burroughs is even wearing a black bowler, a sort of British-banker effect — a deliberate costume. He's absenting himself in his disguise. Hal Chase, whom I never met — the one who introduced them all to Neal Cassady — looks like the sharp kid about to save the situation with a joke. Allen is all adolescent gawkiness and misery. He has shut his eyes, as if the taking of the picture is an intolerable intrusion. And there's Jack in the center. No overcoat, just a cheap baggy suit in which his football-hero shoulders look enormous, loud tie pulled askew. He's stretched his arms over Chase and Allen, so that his fingertips reach Burroughs's shoulder. A cigarette dangles from his mouth in the romantic style of jazz piano players or hard-boiled all-night journalists in movies. He's grinning directly, warmly, at the photographer as the shutter clicks. The only one of them totally connected to the moment.

*

There are people missing from this group portrait. Lucien Carr, who at nineteen had a blond, demonic beauty, is serving a jail sentence for what the newspapers of the previous summer called an "honor slaying." On 116th and Riverside Drive, on the narrow strip of grass between the West Side Highway and the river, he had killed the man who wanted to make love to him there, who had dogged his path, haunted and frightened him ever since his boyhood in St. Louis. With his Boy Scout knife, Lucien stabbed Dave Kammerer twice in the chest, bound his hands and feet with shoelaces, and pushed the body, weighted with rocks, into the dirty waters of the Hudson. Some hours afterward, he had gone to find Jack, and together they'd buried Kammerer's glasses in Morningside Park and dropped the Boy Scout knife into a sewer. Then they spent an odd day out of time, as people often do in the unreality that follows catastrophe — roaming the city, taking in the movie *Four Feathers* before Lucien turned himself in.

The newspapers intimated that Lucien had been under the influence of literature. There were references to William Butler Yeats's *A Vision* in the *Journal-American*, and to Rimbaud's *A Season in Hell*. Ten years later, when the gratuitous act was in fashion, the apocryphal tales I heard about the incident had come to have a Gidean flavor. "If you don't love me, then kill me," Dave Kammerer was supposed to have said, kneeling down on the grass, and so Lucien "had the grace" to kill him.

As for the two girls, Edie Parker and Joan Vollmer, I've never seen pictures of them anywhere. They were best friends, roommates for a while, connective links between Jack and Burroughs and Allen and Lucien. Jack and Edie had been living together off and on since 1941. It was Edie who borrowed money from her family and bailed him out when he was held on suspicion of being Lucien's accomplice, claiming she was pregnant and that they were to have been married that very day. They did in fact run down to City Hall for an hour and go through the marriage ceremony with the permission of the cops. Later Jack ended up going with Edie to live in her parents' house in Grosse Pointe, Michigan, while he worked off his indebtedness to the Parkers in a ball-bearings factory. It was all over between them, though, by January of 1945, and then Edie vanishes — at least from the literary histories — writing a pathetic letter to Allen Ginsberg, imploring him for a list of books "like the ones you first read," as if by becoming an imitation Allen, intellectually, she can prove herself worthy and get Jack back. She's so desperately hurt, she even threatens to expose Allen's homosexuality if he doesn't help her.

Despite this letter, I've always had an image of Edie as one of those girls who tries almost fatally hard to be a good sport. You can't help liking her, though. She's even cute in the way girls aren't cute anymore, a sweater girl in saddle shoes, her light brown hair in a pompadour. There's been something determinedly spunky in the way she confronts bizarre circumstances, trying on a life that doesn't fit her. What became of Edie? Eventually she recovered, I hope, in her next three and a half decades.

I know what became of Joan Vollmer. In 1944 and '45, her apartment on 115th Street was an early prototype of what a later generation called a pad — a psychic way station between the Village and Times Square, or between Morningside Heights and the Lower Depths, in the mental geography of those who came together there, lived there sporadically, made love, wrote, suffered, experimented with drugs, in those six big rooms where Joan had lived alone with a newborn baby until Edie introduced her to Jack. And Jack — seeing an affinity between Joan's sharp, glittering wittiness and Bill Burroughs's — introduced her to Bill. And Burroughs, having lost an apartment anyway, moved in, taking over one of the bedrooms but not always necessarily preferring to sleep in it alone. Then came Allen, Hal and Jack, also Edie very briefly before the split-up of the marriage.

Joan did match Burroughs wit for wit, and in other ways. She seems to have become a great reader of Korzybski,

Spengler, Kafka, etc., startling the men by holding her own in their discussions. She matched him as well in her growing interest in drugs, staying high all day on Benzedrine-soaked cotton from nasal inhalers. Perhaps Bill first showed her how you could crack open the inhaler case like a nut and get out the little pad that could be swallowed down whole with your morning coffee, quite transforming the wintery grey courtyard light and the littered kitchen and the piercing, demanding wails of the wet infant.

There on 115th Street, in the rooms that had been like six empty shells before Bill and the others came, there was now a never-ending magical intensity, brilliance refracting against brilliance. There must have been moments for Joan when her own electricity seemed almost palpable, when her inner radiance overflowed so that even a stranger like Herbert Huncke, an addict Bill brought home from his newly discovered Forty-second Street hangouts, was struck by it and remembered Joan later as "one of the most beautiful women I have ever known."

Huncke too became part of Joan's newly created family in that legendary apartment, a guide to the underside of life that increasingly fascinated all of them. There was surely some hidden rock-bottom truth in that treacherous, all-night world of pushers and addicts, thieves and whores, that you couldn't get at by reading Dostoevski or Céline — it had to be experienced directly.

Burroughs, the aristocrat of the bunch, the heir to the Burroughs Adding Machine Company millions, went into it all the way, much further than Jack or Allen. He bought himself a submachine gun and became a dealer in morphine Syrettes. He married Joan in January 1945. By then she'd become a little paranoid from all the Benzedrine — and possibly she'd gone on to morphine as well. She would have followed Bill into anything — and did.

She died in 1951, several years before I ever heard her name. But the radiance had died even sooner. A visitor to the ranch in New Waverly, Texas, where Bill and Joan Bur-

4

roughs lived and grew marijuana in 1950, remembers her as slovenly, limping, braless, her thinning hair untidily pulled back. She looked, he said, like a very drab housewife and also somehow like a child. It took eight of those little nasal-inhaler pads a day to keep her going, and because it was hard to get them in Texas, she and Bill moved to Mexico City for the last months of her life.

Joan Vollmer Burroughs's death is much more famous than she is. Like Lucien's story, it's part of the prehistory of the Beats. And even unattached to that, it's the kind of bizarre anecdote you'd never forget if you heard it, as I did, around certain Columbia University circles in the mid-fifties. Like Lucien's story, there was something coldly stylized in the telling — a lack of affect that came close to the blackest of humor.

Ever hear the one about the man who played William Tell with his wife and missed?

Maybe it was the old daring witty spirit that flared up in Joan one last time that hot September evening in Mexico City. For many hours she and Bill had been drinking gin in their apartment with two new friends, expatriate ex-GIs. Did the gathering remind her of 115th Street and the more ecstatic days of the past? She suddenly put her glass on her head, this drab housewife, and teasingly challenged Bill to shoot it off with his .38. He was a crack shot, and maybe they'd even gone through this William Tell routine on other festive occasions. Or maybe they hadn't. Maybe it was a knowing, prescient act of suicide on Joan's part, the ultimate play-out of total despair.

But look at it another way. It could well have been a demonstration of her faith and trust, of her blind devotion and belief. A final gift to Bill — whose aim was off that night.

I might have loved Joan if I'd known her, so I make that guess. She's as familiar to me as another woman very like

5

her whom I once knew and loved, and as alien as the person who still lives on in the most dangerous depths of myself.

I look in the index of the book with the snapshot of Jack and Allen and the others, and there I find: *Joyce Glassman.* And half a dozen page references, having to do with approximately one-twentieth of my life, 1957–59, when I used to have that name.

NINETEEN FORTY-FIVE WAS the year we moved into the city, not far from Joan Vollmer's apartment. One-hundred-sixteenth Street, where I grew up, is a wide windy block lined with old apartment buildings, sloping down toward Riverside Drive. Looking uphill, you can see Barnard College on the corner — and across Broadway, the high iron gates of the university, the library domed and columned like a Roman temple, and the brick walks so different from the surrounding pavements of the city.

I used to trespass on the campus and imagine people wondering what I, a mere ten-year-old girl, was doing there. Suppose they took me for a genius actually enrolled in classes? Sometimes in my true identity I roller-skated around the library fountains. Too bad I'd missed their poetic transformation into fountains of wine a year or so before, when Allen Ginsberg had put red dye in their water systems.

Sometimes I roller-skated on Riverside Drive or sat on a bench there reading *Ivanhoe*, *Little Women*, *Little Men*, weeping over *Black Beauty*. I was never allowed to go by myself down the stone steps into the overgrown, weedy, wilder regions of the park, which my mother — who had most likely heard of last summer's killing by the river — called Down Below, just as she did an otherwise unnamed region of my body.

The unparklikeness of Down Below attracted me. One day I broke the rules. I ran down the hills of uncut grass, climbed over a small wooden fence, ducked the traffic on the West Side Highway, and got all the way to the river. I was disappointed with what I found. Just some flat greyish rocks and brownish slow-moving water and a heavy sweetish smell that reminded me of basements. What pleased me was my secret exploit. I didn't go back again for a long time.

It's weird to think of us all in the same neighborhood — the apartment on 115th Street closer than my mother knew, the possibility that we passed each other hundreds of times in our everyday comings and goings. That Joan is the thin, dazed young woman wheeling her baby across Broadway; that it's Jack buying beer and cigarettes at Gristedes when my mother sends me out for tomato juice; or Allen with a notebook of early poems in his pocket ringing the doorbell of the famous professor Lionel Trilling, a man as silvery grey as his name, who lives on the ground floor of our apartment house.

But no more weird, I suppose, than to be on a plane between London and New York some thirty years later, thinking subversive thoughts about the depressing conservatism of young people as I look at the kid in the seat next to me — a totally foolish-looking kid with two expensive cameras dangling around his neck, all decked out in a blatantly tweedy, three-piece suit obviously bought in England — and to have this same boy take out a book that turns out to be: *Lonesome Traveler* by Jack Kerouac.

Simultaneities. Take the West End, for instance — it's still there, as a matter of fact, on Broadway and 113th. A combination cafeteria and bar was what it was originally. Steam tables full of cheap food. Corned beef and cabbage, knockwurst and mashed potatoes. A plain bar of dark wood and no particular charm, bottles lined up on mirrored tiers. A white-tiled floor sprinkled with sawdust. One of those non-descript places, before the era of white walls and potted ferns and imitation Tiffany lamps, that for some reason always made the best hangouts.

In 1944 Edie Parker likes to go there. Jack, who's been shipping out in the merchant marine, is often away at sea for months, and she's at loose ends. There's a young Columbia student at the bar every night, so gorgeous she can't take her eyes off him. A drunken golden boy with straight white-blond hair falling down over his forehead into his narrow green eyes, and a wildness that she recognizes. Maybe there's something about Lucien Carr that reminds her of Jack. At any rate, it's Lucien that Edie picks out of that entire West End crowd and makes it her business to befriend. She doesn't fall in love with him herself. She seems to have saved up this friendship to bestow it elsewhere. "Jack, you really have to meet this Lucien kid." (After all, she's slightly older than Lucien, with her own apartment and a couple of years of experience, so she's earned the right to sound maternal.)

In June, when Jack's around again, she makes him come with her one night to the West End. Jack's skeptical, maybe even a little jealous of this Lucien he doesn't know, this rich, dangerous St. Louis boy with the wicked mouth who's already been kicked out of Bowdoin and the University of Chicago, who's amassed a whole dissipated history by the age of nineteen. But perhaps Lucien is what he's looking for — the friend who'll be a darker mirror image of himself. It's not enough to just have Edie. And this is something Edie knows, most likely — an unarticulated sadness. That Jack, despite her dreams of marriage and "Oh, we'll have our Bohemian period and then we'll settle down and he'll write his books and we'll love each other forever," is unpossessable. Edie's got her resourceful spirit, though. She's even had her own adventures, working as a longshoreman while Jack's at sea, and as a cigarette girl on Forty-second Street. You can weave such an exciting ambiance around a man he'll hardly know he's being held by it.

She turns out to be right about Lucien.

The friendship of Jack Kerouac and Lucien Carr ignites upon their recognition of each other like a Chinese firecracker. They mask their embarrassment with insults — Lucien's "the aristocrat, my deah," Jack's an "oafish jock," a "dumb hick Canuck." This will be their style with each other for about the next twenty-five years. Lucien's the real genius at it — very quick to find the soft spots, always drawing a little blood. Is he tormenting Jack or pinpointing his secret shames?

At first it must look to unbelieving Edie as if the two of them are going to fight, have one of those messy West End brawls that'll end with everyone kicked out on the sidewalk. Oh God, there's nothing dumber than men!

Jack's got his head bowed under the barrage of epithets. But he's not hearing what Edie hears. He's caught some music in this vicious kid's language that's making him laugh in wonderment. He raises his head, still laughing, and serenades not Edie but Lucien with the new song on the hit parade — "You Always Hurt the One You Love."

"Let's go home now, Jack." There's something confusing here for Edie, but she probably hasn't turned jealous yet. "Oh, Take Me Home Again, Kathleen" might be the song she gets back loudly, rudely, from Lucien.

Johnny the bartender comes over in his official capacity and says, "Pipe down, son!" But he grins at Jack, with whom he's had the most remarkable discussions about football — uncanny what that boy remembers, every pass, every play. The next round is on the house.

It's practically dawn when Lucien Carr and Jack Kerouac stagger out of the West End together, presumably followed by Edie Parker, although none of the books say. Legend takes over at that point, refining out incidentals. After all, what's happened is so momentous, leading on into the future lives and times of the Beats, to the immediate rushing in of other major characters — to the Columbia freshman poet from Paterson, Allen Ginsberg, whom Jack will also meet that week; to Burroughs, who happens to be one of Lucien's odd St. Louis acquaintances; to Lucien's crime on August 14; and

10

on into literature and the chemistry of mutual influences and the Duluoz/Kerouac saga in which all of them will appear and reappear and reencounter each other under their invented names. I remember Jack once saying he wrote his books so that he'd have something to read in his old age — although of course he never had any and maybe never believed he would.

But all of this was first set in motion by little Edie Parker, still with her futile hopes of holding on to Jack that night in June 1944.

One night Lucien Carr found an empty barrel and rolled Jack Kerouac home in it — that's a solemnly recorded fact. As it crashes along Broadway through the hot, empty streets with Lucien attempting to push it faster and faster, I see Edie Parker running after it a little off to the side. She's telling herself she's having a swell time as she looks out for cops over her shoulder.

There were sometimes light, nothing-to-do summer evenings when I strolled with my father down Broadway to the newsstand at 110th Street. It was the walk he usually took by himself after dinner, when he smoked his one cigar considerately away from my mother's living room and indulged in his one vice, betting. He does this modestly, the way he does everything else, placing a daily two-dollar bet with the man selling papers. I'm not supposed to know this, but I do. And whenever I ask, "Did you win, Daddy?" he'll tell me he broke even. Nothing dramatic ever seems to happen like Daddy having his ship come in and buying everyone presents, or losing his shirt. Sometimes he goes all the way out to the track with his lunch in a bag, and then he'll say sadly, "Well, I made back my expenses." Still, it's the part of my father's life that seems tinged with glamour — something faintly illicit that's mysteriously his. I'm thrilled to be invited into it. I cling proudly to his arm — the gambler's daughter. With admiring interest I watch the transaction at the newsstand — the casual buying of the *Daily News*, Daddy's discreet words of instruction, the bills going into the pocket of the bookie's canvas apron. "Want a Good Humor?" My father winks, giving me a dime.

Once — and I never tell my mother or my aunts — he makes a stop along the way back at a place called the West End Bar, and tells me to wait outside. "This is no place for little girls." I peer in through the window and it's dark and big with long gloomy booths full of men in shirt sleeves and definitely no children, and a dank, beery smell wafts out the open door through which my father disappears. Instantly I feel even more self-conscious than I do on the campus, as if any minute I might be called upon to justify why I'm even standing outside this place that's so bad I can't go inside it. "I'm waiting for my father," I'd explain, but I feel there's something not right about that answer and that Daddy's gone too far leaving me out here — become someone I don't quite know. He comes back, just as he promised, in a few minutes. "Oh, you've finished your Good Humor," he says affectionately as we turn up Broadway in the direction of home.

2

I'M THINKING, PAINFULLY, of a room. It has a red couch with a green slipcover, a gold-upholstered chair covered in maroon, a needlepoint piano bench also covered in green — hunter green, it was called. The Oriental rug, bought just before the Depression, is red and blue and gets vacuumed every day. The table with curved bow legs — used only for important family occasions — is in the style known as French provincial. A lamp stands on it, Chinese, on little teak feet, its silk shade covered with cellophane.

The piano dominates everything — a baby grand, bought while my mother was still working, before I was born. It's a Steck, an obscure make that's supposedly every bit as good as a Steinway. For years she'd saved up for it out of her small, secretary's salary. Her picture as a young woman, placed on the polished lid that's never opened except when the piano tuner comes, is in a heavy silver frame of ornate primitive design brought by my uncle from Peru. She's slender and so pretty, graciously smiling in the long organza dress she'd made herself, white camellias pinned to the flounce on her shoulder. She could very well be what she never became, a concert singer, but she's engaged to my father, who stands beside her in a dark suit. He's a small man, round-faced like I am, with a sweet, serious look. Above the piano is an oil representation of me done by an artistic neighbor when I was eight — the golden era of my career as a daughter. I had to hold my head in one position for hours and hours, dreaming of the chocolate eclair I'd always get at the end of the session. And after all the sitting still, I never liked the portrait of the stolid child in the flowered pinafore dress with two fat blonde pigtails.

There's the terrible poignancy in this room of gratifications deferred, the tensions of gentility. It's as if all these objects — the piano, the rug, the portrait — are held in uneasy captivity, hostages to aspiration. If the slipcovers ever come off, if the heavy drapes are drawn aside letting in the daylight, everything that has been so carefully preserved will be seen to have become frayed and faded anyway.

You could just as well have gone to hell with yourself and enjoyed all that naked upholstery from the start.

I saw my first tenement apartment when I was twenty — top floor of a six-story walkup in Yorkville. Four very small rooms leading into each other railroad style, cracked walls and old tin ceilings that sagged a little. My best friend Elise, who had just moved in there, had painted all of it white, even the linoleum on the floor. What I remember is the amazing light in that place, how it flooded in as if there was no real separation between inside and outside, and everything — what little there was — seemed to be set afloat in it. A light that was almost Mediterranean, giving the scarred, patched walls a chalky thickness like the walls of Greek villas, beatifying the mattress on the floor, the Salvation Army table, the chairs carried in from the street.

I saw that same extraordinary light in the early apartments of other friends. Why there? The defiant absence of anything over the windows, I guess. Maybe it was just as simple as that.

I sit on the needlepoint piano bench every day for two hours and play Scarlatti sonatas, Beethoven's *Für Elise*, Czerny scales. *Für Elise* — prophetically named, come to think of it — is my favorite. I play it with somewhat more pleasure and confidence than other pieces, and with it I flunk the entrance test to the High School of Music and Art.

Still my mother the optimist refuses to recognize that I am not actually musical. In any case, it isn't her plan for me to be a mere pianist. I'm to be something more exalted — a great woman composer. An eminence I'm to achieve if possible before I'm twenty-one or before I throw it all away on marriage — a state she hopes I'll avoid as long as possible. Perhaps I'll enter into it sensibly in later life, after I've written several operettas. Meanwhile, fortunately, I'm only twelve and have already composed a full-length musical comedy, both words and music. A junior Rodgers and Hammerstein combined!

As I sit at the Steck baby grand, she vacuums in another part of the apartment, the drone a counterpoint to what I'm playing. When I start picking out a new tune I'm trying to make up, she switches off the machine and listens. "That's nice, dear!" Even at twelve, I feel uneasy about my musical compositions, as if I'm getting away with something by managing to produce them. How can I become a great composer if I can never make music up in my head? I can't even read the notes in a score and have them translate into sounds. I'm confined to whatever I can wrest from the keys of the piano — and there I'm up against my limitations as a pianist. It frightens me that so far my private teacher, Mr. Bleecker, hasn't found me out. "*Lovely*, dear!" my mother calls enthusiastically. "You're on the right track!" She really believes it. She switches on the vacuum again and is perhaps at that moment perfectly happy. She is living her second life.

Unexpectedly my mother appears at my school one morning. I'm called out of history class to go down to the principal's office where she's waiting. I'm pretty scared as I run down the two flights of stairs. But I can't remember what transgression I may have committed.

She's sitting on a visitors' bench in her brown mouton coat, clutching her big handbag. She smiles at the principal's secretary as I come in — it's her gallant, times-of-crisis smile, June Allyson smiling through tears. "Thank you very much," she says in a low voice to the secretary. She takes my arm and gently hustles me out of there.

In the hallway, she whispers, "We have to go into the ladies' room." When I ask her why, her face gets very red. "I'll tell you in a minute."

In the girls' bathroom, she delivers an announcement that makes no sense to me: "I found blood in your bed this morning."

Blood? I can't remember cutting myself.

My mother's opening her handbag and taking out something wrapped up in many Kleenexes. "I brought this for you to put on." She's brought some kind of belt, too, made of pink elastic, so I figure all this has to do with Down Below.

So far this is going very badly. But my mother can't help herself. Her love for me is the all-consuming passion of her life. She recognizes no boundaries between our separate beings. She only wants to protect me from everything the way she protected me from drowning when I was little by not teaching me to swim, or from irrevocably scarring myself by discouraging me from climbing or running or riding a two-wheeler in the park. This, however, is different. There's no warding off womanhood, although she tries.

She's all flustered as she looks into my astonished face. "It's just the body's natural way of getting rid of bad blood."

I'm trying to digest this overwhelming information. I have never heard of the body doing such an alarming thing.

She tells me it's something that will happen to me now for the rest of my life. "But it's nothing you have to worry about," she says.

THERE'S A SCHOOL of wisdom about love that says the surest way to lose someone is to hold on to them too tightly — as demonstrated over and over again by the split-ups of lovers, but also by parents and children. Although there it's more complicated by far. Lovers, initially strangers, become strangers again; the tie between parent and child pulls and twists for a lifetime, taking on the strangest forms.

Who would ever have imagined that Jack Kerouac would encounter death at forty-seven in his mother's house in St. Petersburg, Florida, as *The Galloping Gourmet* played on the television? He put down his can of beer, went into the bathroom and vomited blood. Hours later, having refused all doctor's care until it was too late, he gave up the ghost in a hospital filled with the elderly. The old lady, paralyzed by a stroke for years, survived him. Jack was the second son she buried. The first, Gerard, had died at the age of nine, when Jack was only five.

There are losses for which no consolation is ever enough. I can see how she must have clung to the younger boy, taking him into her bed night after night for comfort — breaking all the Freudian rules. But what did Gabrielle Kerouac know of such sophistications? There was her own need, the warmth of her small son's light little body curled into her own, the dreamy fragrance of his hair.

17

I cannot imagine surviving the death of my own son except as an empty physical shell. Anything but that! I catch myself automatically clutching him by the hand as we cross the street, although he's fourteen and a full head taller than I am. The hand, which hasn't quite lost its childish softness, still feels like the enlarged hand of the toddler.

He was nine when I first let him take public transportation to school. I remember standing at the window that first morning watching his small, navy-blue, bright-haired figure trudge in quite a businesslike way across West End Avenue and up the block to Broadway eight stories below. It was like that moment when the plane you're on leaves ground and you know that whatever happens there's no changing your mind and getting off. That's the way you send children away from you into the world — a blind accommodation to fate.

Voices were never raised in the apartment on 116th Street — that was a point of pride. We were gentle people, genteel, Gentile almost — unlike my mother's cousins who still lived in Flatbush, whom we'd sometimes see on Jewish holidays, traveling out there on the subway with boxes of cake. They were loud, unrefined, yelling good-naturedly or fiercely across the mountains of heavy food on the table, always putting more on your plate than you could possibly eat, crowding out the specter of leaner days. They ate, they accumulated flesh, became thick of arm and thigh, produced chubby, red-cheeked, nearsighted children who studied Hebrew after school — dutiful sons, daughters who would learn the facts of life in the marital bed at an early age.

This was the life from which my mother as a young woman had struggled to escape — pursuing culture and the finer things, studying Schubert *Lieder* until the Depression wiped out her slender hopes of ever being more than a secretary, and marriage to an adoring, mild-tempered man seemed a deliverance from stenography. It was her singing that had first attracted him. My mother was sitting in a rowboat out on a lake in a low-priced resort frequented by young office workers in the thirties; she was all alone, singing, trailing her fingers in the water, surrounded by lily pads. He had stood on the shore, entranced.

He was the most perfect gentleman my mother had ever met — maybe because he hadn't grown up in America but in England. The job he had didn't seem right for him at all — auditor for an outfit called the Metropolitan Tobacco Company. But of course it was only temporary. With his personality and mathematical ability he was bound to go much further. It was a job that would be as temporary as his life — both ending in 1960 — and as permanent as my mother's disappointment.

Thirty-five years my father worked there, eight to five, half days every other Saturday, two weeks' vacation in the summer, never advancing, always underpaid. It was the first job he'd found when he came to the States. I have no complete explanation for his lack of ambition. He was a very recent immigrant, and then the Depression came along so soon, closing off opportunity. You clung to whatever you had, took no chances. His salary was cut right after I was born — and still he stayed. Loyalty and pride, I think, strangely enough came into it. He kept the books of the Metropolitan Tobacco Company impeccably, filling in infinite columns of numerals in his fine handwriting. He'd acquired an ulcer by the time I was ten. A man like my father would ultimately have been replaced by a computer.

He subsisted on very small pleasures. A few cigars, the races. The ball game drones through my childhood like my mother's vacuum. I can locate affection in my memories of that household, but not passion. I see two single beds chastely made up with chenille spreads, the Colonial maple lamp table in between. I wake in the night to absolute soundlessness. Nothing stirs from their bedroom, where the door is always left open. He kisses my mother when he leaves for work and when he returns. When I was seven, I suggested to my father that he and I run away together. He hit me — and then overcome by remorse, apologized, warning me, though, that I must never say such a thing again.

The mass of men lead lives of quiet desperation. It was my father I thought of immediately when I first read that line of Thoreau's in an English class at Barnard. I thought of my mother, too. I thought that personally I would rather die than be like "the mass of men." But adolescents think in such extremes, in such stark choices.

Up until the time I was thirteen, I had taken it for granted that the three of us were happy. I based this belief on the notion of love as something that was all-justifying. True, we didn't have as much money as other people, but at least we all loved each other like the March family in *Little Women*. My mother seemed an artist whose medium was thrift. With apparent zest, she combed department stores for bargains, toured the local supermarkets seeking out "specials." She was an expert in the comparative prices of brands of tomato juice. Garments made of remnants of good fabric — she never bought any cloth that wasn't "fine" — issued from her sewing machine. All my sweaters were hand-knitted. In her creations, I was much more formally, thus "better," dressed than other girls. I didn't look "cheap" like they looked in their store-bought garments. I wanted to, though. Secretly I wanted to.

She kept house all those years, she told me only recently, on twenty dollars a week. All through the postwar boom and even into the affluent fifties, she managed to make everything come out of that. More and more the effort consumed her energy, her intellect. She hardly ever touched the piano herself, except to dust it.

We existed in a kind of cultural loneliness that I began to feel acutely as I grew older and more conscious. It was as if my mother had taken upon herself the power to stop time, freezing us into a Victor Herbert operetta in which the furnishings and music were vaguely "classical," the values sentimental, post-Victorian.

She was the severe arbiter of everything new that came into the house — ideas, articles of fashion, the friends I occasionally brought home from school. She found very little that met her standards. We were on some higher sphere than the brassy world outside us with its shiny, impermanent items that we couldn't afford. I was to be guarded from the contaminations of everything "popular" — chewing gum, soda pop, comic books, the Bobbsey Twins, Frank Sinatra ("He's dissonant," my mother would say anxiously, switching to the Schubert on WQXR). My specialness was defined not only by the exquisitely sewn dresses I wore but by her overwhelming expectations of what I would achieve as a child prodigy. I knew my enormous value somehow flowed from her. Without that flow, I'd be an empty vessel, a cheap trivial item — just a very ordinary person, perhaps.

3

$\mathcal{J}$ACK KEROUAC WENT on the road in the summer of 1947 — from Ozone Park, Queens, of all places, to the Pacific, stopping off in Denver to see a new friend, Neal Cassady. As the saying goes, he was traveling light. None of the specialized equipment of latterday hitchhikers and wanderers. He had about fifty dollars in his pocket saved from veteran's benefits, a canvas bag "in which a few fundamental things were packed," and was wearing the wrong shoes — Mexican *huaraches*, the mark of the New York Bohemian intellectual back then.

It seems to have been a journey undertaken empirically, in mingled hope and desperation — an attempt to seek out a brand-new reality to match fantasy. He was looking, he said, for "girls, visions, everything; somewhere along the line the pearl would be handed to me."

It's strange, come to think of it, to go looking for visions. It seems more in the nature of visions to come upon you, seizing you unawares. If you look for them, they tend to recede, lead you a little further on. As for girls, there was uneasy flippancy in putting them at the head of his list — although looking for girls, in that sense, is not so much looking for love as for experience. The "everything," of course, was not to be found. Jack would find something out there, though. Sheer, joyous movement. If it had been possible to remain in motion forever, never tiring, speeding away from each new encounter while it was still unsullied by the flagging of the first excitement, he might have been happy. As happy as Neal Cassady, who'd recently blown through the dragged-out end of the Columbia scene like a fresh wind from the West. A joy-riding car thief, a yea-saying delinquent, a guiltless, ravenous consumer of philosophy, literature, women — all varieties of sexuality, in fact. An undecadent alter ego, Neal seemed. He even uncannily looked like Jack — Jack the dark one, Neal golden like Lucien, but so different from him or any of the Columbia crowd. He seemed as familiar to Jack as the boys he'd grown up with in Lowell before he ever came to the city: "I heard again the voices of old companions and brothers under the bridge, among the motorcycles, along the wash-lined neighborhood and drowsy doorsteps of afternoon where boys played guitar while their older brothers worked in the mills."

Jack spent the months preceding his departure holed up in his mother's house — a retreat foreshadowing other retreats to come, in other houses to which he'd move Memere and all her pots and pans and furniture, as if home could be pitched like a tent — in Denver, Colorado; Orlando, Florida; Rocky Mount, North Carolina; Berkeley, California; Northport, Long Island; even Lowell again. In Ozone Park, the evenings were as drowsy as his memories of boyhood. In the eternal, spotless order of his mother's kitchen, a long subway ride from the all-night haunts of Times Square, he spread maps out on the table after the dishes were cleared, and like a navigator plotted the route of his contemplated journey. The western place names were magic words of incantation. Cimarron, Council Bluffs, Platte, Cheyenne. Thoughts of Neal stirred in him, merged with romantic images of plainsmen and pioneers. Cassady loomed in Jack's mind as archetypal, both his long-lost brother and the very spirit of the West in his rootlessness and energy.

Jack himself was never successfully rootless. His roots in

23

fact were like iron in his soul, binding him to Memere for good, rendering him inert in the times between his wanderings, when he'd return to her and try to be the son she wanted. I hear Memere's suspicious whisperings behind the scenes in the first pages of *On the Road* when Jack refers to Burroughs, Allen, Joan, and other members of the Columbia circle as either criminals or sneering, negative intellectuals. Having fully shared their lives in the frantic cycle that has just ended, he sees them guiltily, angrily, now as other. On the road from Memere to Neal what he was seeking was perhaps redemption.

It was July when he took off. The road he'd chosen was Route 6. On the map, a red line from Cape Cod to Ely, Nevada — the straightest and most direct of all possible routes. In reality, frustratingly unlocatable, all accesses to it closed off. Having set his course, though, Jack was determined to follow it. He even wasted a day attempting to do so, lamenting all the good times he was missing. Visionaries are stubborn people.

Fifteen years later kids went on the road in droves, in the context Kerouac and others had supplied for them. But in 1947, to be a college-educated hitchhiker was to be anachronistic. The Depression decade, when millions of the hungry, homeless, and unemployed had roamed the U.S. landscape, hopped freights, slept in open fields, was still grimly, unnostalgically alive in people's memories. Status and security had been so recently won and still seemed tenuously held. People did not walk the highways unless the cars they drove — preferably the latest models — had flats or ran out of gas. In Council Bluffs, where great wagon trains had gathered in the nineteenth century, Jack came upon a depressing vista of "cute cottages of one damn kind and another." In Cheyenne, he found Wild West Week being celebrated by "fat businessmen in boots and ten-gallon hats," in whose eyes it would have been an act of incomprehensible perversity for a young man to become deliberately classless if he had other options; in another few years, they would see it as positively un-American.

Already what was left of the true West, as envisioned by Jack in Ozone Park, could no longer be found in the places with the legendary names, but in the open, empty spaces in between — a spirit to be grasped fleetingly from the back of a truck filled with migrant workers speeding across the prairies at midnight.

IT'S THE SPRING of 1949 and I'm thirteen and a half. With my best friend Maria, I am sitting in the very front seat of the top deck of a double-decker bus as it makes its way down lower Fifth Avenue toward Greenwich Village, which I've been assured is the very last stop — thus impossible to miss. Suddenly we see it, the famous arch that's supposed to be the entrance to Washington Square and to lots of other things — perhaps a life of romance and adventure — that I've heard about from four older, very knowledgeable Trotskyite girls whom I've met in the basement of Hunter College High School. Juniors who disdain the bourgeois cafeteria upstairs, they lunch secretly on yogurt deep in the locker room. They carry bags of knitting under which there are copies of the *Militant*, which they hawk around Fourteenth Street nearly every day after school. They have Trotskyite boyfriends whom they make sweaters and argyle socks for and endlessly discuss. They never quite explain to me what *Trotskyite* is, but it seems that if you are one, you're headed for trouble not only with the fascists but with detestable teen-age Stalinists who've been known to harass sellers of the *Militant* and even beat them up. I admire the daring of these girls tremendously, their whole style, in fact — dark clothes and long earrings, the cigarettes they smoke illicitly, the many cups of coffee they say they require to keep them going.

26

Friendly as they are, however, they never invite me on their rounds. With Olympian disinterest, they delineate a territory that it's up to me to explore for myself.

As the bus lurches under the arch, Maria and I are leaning all the way forward in our seats, clutching hands. It's that moment when fantasy and expectation collide with reality, when what you've been told exists really turns out to be there — not quite as you've pictured it, but close enough. Here is the arch, as described by the Trotskyite girls, and there is the fountain, the circle in the square where, according to them, people gather every Sunday to sing folk songs. I'd imagined hordes of people, a whole guitar- and banjo-strumming population, their music ringing through the park — but hadn't trusted the glamour of that picture in my mind. I'd thought we mightn't find anyone at all.

Actually today there are about six of them — a few young men in old army jackets, a tall, blonde girl in faded jeans, a man in a wheelchair. They look a little drab, in fact — perhaps because it's also begun to rain. The drops fall on Maria and me as we rush over to them from the bus. Washington Square is emptying out fast. Wouldn't you know it — we've arrived just too late. In another moment they'll be packing up their instruments.

They stand their ground, however. The men turn up the collars of their jackets. As their audience vanishes, they launch into a new and appropriate song, "Let the Circle Be Unbroken," which they sing as loudly as possible into the wind that thins out their voices, disperses them like so much smoke. The rain rattles down harder. I wouldn't move out of it for anything.

I've fallen in love with them all. It's as though a longing I've carried inside myself has suddenly crystallized. To be lonely within a camaraderie of loneliness.

I watch them intently, especially the blonde girl, as if I could wish myself into her. She can't be *that* much older than I am, maybe sixteen, and yet she's been accepted by these grownup-looking men. (At that time in my life I have the strange conviction that the last person any adult male would be interested in is a young girl.) She has glasses and long pale stringy hair and a skinny body hidden inside a man's shirt several sizes too big for her that's torn at one shoulder — *my* mother would never let me out in anything that was torn. You'd think she was beautiful, the way she acts. And maybe she is. The more I watch her, the more I come to believe it.

She's shivering and laughing in the rain, twisting her hair into rope like wash she's wringing out. One of the men holds open his jacket and she ducks into the shelter of it, standing pressed against his side in a warmth I can only imagine with despair. Even now I only look eleven — that's my curse. My outside doesn't reflect my inside, so no one knows who I really am.

With my friend Maria, it's a different story. Maria's outside has that eerie agelessness some girls get so quickly and mysteriously, blooming overnight into child-women. Maria's baby fat has given way to definition — cheekbones, sharp little breasts; the slant of her eyes hints at experience she hasn't yet lived. It's Maria who connects us to this group of strangers.

The rain is getting serious, the sky is definitely black. Calling it a day, the young men snap their guitars into cases. Maria just walks up to one of them. "Where are you going now?" she says to him. "Are you going to sing somewhere else?" If it were left to me, I couldn't have gotten out one word.

He looks at her and smiles at this dark, eager, rather exotic, willowy kid. ("Did anyone ever tell you," more and more people keep telling Maria, "you look just like Gene Tierney?" "That's because my face is so Russian," she explains modestly. "Both my parents are Russian, you know.") "Are you going to come back next Sunday?" she asks. "My friend and I are learning the guitar."

"Is that so?" he says. "Maybe next time you'll bring yours."

"But we don't play very well yet."

This young man's still smiling at Maria in the most extraordinarily friendly way. "Why don't you come along and have some coffee? We're all going to the Art Center. Your friend, too," he says.

That's how easy it was.

I got home that first Sunday just in time for dinner. What did I tell my parents that night? Maria and I spent the afternoon doing homework? We went to the movies? Did my mind race guiltily through the current attractions, picking the one we saw? I knew the truth would be fatal. We took the Fifth Avenue bus to Washington Square. We talked to strange men. We went with them to the Art Center — which was not a center of all the arts, as I'd first thought, but a luncheonette on Eighth Street — a classic greasy spoon that would be rechristened The Griddle less misleadingly two years later. There we had coffee, which I was not allowed to drink at home. It seemed as wicked to drink coffee as to drink a martini. I had to put six sugars in mine to get it down. The men talked to Maria, really, rather than to me. Mostly they talked to each other about versions of folk songs that they wrote down in little notebooks, and someone called Pete Seeger, and there was a joke ending with the punchline "What's the party line on that?" which made them all laugh. The blonde girl necked with her boyfriend; she kicked off her shoes under the table. The man in the wheelchair was a doomed millionaire who lived on Park Avenue. He was a hemophiliac, which I had never heard of — Maria whispered to me it meant that if he got even a tiny scratch he'd bleed to death. He was bloated and greenish pale with brown circles under his eyes, and quite irritable, which seemed understandable under the circumstances. He collected — guitars, banjos, hundreds of folk and blues records; people, too, these people, for whom we heard he gave parties uptown, astonishing the snooty doormen with his guests. Would Maria and I ever go to any of these parties?

What all this seemed to promise was something I'd never tasted in my life as a child — something I told myself was Real Life. This was not the life my parents lived but one that was dramatic, unpredictable, possibly dangerous. Therefore *real*, infinitely more worth having. In trying to trace the derivations of this notion of experience, I come into blind alleys. It was simply there all of a sudden, full-fledged, like a fever I'd come down with. The air carries ideas like germs, infecting some, not others.

Real Life was not to be found in the streets around my house, or anywhere on the Upper West Side, for that matter, or in my school of girls grubbing joylessly for marks, hysterical about geometry exams and Latin homework, flirting ridiculously with the seventy-year-old elevator operator, the only male visible on the premises.

Real Life was sexual. Or rather, it often seemed to take the form of sex. This was the area of ultimate adventure, where you would dare or not dare. It was much less a question of desire. Sex was like a forbidden castle whose name could not even be spoken around the house, so feared was its power. Only with the utmost vigilance could you avoid being sucked into its magnetic field. The alternative was to break into the castle and take its power for yourself.

We go down to the Square the next Sunday and the one after that and the following one. The weather gets warmer; the fountain in the circle is finally turned on; people come out of cold-water flats and into the sun. New musicians arrive and either become regulars or make memorable one-shot appearances — like the man who came all the way down from Harlem with his washtub and broomstick one-string bass, or the old white-mustached Italian mandolinist who tremoloed his way one afternoon through "Oh Mary, don't you weep, don't you mourn" and "Take This Hammer" and "Put it on the ground/ Spread it all around/ If you dig it with a hoe, it will make your *flow*-ers grow." Proletarian musicians cause particular excitement. Although we sing the music of "The People," it is *they*, after all, who are the genuine article.

My whole being during the humdrum week is focused on these Sundays. At night I shut myself into my room and strum the guitar incessantly, singing the songs I've learned under my breath so as to escape my mother's critical ear. "Why are you spending so much time on that? You should be playing the piano more if you want to get anywhere." But the guitar, not the piano, is my passport to the world down-town.

Besides the music, I'm learning a great many other things very rapidly, such as the fact that America is a place of enor-mous injustice and inequality, where the little children of miners starve in shacks and where Negro men are lynched or jailed for crimes that are not even crimes, such as whistling at a white woman. In the South there is one such prisoner facing execution named Willie McGee, and I put little stickers saying "Save Willie McGee" on the walls of every subway stop on the way to school. I learn that a picket line is something you never cross, lest you become a fink, and that espresso is black and bitter so it's much better to order cappuccino made with steamed frothy milk and cinnamon. And that soul kissing — which I only hear about and do not experience — is letting a man put his tongue in your mouth, in direct violation of all sanitary taboos such as not letting another person ever use your toothbrush. And that going crazy is not something frowned upon in the Village but sort of respected if done by artists.

I long to turn myself into a Bohemian, but lack the proper clothes. Oh, the belts I see in the Sorcerer's Apprentice, which is tucked away in a little courtyard off Eighth Street, like a cobbler's shop in a fairy tale. That's where everyone gets them. There are two styles that are popular. One laces up the front like the girdle of Lena the Goosegirl; the other fastens dramatically with a spiral made of brass about the size of a saucer. Such a belt — aside from enhancing your appearance, which I was sure it would immeasurably — is a badge, a sign of membership in the ranks of the unconventional. The way is smoothed for the wearer of this belt, or of the dirndl skirt of lumpy handwoven material that usually goes with it, not to mention the sandals crisscrossing up the ankle, or the finishing touch of a piece of freeform jewelry like a Rorschach test figure dangling down to the midriff by a thong. The way is smoothed because the problem of outside matching inside is so beautifully resolved by this simple means, which only costs money. I'd have been humiliated if anyone had told me that the desire to possess these items was, within a different context, like the desire to possess a certain kind of baseball jacket.

Somehow, early on, I do manage to acquire a pair of long copper earrings. They clank reassuringly against my neck in the slightest breeze, and pull at my ear lobes. I carry them with me at all times in case I need them. They constitute my downtown disguise. Peering into the dirty mirror of a gum machine in the West Fourth Street station of the IND to see how different they make me look, I put them on before I walk over to the Square.

I'm cool and clever as any double agent needs to be. No one on 116th Street would guess my destination. I have switched my route to the subway, so much faster than the bus. I can get to the Village a whole half-hour earlier, and wait till the very last minute to go home to make my seven o'clock curfew. Sunday by Sunday my "last minute" gets later, pushing the outer boundaries of safety. At 7:15 I can still walk in the door with some innocuous excuse for my mother; a 7:30 arrival will bring a storm of frantic where-were-you's upon me. I shoot for the area in between.

Nothing seems crueler than my curfew. I feel I'm missing Everything — whatever Everything it is that happens after seven o'clock. Maria's always going to different places with people for cappuccino because her mother, a divorced ex-actress, doesn't seem to care when she comes home.

By 6:15 I start getting ready to tear myself away for another week. As the seconds bleed from the minutes, I'm in an odd state of heightened longing and anxiety. I feel much the same in later years whenever I part from a man I love. The anxiety is not so much over leaving as over an impending fading of identity.

*A*T A PARTY THAT fall in a loft on Fourteenth Street decorated with red bunting left over from May Day, I met the guest of honor, a genuine coal miner from Tennessee. His name was Tommy Geraci, and he'd been brought up north by some group or other for fund-raising purposes. He was thick-necked, burly, and very dark. But his darkness did not seem derived from exposure to the sun. It was greyish, as if coal dust were engrained in the pores of his skin.

The party was like a few other parties I'd already been to by then. People would come in and take off their shoes. Sitting cross-legged on the bare floor, they'd sing their way through the contents of the *People's Song Book*, or Cecil Sharp's *Old English Ballads*, for the sake of variety. Whatever Tommy Geraci had expected to find on his trip to New York City and Greenwich Village, I don't think it was anything at all like this gathering, which was as blandly festive — I realize now — as a church social, and through which Tommy Geraci wandered in a rather lost and belligerent way, taking consoling swigs from a pint of bourbon. He'd walk straight up to people, stare at them wordlessly and ferociously, and then move on. To my alarm and delight he walked up to me. Swaying a little, he gave me a solemn once-over with eyes that really did seem black as coals. His shoulders strained at the seams of his shirt. He reached out a large hand with

33

black-rimmed nails and suddenly squeezed my right hip. "Someday," he said, "you will be a woman."

Although this was not a startling deduction on his part, it seemed the kindest and most profound thing anyone had ever said to me. To be seen as a woman, at least a future one! I couldn't get over it for weeks.

I've become the chaperone/protector of Maria, whom needless to say I don't protect with my brute strength. It's my insignificant and unwelcome presence that acts as a deterrent to the advances of various grown men who fall under her spell and behave rashly. Why this happens so frequently is inexplicable. Before all this attention, she was just Maria. Now it's as if there's a shining aura about her that sets her apart from me. There are circumstances in which it would be better not to shine so brightly, but it's not even anything she can dim if she wants to. Having all this new power, she becomes more helpless. I have to accompany her everywhere — "Is it all right if I bring my girlfriend with me?" *Two's company, three's a crowd.* I am the crowd.

I wish Maria would definitely say no to a couple of her would-be boyfriends, but she never can. She says she's afraid of hurting their feelings. The most sinister one is Billy. He's an ex-convict, which only makes her sorrier for him. He has one little gold earring and a scar across his left cheek and a knife in his pocket, which he says he needs for protection purposes. There are streets in the Italian parts of the Village that he can't walk down safely, and he says this is because he's black. And it's also because he's black that Maria has to love him. She *has* to, she *must* — or it somehow won't be fair. He says he's going to get a car someday and come uptown and steal her, because she drives him so wild. It's from him we learn that a man's longing is like an actual physical pain. Having created it even unintentionally, it seems you're responsible for its assuagement.

"I don't know what to do about him," Maria whispers to me in algebra class. "I don't know how I really feel." Coming out of school together, we case the street, half-expecting to see him waiting in his car.

Sometimes on weekdays it's as if we've only dreamed that we go to the Village and know anyone like Billy. You can put the Village away like I put away my copper earrings and have problems about things like losing your gym suit on the cross-town bus.

In English, we are reading *The Odyssey* and are dazzled by the sarcastic brilliance of our teacher, Miss Kirschenbaum — *"Poor* Odysseus! All alone on an island with a beautiful woman!"* If Homer cannot escape criticism, then there is hope that nothing is sacred.

But in matters of grammar, Miss Kirschenbaum is no iconoclast at all. She has particular scorn, for example, for sentence fragments, which she says "can *only* be used for effect." So as not to confuse us, no writers who break such rules are ever named. For all we know, Joyce, Stein, Woolf have never been born. SF! she writes in red in the margins of compositions — SF!! SF!!! — routing them out like cockroaches. Effect is something we girls have no right to. Only after years of laboriously equipping each sentence with subject and predicate, as with boots and umbrella, can we hope to earn it. Perhaps not even then.

In gym class, where we do basketball and square dances in which we take turns "being the boy," the fast girls with good figures roll their gym bloomers high on their thighs and tuck the elastics under their underpants; they wear their tops unbuttoned down almost to their bras. They risk demerits to achieve this striking effect. I hear them whisper to each other about dates and boyfriends, with total recall of each touch in or near a forbidden location. One girl sets off a fever of giggles by telling how she noticed that her boyfriend carried "one of those disgusting little raincoat things" in his wallet. How anyone could get a raincoat into a wallet is a mystery to me, but to ask would be to expose a gap in my sophistication. Maria says she was probably making it up.

I do continue to wonder about it, though. Do all men carry little secret raincoats?

A person pursuing Real Life must always be on the alert for fragments of what may seem meaningless information. From these fragments, which can only be gathered accidentally, one may eventually construct a whole piece of knowledge.

Frigid, for example, is a word Billy starts using against me when week after week it is always *three* people and never two sitting at his table in the Waldorf Cafeteria off Eighth Street — which is where he always wants Maria to go with him, so that at least if he cannot have her, he can show her off. Don't I have better things to do than always hanging around, ruining his chances? "What's the matter with you, girl? You frigid?" By his contemptuous tone, I know it's the meanest thing he can think of to say to me, so cruel that if I actually knew what he meant I might burst into tears and leave him alone with my friend. Although I hate Billy, I have a fascinated respect for him. Does he know something awful about me I don't know myself?

To be with him and Maria has become more and more a strange sort of test. It's like standing high on a ladder with someone rocking and shaking the bottom of it so that you'll get dizzy and fall. The balance is somewhere inside yourself, where you feel nothing but only see. You can even see your own face getting all hot and red. And you say "I am *not*," and you won't leave, and the balance becomes a kind of exhilaration.

"I'm going to fix you up," he threatens finally. "And then we'll find out. Next week I'm gonna bring Russell. You want to meet Russell?" he says. "I'll bet you don't know what being with a man is. You so frigid, anyone can see that."

It's a dare, so I have to agree to meeting Russell. In my fourteen years, I've never been out on a date of my own, just Maria's. Russell is a friend of Billy's from jail. He's thirty-two years old, so handsome he doesn't even need anyone like me, but he does what Billy tells him to, Billy says.

As much as I don't want to meet Russell, I have secret hopes about this date. I imagine Russell as someone nice like Tommy Geraci who's been unjustly imprisoned. That wouldn't be so bad. When the following Sunday comes and Maria and I walk over to the Square, I'm feeling excited as well as scared that he won't like me.

There's a tall man waiting with Billy who has funny yellow metallic-looking hair, all stiff as if it's been painted with something. His face is bright pink, and there's something odd about his features. It's not that he isn't handsome, it's just that you can't help feeling his face has sort of died. "Hel-*lo*," he says carefully to no one in particular, as if it's a word he's just learned. He looks at Billy to see if he's done the right thing.

"Hey, man, this is the little girlfriend I found for you," Billy says loudly.

With enormous concentration, Russell smiles.

I'd rather be frigid than go anywhere with this Russell.

I look around the Square and even though the sun is shining and people are singing, it all seems suddenly sinister. The brightness is only the top layer of something very dark. It's as if being afraid of Billy before had only been playing — the way you could scare yourself by listening to broadcasts of *The Shadow*.

I remember I started walking away, and the next thing I knew, Maria was right behind me. And then we both started running, our guitars rattling in their cases. I lost an earring somewhere on Eighth Street. We ran all the way to the subway, and we didn't come back for two whole weeks.

*B*Y ANY STANDARDS, the Waldorf Cafeteria, to which Billy first took Maria and me, and which I later began to visit a great deal by myself on weekday afternoons as well as Sundays, was a dreary-looking place. I remember it as being a uniform grey-brown. It had none of the chrome-and-brass art-deco fittings of the Automat, or the bountifulness of Jewish cafeterias like Hector's near Times Square, where fountains dispensed seltzer and where the rich juices of turkeys flowed onto wooden slabs behind steam tables serving up a dizzying "choice of vegetables" — everything in a nutritious spectrum from the orange and red of carrots and beets to the creamy whites of cauliflower and mashed potatoes. No, there was something poor about the Waldorf, despite its ironic name.

Was the name of the Waldorf responsible for its success? And was the nature of its success as a hangout responsible for its approaching financial failure and disappearance?

No doubt the owner was an actual businessman named Mr. Waldorf. But I'd much rather believe that *Waldorf* was chosen deliberately during the great cafeteria movement of the Depression, when the place first opened its doors to an articulate but broke clientele who needed a well-heated place in which to kill time.

On any given late afternoon during the two years that I

38

went there, it was always crowded with interesting grownups who had no visible means of support: artists, poets, communists and anarchists, guitar-pickers, jailbirds, scavengers.

Come to think of it, I never ate a meal at the Waldorf. A friend of mine, who during her Bohemian period then was a student at City College, says she never did either; and furthermore, no cash register rings in her memory collecting the nickels she surely must have paid out for countless cups of watery black coffee.

I'd hang out around the edges of the crowded tables, listening, looking, not really participating. Ideas flashed by like silver freight trains that wouldn't stop at your station to unload but had to push on to a vanishing point in the distance. What was Jungian? Existentialist? Abstract expressionist? In a garbage can near my house, I found a magazine I'd heard mentioned in the Waldorf — *Partisan Review*. I'd never seen a magazine without pictures. I read the whole thing from cover to cover, awed, miserable, and deeply bored. My ten years of education had certainly not prepared me for this. Would I ever be wise enough not only to understand *Partisan Review* but perhaps even to love it the way I loved *David Copperfield*?

A long time after the fact, I learned "Why, *everybody* went to the Waldorf!" This *everybody*, of whom I'd been quite unconscious, makes the Waldorf sound like the Deux Magots of Eighth Street: e. e. cummings, W. H. Auden, Maxwell Bodenheim, Delmore Schwartz. Painters like Hans Hofmann, Jackson Pollock, and Franz Kline. Obscure younger people, too, like Allen Ginsberg, who moved downtown to the Lower East Side before he followed Jack's route westward in pursuit of Neal Cassady. And certainly, before his wanderings, Jack himself — who often in the Duluoz Saga would celebrate cheap eateries so gorgeously, capturing the precise coloration of the light, the density of steam on the windows in winter, the white, thick chipped crockery, the aroma of eggs and potatoes fried in grease.

But for struggling young people like Allen and Jack, and many patrons of the older generation as well, the Waldorf was only the afternoon stop on the circuit of places that made up the tantalizing night life of the Village, from which I was excluded by my mother's curfew. From the Waldorf one could go on to the San Remo on MacDougal Street, where the caffeine of the daylight hours became charged with alcohol, making the discussions so boozily heated that actual fights would erupt, spilling out onto the sidewalk. Or there was the dangerous Pony Bar, a mobster-protected lesbian hangout of legendary toughness. Or Julius's, preferred by the earnest folk-singing crowd, decorated by wagon wheels covered with a twenty-year accumulation of dust. And after all these places, the final sobering stop in the small hours of the morning was the Jeff (short for Jefferson) Diner on Sixth Avenue, where, sitting on a stool — perhaps next to one of those strung-out, laconic twilight figures for whom the designation *hipster* was about to be invented — one could observe the coming of dawn over the rooftops of the Village through grimy windows.

Over a decade after the Waldorf closed, a man I was sure I'd never seen before walked up to me at an artists' party and said, "Why do you hang back?"

This was Jim Johnson, whom I was shortly to live with and would marry nine months later. He'd been twenty-four in 1950 — a still-dazed survivor of two and a half months of continuous shelling on a mine sweeper at Anzio — studying painting at the Art Students League with Reginald Marsh. He'd lived in a tiny furnished room on Eighth Street on one meal a day. At night he'd often wander, if he could afford it, into the San Remo, where he had some incoherent but strangely inspiring conversations with a middle-aged, alcoholic painter named Jackson, whom he escorted home on one occasion — "He was so bombed, he wasn't going to make it otherwise" — holding him up under the armpits. A few years later Jim had realized he'd known Jackson Pollock.

Together we'd make a similar discovery that seemed equally wonderful to us. We kept having the kind of all-night talks about our pasts in which it seemed that everything must be made known all at once. During one of them, we figured out, by comparing dates, that we'd both been in the Waldorf during exactly the same period. That was where Jim had gone each day to eat his single meal. We might even have sat at some of the same tables.

The Waldorf was one of the places where I began to acquire the habit of hanging around and back at the same time, which my future husband first amazed me by noticing with his stranger's eye.

Invisibility had become my unsatisfying resolution of the outside/inside problem. Moving back and forth between antithetical worlds separated by subway rides, I never fully was what I seemed or tried to be. I had the feeling I was playing hooky all the time, not from school, but from the person represented by my bland outward appearance — the only child of Mr. and Mrs. Glassman, under whose second-rate identity I got good marks in everything except math, still took piano and composition lessons with Mr. Bleecker, and still nourished my mother's extravagant dreams that I would achieve fame before I was in my twenties by laboring over musical comedies whose imitative sentimentality was already beginning to embarrass me. On a more realistic plane, my mother had now set her sights on Barnard College — where, she said, few Jewish girls had ever been accepted and where she was determined to send me before I finished out my four years of high school. Why shouldn't I make my mark upon the world as soon as possible?

Yet in that greater world, which I had discovered for myself without her knowing it, I had the distinct feeling that as a young girl I was inconsequential, neither brilliant enough nor beautiful enough to make any mark whatsoever.

Hoping to crack the secret of Maria's appeal, I tried out some of her mannerisms. The way her shoulders would always go up in a small and charming shrug when there was something she didn't understand. The rather singsong inflection of her voice. "You're beginning to sound like your *friend*," my mother said disparagingly.

Billy had given up on us and disappeared. Once I tried to describe him and some other habitués of the Waldorf, as well as a fistfight I'd seen on MacDougal Street, in an assignment for English on "colorful characters," but Miss Kirschenbaum said I should only write about things I knew.

Maria's latest Village boyfriend was so terrific she no longer wanted me along for protection. He was a poet and member of the Labor Youth League named Brian, with curly brown hair and blue eyes and a face pitted by acne, which strangely made him look rugged. He told us he was twenty-five. He made Maria the gift of one of his plaid flannel shirts, which she faithfully wore even as the weather got warmer Their feeling for each other reached such a pitch that they began to discuss marriage. Quite properly she decided he'd better meet her mother, which turned out to be a big mistake. Maria's mother took one look at this twenty-five-year-old Brian, and, abandoning her previous laissez-faire policy, packed Maria off for the rest of the summer to be a baby sitter for three little boys in Glen Cove, Long Island. All communication between the betrothed was forbidden. It was Romeo and Juliet all over again. I played the role of Friar Lawrence, passing on Brian's letters to Maria, enclosed in my own, and vice versa.

Sometimes on Sundays, Brian and I would take long, silent, gloomy walks together. "You are one great kid," he said to me once. We were on Gay Street, which was one of my favorite places in the Village because it was tucked away and slightly crooked, with little wisteria-covered houses that looked very, very old — I planned to live there when I grew up, but have not yet realized this dream. It was right there on Gay Street that Brian kissed me. His tongue went gently between my lips and almost all the way into my mouth, but then thought better of it and pulled back. An almost-soul kiss!

But not a real one.

7

'M HOLED UP IN my room at my Royal portable type-writer that my aunts gave me when I graduated from grammar school, writing Maria — still exiled in Glen Cove — an account of the momentous two-week vacation I've just spent with my parents. With my right index finger I type and type as the letter shakes loose, without my really even thinking about it, from what could strictly be called fact. With heightened truth, I'm telling the story of how I finally found romance, at a farm resort for middle-aged couples in New Jersey, with Aaron the lifeguard, the only person not middle-aged besides me.

He was a twenty-year-old college student who'd presided over the deep end of the pool. (I describe him, simply, as "older.") Gripping me around the waist and counting while I laid my face in the water for him and held my breath, he'd given me the first swimming lessons I ever had. We'd also done things like crawling under a porch to find some newborn kittens, and I'd told him I was very Bohemian but I couldn't be with my parents around, and he'd taken a picture of me with my guitar and asked if he could visit me in the city. He had a bad limp due to having had polio, and one leg was much thinner than the other, and I hated it when the middle-aged couples said "Such a nice boy. It's a shame," because I knew he'd be angry if he heard.

I relate all of this to Maria, allowing myself plenty of sentence fragments. I'm building toward my climax, which is when my parents and some other couples are taking their slow evening walk down a dirt road just as it's getting dark and they're swatting at mosquitoes and turning on their flashlights, and Aaron grabs my wrist and says, "Let's take a short cut." He's pulling me after him, and we go over a fence and across a dark field full of cow flops and into a patch of woods that are darker still — and all that happened in reality was that we came out onto the road on the other side. But this is not what I say. "And so Aaron took me into the woods," I write, and I type an ellipsis six dots long.

I'm astonished, as I stop and look at the page in the typewriter, by the power of these dots. How much more you can say without saying everything! And at that point my mother calls me into the living room, where she and my father have been listening for the past hour to the Evening Symphony on WQXR. There's something she wants me to take to my grandmother and aunts, who live upstairs in the same apartment house.

I can't remember how long I was gone — ten or fifteen minutes, maybe. But when I return, the radio has been silenced, and my parents are sitting side by side on the living-room couch with oddly stricken faces, as if they've been waiting for me to come back so they can tell me some bad news. I give them some message or other from my grandmother, and they pointedly look away. "Go into your room," my father says, clearing his throat.

I go into my room but I don't see anything different about it. Then I look at my desk, and the pages of my letter are spread out all over it, and across the one in my typewriter, scrawled in black crayon, are the words: WE HAVE READ THIS. AND IT MAKES VERY INTERESTING READING.

I stare at the heavy black marks these words make on the page without believing them. I feel numbly giddy, as if all the air has been sucked out of the world. But they've walked in behind me and are yelling, "What did you *do*? What did you *do* with him?" They're breaking all the rules about never raising voices. "What did you *do?* Did you let him? Did you?"

I'm sobbing and shaking. "I didn't do anything! I didn't do anything!"

"Yes you did!"

"No I didn't! I *didn't!*" I repeat this over and over, sobbing wildly into my hands. They are screaming, I am screaming. Some terrible energy has been released in them by my letter. Lifetimes of anger inflate them to enormous proportions. I can't recognize them as my parents.

Calming down a little, my mother becomes a cold interrogator. "Then why did you write such things? Would you care to tell me?"

"I don't know!"

It was my mother, I learn later, who read the letter. Sitting in the living room, she'd been pleasantly aware of the clack of the typewriter and thought I was doing something "creative." When I went upstairs, she couldn't resist the opportunity to take a peek.

"You didn't know that you were lying?"

Silence.

"If you weren't lying, then you did do something with that boy."

I'm no longer weeping. I've begun to know that soon we will all go to bed and that when we get up in the morning everything will be much as it was before. All I have to do is say that I was lying — they even *want* me to say I was lying — and so I say Yes, I lied.

"So we have a little liar for a daughter," my mother says with relief.

My father walks into the bathroom and vomits.

One Saturday afternoon in the fall, Aaron did come to visit. He brought the picture of me he had taken that summer and developed himself. Painfully smiling as if keeping up a front of secret amusement, my mother put a plate of Fig Newtons and a pitcher of pink lemonade down on the table in front of us and walked, almost tiptoed, out of the living room. He asked me about school, I tried to think of things to ask him about college. As if he'd been my camp counselor, he said I really should keep on with my swimming, since I'd made such a good start at it. The Indian-summer heat baked the Oriental rug. We ate the Fig Newtons, which grew progressively soggier. Of the Aaron of my ellipsis, there was no trace at all.

Also that fall, Maria transferred to a coed high school — Bronx Science. On her first day there, she walked into the cafeteria and was shocked to find Brian. "What are you doing here?" she demanded, although she immediately had her suspicions. "Oh, I'm an English teacher." Some teacher! It didn't take her long to uncover the truth — Brian was only seventeen. Naturally she broke off with him immediately, which I agreed was certainly the only thing to do. Our standards were very high.

4

I STARTED AT Barnard College a few weeks before my sixteenth birthday. It was the fall of 1951. Putting on a pleated Black Watch plaid skirt that fastened in front with a large safety pin, dark-green Bonnie Doon knee socks, and matching lamb's-wool (lamentably not cashmere) sweaters, I packed a small suitcase and moved across 116th Street to Hewitt Hall for three days of freshman orientation. Exhausted by my efforts to lead a double life that would not be detected by my parents, I was giving up Bohemianism, which I now saw as childish. I believed I was ready for an instant transformation in which I would become "collegiate." I did not at all want to be perceived as odd. I'd go to proms in strapless gowns of pastel tulle, and perhaps even learn to take an interest in football, though that was probably going too far, I thought. My idea of the life that would await me in college was a composite of images from three main sources: the works of F. Scott Fitzgerald, *Mademoiselle* magazine, and the campus department of Lord and Taylor.

Barnard seemed restfully quaint, almost pastoral, with its trees and bricked paths, and the delightfully overgrown area behind the tennis courts known as the Jungle, and the beau parlors in the dorms, which were miniature living rooms without doors in which girls were allowed to sit with their dates. It was like a city garden, unsuspected until you walked

47

through its gates and stood within its walls that so mysteriously created the illusion of distance. Distance from the buses and subways rattling down Broadway to less-exalted destinations, and from the edges of Harlem only six blocks away, and from Eighth Street, where the Waldorf Cafeteria had recently been boarded up — the first of my lost landmarks. Distance even from Columbia and its troublesome men, who once a year in a rite of spring would surge across Broadway and tear down the green wooden fence surrounding the Barnard dorms, then pay to have a new fence erected.

It was the era of the ivory tower — and Barnard provided its maiden version. A retired general named Dwight D. Eisenhower was the president of Columbia University. A retired commander of the WAVES, Millicent MacIntosh, was the dean of Barnard. It was the era of Senator Joseph McCarthy, Roy Cohn, and G. David Schine. You could buy a copy of *Red Channels* in any candy store. In the house I lived in with my parents, there were rumors that the superintendent was paid by the FBI to sift through the garbage of certain professors. It was also the era of the beginning of television. A television set in operation in any shop window would draw a fascinated crowd. My aunts got a set a year or so before my parents. In the dimmed light of their living room, surrounded by bookcases full of the no-longer-read works of George Bernard Shaw and Henrik Ibsen in complete matching sets, as well as oddities such as books by Lafcadio Hearn, Balzac's *Droll Tales*, and *My Life* by Leon Trotsky, the family would gather to watch Milton Berle, and Ted Mack's *Amateur Hour*. On the campus, however, tradition reigned supreme. Prufrockian professors walked the brick paths in neutral tweeds. Every self-respecting Barnard English major claimed to be passionately interested in the seventeenth century. At Columbia it was Lionel Trilling's course in the Romantic poets that drew the brightest and most ambitious students, or Mark Van Doren's course in Shakespeare. Both men had taught Allen Ginsberg and Lucien Carr during the more turbulent wartime period. Their new crop of students — my generation — was called the Silent Generation. Our silence was common knowledge and was often cited in the pages of *Time, Life,* and the Sunday magazine of the *New York Times.* We were also called "other-directed" by David Riesman in *The Lonely Crowd.* We were considered passive, conformist, seldom individualistic or given to acts of rebellion. For us, that middle-aged line of T. S. Eliot's, "Do I dare to eat a peach?" had an especial poignancy. To our shame, we knew we usually didn't.

Just as the fifties had begun, an event had occurred of no immediate interest to the Silent Generation and of trivial importance to the reigning literati. This event — nonevent, really — was the publication of a novel called *The Town and the City* by an unknown writer named John Kerouac. In his jacket photo, John Kerouac looked much as an up-and-coming young intellectual of the time was supposed to look — well-kempt, wearing a dark suit, white shirt, and neatly knotted tie; his face was handsome and poetically melancholy, betraying a writerly intensity. The reception of his book could best be described as "mixed" — a word that to publishers means "damned by faint praise," which ultimately translates into low sales. The great reading public is not necessarily on the lookout for a "rough diamond of a book," which is what the *New York Times* reviewer called *The Town and the City;* it would rather save its money for gems with a lot of glitter.

Rough diamond is usually a term used to describe promising young men (but strangely, not young women) of working-class origins. (The young Welsh miner rescued from the pit by the efforts of the refined spinster schoolteacher in the 1940s best seller *How Green Was My Valley* was certainly such a diamond.) It was not a particularly happy thing to be in the 1950s, when the proletarianism of the thirties and the democratic leveling of the war years had given way to a rather frantic scramble for polish.

Allen Ginsberg's former classmate Norman Podhoretz, a boy from the Jewish slums of Brownsville who had attended Columbia on a scholarship, confessed to this with a self-consciously shameless shame in his autobiography, *Making*

It. Proclaiming himself a member of "the country" called the upper middle class, "less by virtue of my income than by virtue of the way my speech is accented, the way I dress, the way I furnish my home, the way I entertain and am entertained, the way I educate my children — the way, quite simply, I look and live," Podhoretz then disclosed, "It appalls me to think what an immense transformation I had to work on myself in order to become what I have become." He had evidently felt less appalled in the early fifties, when, with the encouragement of Lionel Trilling, he went all the way to Clare College at Cambridge to be polished into assimilation with WASP gentility.

Podhoretz makes the declaration that "One of the longest journeys in the world is the journey from Brooklyn to Manhattan." But Jack Kerouac (another Columbia scholarship boy) had taken a much longer journey from his French-Canadian factory workers' neighborhood in Lowell, Massachusetts, to Morningside Heights. That cultural and psychological distance was never to be fully traveled, however. The John Kerouac who could be seen in conversation with Gore Vidal and Alfred Kazin at various literary cocktail parties in the spring of 1950 was also always, both proudly and with some anguish, the Jack of Lowell. Just as it had been the Jack of Lowell, with all his conservative values and even a shy puritanical streak, who had taken the Dostoevskian midnight subway with Herbert Huncke to the low-life haunts of Times Square. While Podhoretz was obsessed with maintenance of distances, John Kerouac knew that all realities are contiguous, even life and death.

I was among the millions who didn't read *The Town and the City.* Around the time it was published, I was reading the novels of Thomas Wolfe. I read all of them, undaunted by their length. In Eugene Gant's adolescent yearnings to break free of the constricting ties of family I saw my own. Awash in the rocking sea of Wolfe's language, I was stirred by the rhythm of such phrases as "a stone, a leaf, an unfound door." I cherished the Wolfeian word *inchoate,* which suggested a chalky obscurity, and hoped there'd be a passage in my own writing where it would be apropos. But if I'd happened to come across John Kerouac's book in the public library, I might have been equally stirred by "A child, a child, hiding in a corner, peeking, infolded in veils, in swirling shrouds and mysteries," and the novel would have surprised me by being set partially in my own uncolorful neighborhood, as well as in Galloway (Lowell), and even more by its revelation of the Bohemian world you could get to so quickly in the city — the world I was now renouncing with such determination but also with a feeling of incompletion.

During that first weekend at Barnard I met a girl whom my instincts immediately told me to avoid. I was almost sure I'd seen her in the West Fourth Street Station, or around the Waldorf a couple of times, or in the Square. She was even wearing one of those telltale belts from the Sorcerer's Apprentice — the spiral kind — into which she'd tucked a drab and unbecoming skirt and a demure white blouse with a Peter Pan collar, the kind your mother might make you wear in seventh grade, pulled tightly over her large breasts. Her dark hair was ungraciously scraped back with a rubber band, and acne flared under the ragged bangs on her forehead. Behind her black-rimmed glasses, eyes looked out at you sorrowfully and fiercely.

I did not want to know Elise Cowen, who clearly was *not* collegiate and whom I could tell at a glance was even beyond the effort of trying. She introduced herself in such a low voice I had to ask her to repeat her name. But her eyes insisted, "I *do* know you. We *have* been to the same places. And isn't it ridiculous for us to be *here?*" And all the while, in my plaid and lamb's wool, I'd hoped I blended in so perfectly.

I resisted friendship with her for about a month, during which I went to freshman mixers where I fox-trotted pressed stiffly against the suits of Columbia boys who asked me what

I was taking. I even tried out one meeting of the Columbia Zionist organization, where all the nouns and verbs seemed to be in Hebrew and where the president mortified me by shaking my hand at the door and saying, "Thanks for coming. People of other faiths are always welcome."

In my room at home I secretly practiced the Charleston, in case I was ever in a situation where I'd be asked to do it. I'd caught on that among the more glamorous crowd at Barnard and Columbia, it was very much the thing to emulate the customs of the Roaring Twenties. In addition to the revival of the Charleston, this involved a lot of flamboyant drinking and the throwing of wild and lavish parties. The previous spring, thirty students had sold pints of blood to finance a May Wine Festival at the swanky Essex House — on whose neon sign that night the *E* and the first *s* had been totally blacked out, according to later legend. Blood and wine — there was something about the decadent absurdity of that party that captured my imagination. Never had I imagined that pleasure could be pursued with such seriousness.

I saw Elise at only one of the mixers I went to. She was standing in a corner of the Barnard gym, scowling downward as she concentrated on something she was doing with her hands. Later, as I fox-trotted closer, I saw that she was attempting to roll a cigarette while holding the string of a bag of Bull Durham between her teeth. The cigarette, when she finally got it finished, was a horrible-looking thing with long shreds of tobacco dangling from one end. She struck a match and lit up, flicking little sparks off the front of her blouse.

We became friends — because I had run out of music paper. We were walking out of Freshman English together, and I mentioned that I had to run to Broadway and buy some before I went on to my next class, which was in counterpoint. "Oh, don't buy any more after this," she said. "My father manufactures the stuff." The next time I saw Elise, she presented me with a shopping bag in which there were reams of it. Far too much, in fact — the thought of having to fill all those pages with my hated compositions depressed me.

We went and had coffee. I think it was in a lounge Barnard had for day students. There was an hour before our next classes, which we ended up cutting, unwilling to tear ourselves away from a conversation of such inexhaustible intimacy. Most of our conversations were like that during the ten years that we knew each other, so that even now it's sometimes a shock to remember Elise is dead and I can't pick up a phone and speak to her.

ER MIDDLE NAME was Nada — a name of such bleak prophecy it's astonishing to think of anyone inflicting it upon an infant daughter. (Mine, for example, was Alice, conjuring up the looking-glass child, teas in pinafores on lawns.) "Literally it means Nothing — Nothing and Nothingness," Elise said with a certain melancholy pride. Was it her mother or father who chose it? The latter, I think — although if you met the man, there seemed, on the surface, nothing about him capable of *Nada*. A large bluff man with a mustache, handsome in a bearish way, with a touch of showbiz about him due to the nature of his business — the music business — and its connections to Tin Pan Alley. The mother was a skinny woman, all nerves and angles, with tinted auburn hair. "My little mother," Elise used to call her during remorseful periods when they weren't fighting.

The Cowens were what my parents would have called "a nice couple." They had a "nice" apartment on Bennett Avenue in Washington Heights, on the seventh floor of a blond brick house that had been built just before the war. I remember the layout of that place to this day — the sunken living room that made Elise's tiny cube of space, elevated by three steps like the rest of the apartment, seem terribly exposed, as if it were on a stage. The living room had a big casement window, the kind where the panes of glass open out just like shutters. The walls were painted pinkish brown; everything in the room was autumnal in some decorator-color way, and there were vases of dried things arranged on little tables.

The Cowens had much more money than my family. There were trips to Miami, their daughter's visits to ortho-dontists and dermatologists, gala nights out "on the town" with other similar couples. They raised their voices, though, a great deal. Mr. Cowen was given to threats and rages; Mrs. Cowen to recriminations and tears. Elise was the focal point of their high-strung emotions, even of their battles with each other. She was the sore spot, the darkness in the household, depriving her parents of the middle-aged gaiety that should have been theirs.

It had not always been so. In the Cowens' living room there was a color photo of Elise taken during her "good" period, which ended shortly after her thirteenth birthday. An exquisite little slender face with startled intelligent eyes, framed by smooth brown hair that came to a perfect widow's peak on an unmarred forehead. Who wouldn't love such a child? Perhaps *Nada* was mistakenly thought to be romantic, an Ondine-like name hinting at the rather attractive nihilism of the love/death.

The end of the good period, which Elise could pinpoint precisely, was abrupt and catastrophic. An impromptu party for her junior-high-school friends. She'd brought them all home with her and decided to make brownies, although she'd never used the oven by herself. She opened the door after they'd been baking awhile, to see if they were ready, and the oven exploded in her face, singeing off quite a lot of her hair as well as her eyebrows. After this she always thought of herself as ugly.

Her hair grew back, but in a funny, uneven line; there was no more widow's peak. And adolescence was cruel to her, bringing weight and pimples and breasts that were too large and her father's anger at the stranger who had replaced his daughter. A silent, obstinate girl who holed up in her room and read poetry and did not want to go to Florida. A girl who smoked and took no trouble with her appearance and whom he accused of hanging out in bad company and sleeping around like a little tramp. He had wanted a Jewish princess; he would have worshiped such a girl, nothing would have been too good for her.

When she was sixteen, Elise had slept with a boy, she had actually gone all the way to that mysterious stage beyond petting. But she had not slept around. It had been the culmination of a long, single-minded passion, of months of anguish and soul-searching and progressive nakedness. The boy had been someone in her class (she'd gone to Bronx Science and knew Maria slightly). The most brilliant boy in her school, she said. He'd gone on, in fact, to become the president of the Student Organization. This really surprised me — I couldn't imagine Elise loving the president of anything. Years later, though, a classmate remembered them as an idealized high-school couple, "terrific together," and Elise as "so pretty then, and popular with everyone." She'd followed him to a Zionist training camp in Poughkeepsie, although not a Zionist herself, and there in a sleeping bag It had happened. This, however, was the end. He feared they would get too involved.

I'd learned myself by the age of sixteen that just as girls guarded their virginity, boys guarded something less tangible which they called Themselves. They seemed to believe they had a mission in life, from which they could easily be deflected by being exposed to too much emotion.

Elise bore this boy no ill will. In fact, she accepted her pain with a baffling humility. She spoke of his beauty, his shining intelligence, as if she'd only become acquainted with such a person at all through great good luck.

Humility — that was the Nada side of her.

"Pull down thy vanity, I say, pull down . . ." It was she who first read me that line of Pound's, triumphantly, one afternoon in the Barnard library.

She didn't do well at school. Learning was a focusing of everything upon a single object. She couldn't reconcile her intellectual passions with the need to get by through ful-filling requirements. Her Freshman English paper was to be an exegesis of T. S. Eliot's *Four Quartets*. If there was vanity in her, it was in that kind of choice — always something fatally difficult.

Over and over she read those poems, tracking down every conceivable reference attached to an image — and still they would not give up their meaning. It remained sealed inside Eliot's words. "Garlic and sapphire in the mud..." What could you say with finality about that? She handed in the paper weeks after the term was over; the instructor changed her Incomplete to a C.

And then there was Psychology I, where, under the influ-ence of Pavlov and Skinner, she became convinced that it would be possible to condition the mimosa to retract its sen-sitive leaves in response to sound. This could be achieved by coupling the human touch with the ringing of a little bell over an extended period, then gradually using the hand less and less. The gentlest, most poetic of experiments. Perhaps it could even have been successful. But Elise hadn't figured on the mortality of the mimosa, so the results remained in-conclusive.

Her instructor in philosophy, however, was sympathetic. Alex Greer was an anomaly himself at Barnard, a fish out of water. For one thing, he was young, only on the verge of thirty — although to girls as young as we were, that of course seemed old. He was friendly — perhaps too friendly, his de-partment felt — with his students, walking away from his lectures in a cluster of excited girls who'd follow him into his office or into luncheonettes on Broadway, offering up their confidences or, more accurately, themselves — if only he'd notice. But he was married. Unhappily. An interesting air of potential disaster hung about him like the perpetual smoke from his cigarettes, which he was always running out of and endearingly borrowing, and there was a drag in his gait, a suggestion of woundedness. There was debate about his features, which were oddly assorted and also indefinite — you'd remember Alex as much uglier than he was, or much handsomer. He had the pallor of late nights, and grey Chinese eyes, and a way of crumpling up his jacket and slinging it over one shoulder as he walked across the campus. One girl noticed an enormous rip in his shirt all the way down the back.

For five years he'd been completing his dissertation on Kierkegaard, subjecting it to heroic overhauls as new perceptions forced re-examinations of his thesis. His doctoral degree eluded him; his job at Barnard was in jeopardy. It was whispered that his wife was having an affair. He was a thrilling teacher, a born synthesizer — in a single lecture he could invoke Plato and Freud and Proust and B. F. Skinner and even Mahler and Hesse. In one class he made the amazing revelation that he had been raised by his mother as a Christian Scientist, and would have died of meningitis when he was seven if his father hadn't intervened and called a doctor. He directed troubled students to sources of inexpensive psychotherapy, and comforted them with a line or two from Yeats: "And only God, my dear, will love you for yourself alone, and not your yellow hair." Elise was Crazy Jane. To her he quoted: "For nothing can be sole or whole / That has not been rent."

Of course she fell in love with him. But where Alex Greer's other students took in stride the crush on the teacher which was only a little game one played with one's imagination — a game just slightly less a fantasy than picking a movie hero to have a crush on — Elise's passion became tormentingly real, self-abnegating devotion. Since it was unthinkable that Alex could desire her, she offered her services.

His household was in disarray as his marriage splintered: His wife was more and more absent; he needed a baby sitter for his two-year-old son. He couldn't afford to pay her very much, he pointed out. It didn't matter, Elise said in her low, embarrassed voice. She needed to get away from her parents' house anyhow. "Read anything you want here," he told her.

"Borrow any book. Eat anything you can find in the refrigerator."

He had an apartment on the ground floor of a building on 112th Street. It was like an apartment at the bottom of a well — midnight even on a sunny day. The door was never locked. You never knew whom you'd find there. Psychologists, Dixieland jazz musicians, poets, runaway girls, a madman named Carl Solomon whom an old Columbia classmate of Alex's, Allen Ginsberg, had met in a psychiatric ward. I recognized it immediately as a private Waldorf. They came and went even when Alex himself wasn't around. They left ashes and dregs of coffee; they made telephone calls to psychiatrists and estranged parents and had nervous breakdowns on the sagging couch in the living room. A week of dishes accumulated in the sink. The phonograph played "Songs of a Wanderer" and Billie Holiday and Stravinsky. The baby, bare-bottomed, ran from room to room, dragging a dirty teddy bear by the ear; he looked out the window and said, "It's dark in the bye-bye." He clung around Elise's neck and twisted her hair in his fists and said, "Where mommy where mommy where mommy."

Sometimes there would be desperation parties thrown at the last minute, and more people would come. There'd be lots of running out for beer and dancing and Alex jumping up on furniture and waving his arms, drunkenly conducting entire symphonies or running after girls with absurd insistence — never Elise, but aloof debutanteish ones with Frenchified nicknames like "Folie" or "Bichette," always enigmatically just back from Paris. Alex was not immune to the Gatsbyism of the period. He saw himself more as Dick Diver, though. Elise and I read Alex's copy of Tender Is the Night in the same week and were shaken by Dick Diver's fadeout into the increasingly obscure towns of upstate New York. Was that to be the eventual fate of Alex?

Sometimes Alex's wife Sally would return for a few days. Reconciliations would be attempted. They'd lock themselves away from everyone, or they'd decide to attempt going out like a couple on a date — and Elise would come down from Washington Heights to stay with the baby. Sally was the daughter of a college president. She had all the nervous finishing-school charm of the girls Alex ran after at parties. But it was like a glaze over anguish. She'd sit in her own living room like a visitor and chatter distractedly about her recent adventures looking for an apartment; or she'd be the faculty wife for a minute or two and force herself to ask you interested questions about your studies. One weekend, with Elise's help, she painted all the insides of the kitchen cabinets red, but fled abruptly on Sunday night because the baby ran away when she tried to hold him on her lap.

She loved, but was bent on leaving, Alex — no one quite understood why. It had been viewed as one of the brilliant marriages of their circle at Columbia. There seemed an element of willfulness and waste here, something threatening to all the other university couples. It was like hearing friends had been in a senseless accident, and feeling your own vulnerability. She wasn't even leaving him for another man, but for something so crazy and inexplicable she was naturally going into analysis to get at the root of it: the need to be alone.

There is a winter night that from this distance looks inevitable.

Lying under an old army blanket in her sweater and half-slip, Elise is stretched out on the couch in Alex's living room. The skirt she'll wear to classes tomorrow is folded over a chair; her glasses are on the coffee table. She decides finally to remove the sweater, too. She decides — sitting up to yank it off, shivering when she gets back under the blanket. It's so late the heat went off hours ago. Too late even now for her to go home on the subway. She'd told her parents she's baby-sitting for the Greers again, but it's only Alex who'll come in the door eventually.

The call from him had been desperate. Would she come down to stay with the kid? He had to get out of the house, he had to think, put himself in motion. She thinks of him, grey-faced, roaming the streets of the city in the snow that's softly hitting the windows.

She's scared a little — only because she can't measure her own hunger. Sometimes just talking to him, she feels faint with it; her body opens to him secretly. She's only slept with one person so far, and that was two years ago, and this will be different — very. No hope of anything, but just the thing itself.

She's protected, she thinks, by that clarity.

Asking nothing, she will give herself over. Love must be total. If you love someone, you must also love those others he loves, as she for instance loves Sally without jealousy.

She does, she's capable of that larger tenderness. That is her purity and her hidden pride.

5

7 WROTE AN EXERCISE in description for Exposition, Structure and Style, a course I took in my sophomore year:

SCENE: A friend's room.

MOOD: Sordid, shabby, mirroring disgust and disinterest of owner.

RELEVANT DETAILS:

Cigarette butts on floor.

Harsh blue paint flaking off in places, revealing dirty white paint underneath.

Seat of armchair lumpy where springs are starting to come through; floral design of slipcover faded in places to blur of yellow.

Brownish discoloration of wall above rusty gas burner.

Cheap mirror that distorts every image; glass almost black where nearest frame.

Pictures Scotch-taped on wall; one dangling forlornly, hanging by a taped corner.

IRRELEVANT DETAILS:

Pink quilt on bed.

Portable typewriter standing in corner.

Photo of mother and father in Miami on bureau.

The teacher was a storybook professor with a hyphenated name followed by a Roman numeral who wore tweeds of a remarkable pinkish grey, set off by velvet silver-buttoned vests. He wrote in the margin: "Don't you get any joy out of life? Think you're a little existentialist or something?"

The scene described was on the top floor of a rooming house on 108th Street. It was the place Elise had just moved into. My concept of relevance, I see, was rather unformed. Nothing could have been more relevant than the photo of Mr. and Mrs. Cowen.

Elise's room had other meanings for me besides sordidness and disgust. I envied the courage it represented. Nineteen-year-old girls did not leave home except for dormitories or marriage. If you wished to live free, you could not also expect to live well. You entered a world where janitors refused to give you clean sheets and Puerto Rican hookers screamed in courtyards. You were in danger of celebrating Thanksgiving with a solitary Turkey Special in Bickford's Cafeteria on Broadway.

On 108th Street, Elise slipped into amorphousness as if dream life was absorbing everyday reality and she couldn't manage to rouse herself without enormous effort. She seemed to lose entire days, missing classes, forgetting to meet me for lunch at Chock Full o' Nuts, forgetting to show up for the job in the stacks of the Columbia library that was supposed to feed her and pay her rent of $7.50 a week.

Alex's apartment was the most reliable place to find her. They were sleeping together, but it was somehow not a love affair. They were like friends who sometimes huddled together for warmth. There were other men, too, whom she'd tell me about but whom I never saw. One-time strangers she'd meet in the West End or other bars on Broadway and bring back to 108th Street with her — mostly because she was lonely.

Columbia had spawned a large outcast population. Students whose official connection with the university had been severed, sometimes years before, but who could not bring themselves to move away. They inhabited cheap rooming houses like Elise's, or enormous residence hotels, like the Yorkshire on Broadway and 113th Street, that had electric-blue rooms and fluorescent lighting and filthy community kitchens where every quart of milk in the refrigerator had a different name inked on the container. Alex's friend Carl Solomon lived in the Yorkshire. He was a large, alarmingly gentle man who once walked up to me at one of Alex's parties and demanded, "Tell me, how much do you weigh?" as if it were a matter of the greatest urgency. He had published a brilliant account of his time on a mental ward in a magazine Alex showed Elise and me called *Neurotica*. As springtime approached, Carl had tried to get a job as a Good Humor man and was turned down. Shortly afterward he'd flipped out in his room, and was taken away to Rockland Hospital. From then on, I had a horror of the Yorkshire. It was the place people went for crackups, for suicides, for defeats. I vowed I'd never live there, whatever happened to me. But despite my knowledge of the dark side of the neighborhood, my own life was anticlimactically staid.

I didn't even come close to being one of the Charleston crowd. I studied hard and anxiously, I lived at home and never stayed out all night. The repressed boy I picked to fall in love with never went beyond hand-holding and a ceremonial rather than passionate good-night kiss. I was awfully confused by this boy, who never so much as put his hand on my breast even for a second. I was afraid that if I tried to encourage him, he'd think I was disgusting. Frank's parents seemed more enthusiastic about our relationship than he was; it was they who plied me with invitations to come to dinner. To demonstrate their acceptance of me, they'd ask me questions about "the Jewish faith," which they seemed to feel was more colorful than their own. They lived in an enormous apartment on Park Avenue and would always call the livery service around the corner for a chauffeured limousine to take me back to 116th Street.

One Saturday night the limousine took Frank and me to the Village. Our destination was Rienzi's, an espresso place on MacDougal Street. I hadn't been down there in months, and it seemed strange to walk those familiar streets in my high-heeled pumps and my collegiate sophistication. At the corner of Waverly Place, a man in an ankle-length black overcoat covered with dust was going through a garbage can. I recognized him from the Waldorf — a famous Village scavenger known as Swamp Rat. He looked up and smiled at me through his matted beard. "Heidi-heidi-ho!" he said warmly.

"Oh, hi," I muttered.

Frank had dropped my arm and was halfway down the block. "You *know* him?" There was something unpleasantly rhetorical about Frank's question, as if he'd suspected all along that I would know such people.

We broke up after I took him to a party at Alex's. We stood and argued on an island in the middle of Broadway, with cars whizzing past on both sides. "My theme is Growth," he actually said. "Your theme is Decadence and Decay."

I wept over this unfairly contemptuous accusation, but I recognized its truth. I *was* attracted to decadence, if that meant people like Alex and Elise. I had little respect for respectability. I was sure only cowardice kept me on the straight and narrow.

Elise vanished one week that fall. I left notes at the rooming house, looked for her at Alex's — but not even he had seen her. Early one morning I cut my first class and walked down to 108th Street.

There was a light under her door. I kept knocking. At last I heard her steps and she let me in. She was wearing flannel pajamas with little blue roses printed on them. There was a bloodstain on one of the sleeves.

I said, "Elise, what happened to your wrists?" because both of them were bandaged.

She said she'd slipped in someone's bathroom and cut herself on some broken glass — it was really all quite stupid. They'd had to take stitches. She told me all this in rapid, brittle tones. It was like a second voice almost. "The doctor thought it was a suicide attempt. He wanted to call the police. Can you imagine? And isn't it amazing that suicide is illegal when society is so indifferent to human life?"

I agreed. It was amazing.

She'd been sleeping before I came, but every light in that blue room was burning. The torn window shade flapped against the sill. She asked me what it was like outside. There was clothing all over the floor; moving very slowly, she picked up underwear, jeans, a sweater. This was how it was to wake up here. "I wish you smoked, Glassmangirl," she sighed. I said I'd run out for cigarettes but she said no. She sifted through a couple of ashtrays and finally selected a longish butt. "This is an Alex habit," she told me, with a smile that was like a flicker of pain.

When you were hung up on someone, you said his name a lot — it was like a little reference point that was always there. No matter what the conversation was, the name would always crop up in it. If someone you loved didn't love you, would you want to die?

Recently Elise and I had discussed suicide and had agreed that there might be points in your life when it could present itself as one of the honorable alternatives. Death could be your proud refusal to come to terms with the existence that had been meted out to you. Or there was the view Alex had once expressed that one could view self-destruction as the opposite of apathy, the final proof that one could still function. We'd quoted Dorothy Parker to each other on the various methods one could employ to do oneself in, and giggled nervously.

When my grandmother had died the year before, I'd learned there had been a suicide in my own family. My grandfather hadn't died of illness. He'd put his head in a gas oven one day when he was only thirty-five. In Warsaw he'd been a poet and scholar; in this country he'd found no identity, only jobs as a laborer, and he was bad at that kind of work. Some time in 1908 he'd injured his hands — perhaps deliberately. That was when he'd killed himself, leaving my grandmother with four children.

My mother and aunts had always told me, "You're just like your grandfather. He was very artistic." But for fifty years they'd thought of his death as shameful. They burned all the papers of his my grandmother had kept. They said they were "private." And anyway they were all in Yiddish and Hebrew — you'd have to go to strangers to find out what was in them.

I'd thought a lot about my grandfather after that — not as a grandfather so much as a tragic young man like someone I might have known around Columbia. The riddle of his death seemed almost a gift — it was as if I'd inherited a poem.

Still I wasn't ready to believe that suicide could be real. I wanted it to remain literary. A remote, forbidden act that you only heard about, that only a stranger could commit.

We went out to Broadway and walked up to Chock Full o' Nuts. I bought Elise a cup of coffee because all she had was seven cents. I lent her a dollar, which was all I had.

She said she had something to tell me. She was dropping out of Barnard for a while and moving back to Washington Heights. Her father was coming that afternoon with his car, so she had to get boxes and pack up all her stuff.

I couldn't bear the thought of Elise giving up like this — as if her parents, waiting for her to be defeated, had been right all along. "You'll come back, won't you?"

"There's something I have to do first. I'm going into analysis. They're going to pay for it. But they won't if I don't live at home. I can't blame them," she said, with that quick, painful smile again, "for wanting a daughter."

"Oh, how her parents must feel," my mother said when I told her Elise was going into analysis. Because although in circles like Alex's, analysis had the status of a cult, it was considered by most people disgraceful — something one could not mention to the neighbors.

"There's something not right about that girl. I hope you'll have sense enough now to make some other little friends."

"What do you mean, *sense enough?*" I shouted, and

slammed the door of my room. I wasn't sure why I'd told her anyway. Was I obliquely trying to tell her something about myself? There seemed so little truth in our relationship that I felt orphaned.

I didn't see Elise for the first few weeks after she'd moved home. One day she took the subway downtown and met me after classes. She'd put on weight in Washington Heights, and her face had erupted violently. We walked over to Alex's, where she was supposed to baby-sit that night, and let ourselves in. The apartment was dark and empty. We rummaged for clean cups in the kitchen and made instant coffee.

Alex, Elise said matter-of-factly, had a date with someone. But that was all right, she said. It really was. He was going to lend her books she needed. She intended to read all of Freud. What better thing could one do in Washington Heights? In the afternoons she worked in her father's office. She went to the analyst three times a week. She was getting along with her mother — "poor little Mummy." There was the distance, as she told me all this, of the patient observing her own recovery, holding her hands to the light, looking in the mirror to see the bones behind the flesh.

The clinic had a waiting list, but they'd taken her right away — "I guess I convinced them I was an interesting patient." Each session cost exactly the weekly rent of her old room. Elise had doubts about the analyst she'd been assigned to, but knew such thoughts were not constructive. And anyway she'd resolved to study Freud herself — that would make up for any deficiencies in her analyst's perceptions.

I remember saying something to Elise I immediately regretted. "Someday — just to see what it's like — I'd like to go to an analyst a couple of times."

I did mean it. It was as far as I could go. I was always wanting to see what things were like. It was my way of protecting myself against them.

Her face flushed, her voice shook. "You can't ever 'know what it's like.' Not like that, Glassmangirl."

*

To know what life was like. Real life. My very name seemed a metaphor for what I saw at seventeen as my unique apartness. *Glassman, Glassgirl.*

Years later, my ten-year-old son startled me by his description of his feelings during a bus ride he had taken with classmates. Something sort of weird had happened, he said, hard to talk about. He didn't seem exactly troubled by it, more bemused. "See, all the kids except me were horsing around, acting ridiculous. And I just sat there watching. It was like I was looking through a window and they were all on the other side."

I said, "A lot of people feel that way."

"A *lot?*" he said, unconvinced, uncomforted, just as I would have been.

I READ THE WORDS *Beat Generation* for the first time sitting in my parents' living room. It was November 16, 1952. Earlier that morning, my father had gone out for the Sunday *Times,* as he always did, returning also with coffee cake from the bakery. As usual I'd grabbed the magazine section to look through it as fast as I could before he took it over, sitting down with his dictionary and atlas to do the crossword puzzle, which would take him most of the morning and sometimes into the afternoon. It gave my father particular pleasure to enlist my aid in this. As his college-student daughter, I was his literary consultant. "When (blank) wood do come to Dunsinane," he'd call out.

On this particular Sunday, an article by a writer named John Clellon Holmes immediately caught my attention. Entitled "This Is the Beat Generation," it was a declaration of faith in a state of mind that, although new, according to this article, was totally familiar to me: "Everyone I knew," Holmes wrote, "felt it in one way or another — that bottled eagerness for talk, for joy, for excitement, for sensation, for new truths. Whatever the reason, everyone of my age had a look of impatience and expectation in his eyes that bespoke ungiven love, unreleased ecstasy and the presence of buried worlds within."

Of course Holmes was writing about people at least Alex's

age, who did things Elise and I would never do, such as hanging around Forty-second Street, and all of them, besides, were men. But wasn't this "bottled eagerness" exactly what we felt? Could we be somehow more a part of the Beat Generation than of the Silent one we'd been born into chronologically?

That strangely used word *Beat* was immediately arresting. For one thing, it was blatantly ungrammatical. Did it mean "beaten"? Did it mean that there was a whole generation that moved to the vibrations of a particular rhythm — some kind of new music, perhaps, like the bebop Alex sometimes went down to Birdland to hear? The people Holmes described were in fact beaten down — down to "the bedrock of consciousness," achieving a desperate beauty that seemed to be a kind of triumph. Holmes did not take credit for coining the phrase; with great scrupulousness he attributed it to a fellow writer and hipster named Jack Kerouac.

The previous spring the same John Clellon Holmes had published a novel entitled *Go*. Alex had gone out and bought it right away. He'd stayed up all of one night reading it and passed it around to a number of friends, including Elise. He'd actually known a couple of the characters — the poet David Stofsky was Allen Ginsberg in real life; and there was also Agatson, who represented a dead man named Cannastra who'd been famous for giving wild parties during which he danced on broken glass, and who in 1948 had inexplicably tried to climb out the window of a moving subway and been decapitated. Alex never said whether he'd met the young writer Holmes called Gene Pasternak.

Go seemed much more to Alex than a roman à clef. There are books that serve as mirrors in which one catches reflections of oneself. He admitted he identified with the narrator Paul Hobbes, a young intellectual dissatisfied with the middle-class life he's unable to give up, both awestruck and threatened by Stofsky and Pasternak, as well as by a Neal Cassady character named Harte Kennedy, who appear to reject all traditional values. *Go* ends with Hobbes alone with his wife on the deck of a Staten Island ferry the night he hears of Agatson's senseless death; he stands at the railing staring at the darkened shoreline, the myriad lights of Manhattan, asking himself, "Where is our home?" It was the very question which haunted Alex — and for which the Beat Generation and the generations that came afterward would fail to supply adequate answers.

Perhaps in the throes of his excitement over *Go*, Alex — always in the avant-garde of the Columbia community — had arranged an unusual adventure that spring for himself and a few of his friends.

Summoned one evening to Alex's apartment, Elise and several others had solemnly passed around skinny little cigarettes filled with marijuana, which they smoked down to the last ash, choking on the long inhalations. Alex then led them on an excursion to Palisades Amusement Park, where they rode the roller coaster and Ferris wheel. They returned, groggily, to 112th Street, where more reefer was passed around, and a discussion then ensued about food. It was decided to make Campbell's tomato soup, but it was a very long time before anyone actually went into the kitchen and made any. This occasioned a remark by one of the guests that was widely quoted for a while around Columbia: "It takes *hours* to make Campbell's soup." Later Elise explained to me gravely that this observation epitomized a peculiar feature of the marijuana experience — its remarkable and often quite humorous slowing down of time.

The experiment was not tried again. The marijuana experience was another one I only heard about second hand.

*M*EMORY IS STRANGE. If I look at the spring of 1953, I can remember no Saturday-night goings-out in my own life with any specificity. I remember instead a date of Elise's. I recall even what she wore for this occasion: a red cotton dress, sleeveless and full-skirted, primly tight at the waist. It was her favorite dress, although she was self-conscious about the color: "red as the side of a brick shithouse." Her hair was still long then, and she released it this once from its rubber band.

She had met someone at a party at Alex's. A poet. All this unusual preparation was for him.

There's a photo of Allen Ginsberg from around that time, on the cover of his published journals. When I saw it recently in a bookshop, I noticed something that had never struck me before. They could have been born into the same family, brother and sister, they looked so much alike. Their broad foreheads and somewhat heart-shaped faces, the vulnerability at the corners of their mouths, their same darkness. They even wore nearly identical black-rimmed glasses, through which their large brown eyes absorbed the world nearsightedly.

He doesn't come uptown for her. She takes the subway to the Village where he's waiting, and they walk through those blocks that were the geography of my adolescent yearnings to the San Remo Bar, where an amazing number of people seem to know him. This is where the subterraneans are, Allen says — he has the scholarly gentleness of a guide. Here recently he'd had a disappointing encounter with Dylan Thomas, who was much too drunk to discuss poetry with an unknown young man and was merely looking for girls. But there is more to this tour. There is Fugazi's next, on Sixth Avenue, much darker and quieter, where musicians and hipsters sit frozen and drugged on bar stools. The women here, Elise notices, are all beautiful and have such remarkable cool that they never, never say a word; they are presences merely. But she herself is tormented by speechlessness. Why can't she say more? What must he think of her? She's choked in her red dress, stupefied with feeling — quite the reverse of cool, oh not cool at all as finally they walk eastward on Eighth Street, much further east than she's ever been before, crossing the Bowery, which is like the dark, outermost boundary of the Village, the point at which Eighth Street changes its name to St. Marks Place and becomes a little Europe of tenements. He lives somewhere in this unknown area.

In his journal the previous year, Allen Ginsberg had written a self-mocking, capsulized autobiography:

A Novel

At 14 I was an introvert, an atheist, a Communist and a Jew, and I still wanted to be president of the United States.

At 19, being no longer a virgin, I was a cocksucker and believed in a supreme reality, an anarchist, a hipster totally apolitical Reichian! I wanted to be a great poet instead.

At 22 I was a hallucinating mystic believing in the City of God and I wanted to be a saint.

At 23, a year later, I was already a criminal, a despairing sinner, a dope fiend; I wanted to get to reality.

74

At 24, after being a jailbird, a schizoid screwball in the bughouse, I got layed, girls, I was being psychoanalyzed.

At 26, I am shy, go out with girls, I write poetry, I am a freelance literary agent and a registered democrat; I want to find a job.

Who cares?

He met Elise just as his already extraordinary life of many changes was about to change again. He was to give up his attempts to be "normal," give up psychoanalysis and attempts to hold straight jobs or to be straight sexually. He was about to go to Mexico, then to San Francisco, where he would fall in love with a blond eighteen-year-old boy named Peter Orlovsky and where he would break with literary traditions and discover in writing *Howl* his own voice as a poet.

And yet there's something between Allen and my friend Elise, that instant knowing which can exist like a mysterious current between two people. He accepts her in her Crazy Jane-ness, somehow encompasses her — whereas Alex had simply observed.

"He seems to think I'm very deep," Elise remarked wryly afterward, shrugging it off because maybe it was safer not to believe it.

As if they are making a spiraling descent in their slow progress from the San Remo to Fugazi's and then eastward, they stop briefly in the Sagamore, an infamous all-night cafeteria on the edge of the Bowery — a place that like the Waldorf will shortly go out of existence. A cafeteria for the real poor. Nothing voluntary in the destitution of the bums and old people who are its main customers, or the furtive desperation of the petty-criminal types who also pass through there, second-story men, small-time drug dealers.

Allen discovers Elise knows Carl Solomon, and tells her of his own first meeting with Carl three years before in a corridor at New York State Psychiatric Institute, where they were both patients. "Who are *you*?" Carl Solomon had demanded. "I'm Myshkin," Allen answered. Carl had introduced himself as Kirilov.

All his life, Allen has been on familiar terms with madness. His mother, Naomi — once beautiful, once a dedicated communist, a woman who played the piano for her sons — has been in and out of mental institutions since he was a boy; has had shock treatments, been lobotomized. "My mother's in Madtown," Allen says, as if Madtown is no different than Brooklyn or Forty-second Street — a destination you must always count in as a possibility for yourself. Perhaps in Elise he sees Naomi. "I've always been attracted to intellectual madwomen," he confesses in his journal six years later, including Elise in that category.

He takes her home that first night to his apartment on East Seventh Street and they make love — an act his analyst would have approved of and hers might have viewed quite negatively. More wildness, more lack of self-respect and even of self-preservation — this too-quick nakedness, this giving yourself over to a stranger. She's done this too many times before, finding not love but only confirmation of worthlessness.

But this has a different meaning.

Elise speaks of Allen in a surprising way a few weeks later. "Allen is my intercessor," she says.

An extraordinary statement from a girl who was a Jewish atheist. She was still influenced by T. S. Eliot, although she was about to relinquish him; lately she had also been reading some Provençal poet for whom the intercessor was the loved one rather than the Virgin Mary. For Elise, it was Allen who became the holy figure who could intercede in her behalf with a wrathful God. It seemed a dangerous way to think of someone in the twentieth century.

Nonetheless . . . *intercessor.* That was the meaning of Allen in Elise's life, from the very beginning.

She had read *Go*, of course. Maybe that idea of Allen started there, with Stofsky:

> A vision! A vision! The words kept stinging into his consciousness like quickening waves of fever. As he went on, almost running now, he found himself haunted by the odd uprush of pity and rage that had taken control of him during the moment in the bookstore. It was love! he cried inside himself. A molecular ectoplasm hurtling through everything like a wild, bright light! And they were afraid, almost as if they all suspected. He had seen it clearly in an instant of pure clarity: the chemical warm love that swam thickly beneath their dread

For Elise in her own dread of lovelessness, her fear that she will never be found acceptable, never never fit, be outcast even among outcasts; for Elise who feels herself to be a shadow, Nada, voiceless — coming upon this passage as she turns a page in some midnight solitude is like having a window open up inside her, an illumination of hope. If a Stofsky exists, then there are counterparts for herself. Counterparts even in the self-loathing and despair that strangely seem the source of such visions.

> He had had visions! He knew, at last, what his mad, forlorn mother, "who had slept with the devil," had tried to tell him. He had had revelations! And suddenly he was frightened of being alone, as if exercising a last, failing perception of himself. It pained him mortally that he should be alone now, and some of his usual self-consciousness returned. Nobody cared when a man went mad, he thought nonsensically, sadly; but as he threw on his clothes, he laughed and laughed.

77

That tipping of the scales toward life, at the very moment when the self seems nearly extinct! To read this and then meet him! There must have been for Elise a deceptive elimination of that first necessary distance between people — a kind of jet lag of the spirit. Hurtled somewhere too quickly, you can lose your bearings.

Allen Ginsberg believed in nakedness as the best defense against the world. A self-exposure so pure and indiscriminate, so total, that no room would be left for interpretation. No legend but in the passing moment's reality.

Thus Elise was a moment in Allen's life. In Elise's life, Allen was an eternity.

6

In a "DREAM LETTER" from John Clellon Holmes recorded by Allen Ginsberg in 1954 are the words: "The social organization which is most true of itself to the artist is the boy gang." To which Allen, awakening, writing into his journal, added sternly, "Not society's perfum'd marriage."

The messages of the real Holmes seem to have remained consistent with those of the dream one. Even in 1977, after years of a stable and sustaining second marriage, after all the messages of Women's Liberation that so battered the consciousness of the seventies, Holmes wrote in his preface to a new edition of *Go*: "Did we really resemble these feverish young men, these centerless young women, awkwardly reaching out for love, for hope, for comprehension of their lives and times?" And whereas he scrupulously matches each of the male characters in his roman à clef to their originals, the "girls" are variously "amalgams of several people"; "accurate to the young women of the time"; "a type rather than an individual." He can't quite remember them — they were mere anonymous passengers on the big Greyhound bus of experience. Lacking centers, how could they burn with the fever that infected his young men? What they did, I guess, was fill up the seats.

*

It's a crisp September morning, the beginning of yet another academic year. The grey-haired, craggy-faced, perhaps self-consciously Lincolnesque professor enters the small class-room where his girl students await him. There's a proper hush as he takes his place behind the oak table, circa 1910, lays out his sharpened pencils, his roll book containing their names, his two slim volumes of something or other — must be the latest in criticism. Intimidated in advance, the girl students study this man's glamorously American Gothic features, looking for signs of humor or mercy. Can he be gotten around? They will be judged by this Professor X, the big fish in the rather smallish pond that is the Barnard English Department.

Picture this middle-aged man, who no doubt wishes he were standing before a class at Harvard — *that* would count for something. There will be few compensations for the spirit here, much less the eye, in teaching this new frumpy lot of young females — rumpled, pasty girls who've dived into the laundry bag for something to wear to class. Only one slouching beauty with a tangle of auburn hair and a glory of freckles, as well as — perhaps he notices imme-diately — extraordinary knees, can possibly redeem this se-mester for him.

He wrenches his gaze away from her and begins. Ha! Let's try this question on 'em, he thinks. He rises to his full six feet, the more to heighten the little drama of this open-ing moment.

"Well" — his tone is as dry as the crackers in the Amer-ican cultural barrel — "how many of you girls want to be writers?"

He watches with sardonic amusement as one hand flies up confusedly, then another, till all fifteen are flapping. Here and there an engagement ring sparkles.

The air is thick with the uneasiness of the girl students. Why is Professor X asking this? He knows his course is re-quired of all creative-writing majors.

"Well, I'm sorry to see this," says Professor X, the Mel-ville and Hawthorne expert. "Very sorry. Because" — there's a steel glint in his cold eye — "first of all, if you were going to be writers, you wouldn't be enrolled in this class. You couldn't even be enrolled in school. You'd be hopping freight trains, riding through America."

The received wisdom of 1953.

The young would-be writers in this room have understood instantly that of course there is no hope. One by one their hands have all come down.

I was one of those who'd raised hers.

The social organization which is most true of itself to the artist is the girl gang.

Why, everyone would agree, that's absolutely absurd!

By January of 1954, Allen Ginsberg is on the move in the Yucatán. First in Chichen Itza, where lying high on para-codeine in a hammock in the great ruin at El Castillo he stares into the Mayan night and sees "Naomi's face, young and darkhaired, at a piano at a party, close up, facing me, svelte and in rapport with life." The past gets carried along in the form of dreams as the present unrolls in the jungles and lonely mountain roads and crumbling pyramids of ancient cities where every sight is totally new. In Tacalapan, a dream of a party in New York, a "gathering of souls" — Jack, Lucien, Bill, and others — "all posturing terrifically gay or tragic." At Acavalna, a vision of "the word Time — like a great silver wall blocking the sky," and a fleeting recollection of a young blond hustler encountered in the Astor Bar near Times Square.

Broke in Salto de Agua in mid-May. A muddy garden there where meat hangs dripping from the branches of flowering trees. And on across the lunar landscape of Coatzacoalcos to Mexico City, empty now of Bill Burroughs and the dead, witty Joan. The feeling that Joan has somehow been abandoned to this place. Allen walks Orizaba Street looking

81

for her ghost. In all this merging, the wellspring of new imagery.

As he crosses the border into California in June, making the notation "Enter U.S. alone naked with knapsack, watch, camera, poem, beard," he appears to resemble exactly that archetypal male vagabond/writer of Professor X's imaginings, but for *naked*, that angelic and androgynizing word.

J WAS EIGHTEEN in the spring of 1954. For Professor X's writing class, I was keeping a journal. I filled many of its pages with descriptions of Alex Greer and the circle of people who collected around him, whom I called "the community." The enchantment I'd felt when I was sixteen was giving way to a harsher view:

> The members of "the community" are very much afraid. They are afraid of bouncing checks, rejection slips, institutional hierarchies, middle-class backgrounds, sexual failure and schizophrenia. I think it is schizophrenia that frightens them the most; this threat seems to them more imminent than any other. They believe it is entirely possible that anyone of their number may someday "become schiz."
>
> "Did you know that D. was schiz? His mother was too. When he was four, he burnt down the house by setting fire to the baskets she made in occupational therapy. Isn't that fabulous?" The room trembles with uneasy laughter and someone says, "My God, I nearly flipped today myself!"

In another entry I declared:

> I do not want to become too entangled with "the
> community." The people attract me, but, in a way,
> they are all slowly dying, and I do not want to
> die. Yes, I will observe. Elise wants to belong, how-
> ever. She has always needed to be part of some-
> thing. Elise watches wistfully as they play their
> dangerous games, killing time between now and
> the final disaster.
>
> The role of observer has its advantages. You
> may play as much of a part in the group as you
> wish, but when you are drawn in a little too tightly,
> you can always say, "Well after all, I'm just an
> observer," and step back into safety again.

For some months I'd been going steady with a boy who
wasn't a member of "the community" but only another
eighteen-year-old like me. We seemed always to be standing
in hallways, listening for the elevator, with our hands inside each other's clothes.

Our major problem as lovers came down to having no
place to go. In comparison, even contraception seemed con-
querable. Steven, a biology major at Columbia, read up on
the efficacy of condoms, the amazing capacity of rubber to
withstand enormous pressures. He planned, I think, to marry
me after we had both graduated. I don't think I exactly
planned to marry him, although sometimes I really thought
I might. It seemed a progression so entirely inevitable you
could enter into it almost without thinking and wake up
one rainy morning to find yourself a graduate student's wife
in some bleak Sears, Roebuck apartment out in Iowa or
Indiana.

We went to bed at last at Alex's, where ostensibly we were
baby-sitting — fooling nobody. I'd come up with this solution after consulting with Elise. What would Alex think? I
asked. I was perhaps overly preoccupied with what Alex
thought. In some way I wanted to serve notice I was no

longer the child he took me for. Somewhere inside me, waiting to make her appearance any minute now, was the person I really was.

Elise was waiting with Alex that night when Steven and I arrived at 112th Street. What a wonderful opportunity this was to go to the movies, Alex said, although a storm of monsoon proportions was raging outside. He couldn't thank us enough. We all chatted formally, nervously, for a few minutes. It was a little the way you'd chat with parents. "We won't be back before midnight," Alex told us as they left. Elise hugged me and whispered, "We put fresh sheets on the bed."

Alex's bedroom was tidier than I had ever seen it — as if made up for company. Across the hall, his little boy was fast asleep. Steven closed the door and turned out the light, and we took our clothes off in the dark. "Don't be afraid," he said. He took a Trojan out of the little package he'd brought with him and insisted on blowing it up into an enormous pale balloon, so I could empirically see there was nothing to fear.

Between the sheets we explored each other and he lay on top of me as he had in the park. Except the bed and the bareness of our bodies solemnified everything. *"Now?"* he said. I said okay and he put himself into me, pushing and pumping, surprising me by the force of it. My mind jumped to Lorca's play *Blood Wedding*, which I had just read, and the bloodstained sheets hung out the window for all the village to see. He shuddered against me and cried out a little and it was over. Lying there, I was troubled by an entirely new question: Was this all there was?

New York was empty that summer by the beginning of July. "The community" had scattered. Everyone seemed to have some place to go outside New York. Steven had gone to Woods Hole to study marine biology. He wrote me love letters with mournful hound-dog faces sketched under his name. Elise, too, had gone — to be a counselor in a camp for girls upstate, a respite from Washington Heights. We corresponded a lot. We were both reading Henry James, I remember. *The Ambassadors.* Elise lost her copy and I sent her another in the mail so that we could write to each other about Lambert Strether's renunciation of Madame Vionnet, a fictional event that quite overwhelmed the two of us. The notion of the renunciation of passion, the moral ecstasy of self-denial in order to do "the right thing," seemed exquisitely compelling. More and more, as the summer wore on, it seemed as if James's message had peculiar relevance for me.

I had a summer job at a branch of IBM on 114th Street, where I copied numbers onto forms that were put into a key-punch machine. It was an office of middle-aged women who brought their lunches in bags. I went out for mine, sticking my card in the time clock. You were paid strictly by the hour. I got into the habit of dropping over to see Alex, who was also stranded in the city. I had never spent time alone with him before. Returning to IBM, I'd be flushed and wide-eyed in the ladies'-room mirror; I'd sit down at my desk hardly conscious of the numbers swimming under my pen from one piece of paper to another as the clock crept toward five.

My lunches became more and more extended. In the grip of my Jamesian agony, I'd talk to Alex for hours about my parents, my writing, my ambivalence about music — which he seemed to find especially fascinating, always putting on different records as if to find the one that might cure me of it. "Listen," he'd say. His hand would make a conductor's gesture, then come to rest on my shoulder, calling my attention to a particular passage in Shostakovich or Stravinsky. I'd really try to listen in the precise way he meant, but secretly be hopelessly awash in his grey eyes, his thin, amused mouth. Sometimes he'd take me for long aimless walks up past Columbia under the elevated tracks of the subway into the edges of Harlem.

"We have a rapport," he joked once as we waited to cross Broadway, "like Tennessee Williams and Carson McCullers." I was filled with instant confusion and disappointment.

"What kind of rapport is that?" He pulled me to him for a moment. "Oh, you know, don't you? A perfect understanding . . . in certain ways." One day my lunch lasted until four o'clock, and after I clocked back in at IBM, I got fired.

I tried to remember I was in love with Steven. I was Elise's friend, and even though she subsisted now on Allen Ginsberg's cryptic post cards, Alex still seemed in some way hers. He was also twenty-nine years old, undivorced, the father of a child, and not Jewish — a combination of everything my parents would find unacceptable. And there were my own doubts about him, too, which had found their way into a story I'd outlined at the end of the term but never started. In it, an Alex-like character named Michael was forced to play God to a group of rather desperate people, despite his knowledge that he could barely keep his own life running:

> Jane loves Michael and believes in him. It is she, more than anyone, who can make him feel that he is "God." She has assumed the responsibility for the more humdrum aspects of his life, and is actually playing the role of a mother to him, although she feels it is the other way around.

At the end of August there was a middle-of-the-night fire in the Yorkshire Hotel. Everyone came coughing out of their rooms into the street as the engines clanged down Broadway. A girl from my writing class had been staying there. She too had been one of Alex's students as a freshman, and often joked about the mad crush she still had on him. As she was standing barefooted in her bathrobe on 113th Street and Broadway, he suddenly appeared. He'd taken her back with him to 112th Street, and "somehow . . . one thing led to another." She called me the next day to tell me the wonderful news.

How could love be so subject to accident?

Why her and not me? Succumbing to a most un-Jamesian desolation, I told my mother I had a summer virus and took to my bed for two weeks.

A letter came. It was mailed from Florida, where Alex had gone with his son to visit his parents. *Joyce,* it began, with a long blank drawn after my name. The rest of it was a peculiarly detailed description of the plane flight to Miami — including altitudes, vibrations of the engine, even the magazines handed out by the stewardess — all written to someone who had never been on a plane. I recovered and waited.

A week later he called me from a phone booth on Broadway. I rushed out of the house to meet him at a secret luncheonette on Eighty-sixth Street. I knew it was the beginning of my life as a woman.

At the end of the summer, I told Elise everything. She assured me she'd known Alex and I would end up together eventually. "Delight each other," she said — as if it could be that simple.

I N THE 1950s, sex — if you achieved it — was a serious and anxious act. For all the "bottled eagerness" of which Holmes wrote, even the beds of the liberated were troubled. The new self-consciousness about coming or not coming — making it a man's duty and triumph that *both* should come, and a woman's shame if she didn't — brought dread to the question "Did you?"

Solemnly people experimented here and there.

In California, there is the later-to-be-famous three-way marriage of Neal and Carolyn Cassady and Jack Kerouac, then working on the railroad with Neal and living in the attic of his house. "My best pal and my best gal. Have a ball, kiddies, so long," Neal says one day as he splits out the door. Socialist of the emotions.

Sharing is all. This is a notion Carolyn has been fiercely resisting, having shared Neal with all too many women as well as with Jack and Allen, which is even more confusing and negating. Men are always disappearing on Carolyn into the attic, leaving her with the dishes. After her first shock, she thinks it over and decides to take Neal up on his challenge:

> The hope that my gamble would change the pattern of our lives was well founded. Everything appeared in a new light. I began a season of

singing days and nights, I was a *part* of all they did now and I felt like the star of the show.

A temporary domestic harmony results, which may be as close as Carolyn Cassady ever gets to bliss:

> I was functioning as a female, and my men were men. It may have taken two of them to complete the picture generally relegated to one, but so much the better ...
>
> While I performed my household duties the men would read each other excerpts from their writing in progress or bring out Spengler, Proust or Shakespeare to read aloud, accompanied by energetic discussions and appraisals ... I was happy just listening to them and filling their coffee cups. Yet I never felt left out. They'd address remarks to me and include me in the group with smiles, pats and requests for opinions or to moderate an argument.

But it all blows apart in the end, another failed utopia. Neal, despite his generosity of spirit, feels rejected — "Tell the old boy to get his own girl" — and resumes his frenetic wanderings. He can never just stay home with Carolyn and the kids for very long. Jack goes off to an adobe hotel in Mexico City to be alone and lonely and to write tenderly to Carolyn to come to him. But leaves before she can get there.

Somehow they all remain lifelong friends. And even after both men have died, Carolyn never succeeds in making sense of it. "Funny how Jack always seemed to be the cement that bound our little family together," she muses regretfully twenty-five years later.

"I've got it!" a girl screams down from a third-floor window in Hewitt Hall my senior year at Barnard. "Come on up! I've got it!" She has it in a jar that she hides beneath her under-wear in a dresser drawer. It's a little cup made of brownish rubber, dusted with cornstarch lest it crack. She lifts it out and shows it to Elise and me, this illicit thing — contraband. You buy a ring in the five-and-ten before you go to the Mar-garet Sanger clinic, and then you just make up a married name, why the hell shouldn't you? She's ready now. She has the key to everything.

Elise cuts off her hair a few months later and becomes the lover of this daring girl, Sheila. She walks rashly into a Puerto Rican barbershop and asks for "a Joan of Arc haircut, por favor." She wears stiff, ill-fitting Levi's with those girlish blouses her mother bought her in high school; carries a large deathly black handbag like the ones old ladies have, which she jerks by its strap back and forth as she makes her way down Broadway, eyes focused upon distance, upon an arrival that will take place somewhere in the future.

No one looks like Elise, her friend Sheila complains. God, that haircut and that bag! Get rid of that bag! How can a bright person be so dumb about things like that? Otherwise Elise is brilliant and *she's* the dumb one, Sheila would be the first to tell you, just a very average girl from Shaker Heights, so you'll know how suburban she is in case you want to make something of it. They lie in bed in Sheila's room in the afternoons, and sometimes at night foray down to the Grape-vine, a bar where women dance with women, taking along their "escort" — an odd Columbia boy of Elise's acquaintance named Leo Skir, who looks extraordinarily like Kafka and writes stories called "Leo in Mexico," "Leo the Zionist." The two of them gang up on Elise and tease her about her hang-up on Allen, whom she hasn't even seen for a year and a half.

They're more like relatives than friends, Sheila and Leo, in their blunt familial insistence that Elise shape up, in their refusal to understand anything but reality. Elise's obsession, in Leo's view, is as trivial as any of his own. He actually once considered committing suicide over a boy named David. "What's stopping you?" Elise had said. Even she knows bet-ter, sees through herself.

"I'm really sick of hearing about Allen," Sheila says, because Elise should love *her*, after all. But in loving Sheila, Elise is loving Allen too, reaching him in some place in her mind, living his life — loving Sheila as Allen loves men.

There are periods in growing up that seem to be like sleep. The sleeper dreams and tosses but remains in place, lodged in a continuum that's later hard to remember. Thus I've lost much of my first three years at Barnard, but my last one is sharp and clear. The year of Alex. The year of change. The year I quit music, failed to graduate, broke with my family — reclaiming the little girl who took the subway to the Waldorf Cafeteria but who would now no longer have to be home by seven, having orphaned herself deliberately.

I'm in such a hurry at nineteen to finally be the heroine of my own drama. My life fills with the excitement and newness of love. I'm borne up, up, stronger than any bubble, and I know I'll feel this way forever. Looking down I see a few obstacles — my parents, the attention I should really be giving to my studies, Alex's unfinished thesis, his unresolved feelings for Sally, the snobbery of his friends who can't understand why, after being married to her, he's taken up with an insignificant kid — but they aren't obstacles once you've flown over them. Even Elise fades a little, recedes into her own separate existence now that I have mine.

This euphoria is temporary, therefore dangerous. My parents unfortunately interpret danger as the loss of virginity. That's the least of it.

To my parents, Alex is the thief who is stealing their child — or the child they think they have. I've practiced doubleness all too successfully up till now. This new girl they're dealing with is a stranger to all three of us. Uncontainable, openly reckless. Hardly able to sit through dinner, she bolts out of the house with no excuses, returns God knows when.

As I slip in the door at two o'clock in the morning — a pale glimmer from my parents' bedroom. It's my father looking at his watch with his flashlight. My mother stalks me on Broadway, aided by my aunts, and informs me that I have been seen. Seen going in the West End Bar with a man. Seen carrying a bag of groceries — to whom? Seen turning the corner of 112th Street — my hand hidden in my pocket, clutching the key Alex has given me, hastening toward his bed, yes, and nakedness and darkness and risk. Because I can never quite bring myself to go to Sheila's clinic. It's odd what you have courage for and what you don't.

I bring Alex home to meet them once, as though he and I are fiancés, which we are, almost. Although it's not quite the same as being one of the girls at school with the pastel sweater sets and big engagement rings — the act having preceded the promise, in our case. We all sit in the living room and my mother makes an attempt at serving tea. My father, surprisingly, offers Alex a drink, bringing out the rarely opened bottle of Scotch and measuring it into a jigger, then into two glasses, as if to set himself and Alex apart, man to man, from my mother and me. The visit's a disaster. My parents smell out the alien in Alex beneath the threadbare grey flannel suit he's put on for the occasion. *He is not one of our kind.* Not even his credentials impress them — a college instructor, after all, soon to be *Dr.* Greer, a Ph.D. *He's a man who has been married. Not Jewish. A seducer with peculiar ideas.* They know all this atavistically. Doctor them no doctors. *He is not decent.* Like a wolf bellying under a fence, he brings terror into the house. *We have always been decent people here.* Too late they see they've been wrong about my upbringing. All their sacrifices, everything they've denied themselves, all the hundreds of small painful economies, are being reduced to ashes by their daughter. With their aspirations for the finer things, they've pushed me too far. I've been swept out of reach. *If we hadn't sent her to college, this might never have happened.*

The decency of my mother and father is absolute, incorruptible. There's such terrible pathos in it — a smiling-through-tears sentimentality of the kind that seizes you by the throat. They're as prewar as their living room. Their innocence is the great achievement of their lives. It asks to be protected, and ultimately I will have to protect it by leaving.

I'm scared to death, really. Childishly I turn to Alex. I need to know that he'll love me forever. I'm not so unlike my parents after all — I believe in commitments that last a lifetime. Alex is the great liberator of girls like me. Doesn't he tell all his students to leave home? It's the first step toward the sexual freedom he advocates for all. The repression of my parents' generation is beyond anachronism, says Alex — it's illness. He often speaks of the work of a Dr. Wilhelm Reich, whose patients sit in strange science-fiction metal boxes to be recharged with electrical particles of sexual energy. This is something Alex has tried himself, as well as the Freudian analysis that sooner or later I'll have to put myself through. He loves me, it seems, conditionally — looking past the uncertain young girl to the splendidly transformed, self-assured creature I'm going to turn myself into for him very fast, even before I graduate and get my own apartment. In bed we work on the transformation — and there I keep mysteriously failing Alex by always remaining too conscious. It's as if my anxious desire to please him prevents me from "letting go" — the very thing he requires from me the most. I always wait for it to happen and it scares me that it never does, and one day when he asks me if it did this time, I say yes, it did. The lie is such a relief to him, it doesn't seem bad to have told it. I tell it again. It becomes a given in our relationship, this secret that I can't even reveal to Elise. Do many women resort to such subterfuge? As far as I know, I'm the only one.

Love was a state of suspended animation. I cut Experimental Psych and the Eighteenth-Century Novel and Melville and Whitman and Greek Tragedy. I disappeared almost totally from gym. There was some silly antiquated rule about needing credits for attendance in physical education to get your diploma, but I'd never heard of it being used on anyone. Uncollected notices piled up in my campus mailbox — when I walked past, I could see them out of the corner of my eye, stuffed into the pigeonhole with my name on it.

My father rang the doorbell at 112th Street one night. Standing out in the hallway, his voice shaking, he threatened Alex with exposure to Dean McIntosh if he didn't give me up. Hiding in the back bedroom, I heard Alex say coldly, "I can't do that, Mr. Glassman," and close the front door. My father made his way back up Broadway, through the blocks I no longer walked with him in the evenings. He said nothing about his visit when I came home a few hours later. I had the feeling he hadn't told my mother. I waited for the threat to be carried out, but it wasn't. The only result was a change in Alex, a pulling-back that didn't go away. He'd filed me in the category of his "problems."

Adversity didn't bring people together. Wrapped in my sensibility, I wept in the neighborhood luncheonettes. My sadness seemed overwhelming but valuable — the stage you had to pass through to get to some greater wisdom.

Some days I cut classes for the sake of art. It was as if a muffled orchestra played inside my head at such a distance I couldn't quite get all of what it was playing. There were all these tones and rhythms not yet imbued with sense, but suggesting it, calling it into being. I'd write sentences in my notebook and sometimes get very close to this orchestra. Other times it would trick me and vanish around corners, leaving trampled words that made thin, whistling noises when I read them over. I'd be convinced the orchestra would never play again, but then it would resume as if it had never stopped — I'd simply failed to reach it.

Nothing similar to this orchestra of language had ever accompanied my writing of music. This I continued to do in a void, filling up endless pages with the inked notes that were my last offering to my mother — they looked, she said, so professional. I'd exhausted all the composition courses in the Barnard catalogue and gone on to private lessons with the composer Wallingford Riegger. From fugues for the piano I'd progressed to string quartets.

Once a week I'd turn up at Mr. Riegger's apartment and

present my latest output for criticism. He was a man of nearly seventy with a wry sense of humor that he never exercised at my expense. His apartment was the plainest one I'd ever seen. Everything was austere, straight lines and bareness. There were no extras anywhere. Other music teachers I'd worked with had Steinways and carpets and busts of famous composers and signed photos of former students. Mr. Riegger worked in a tiny maid's room on an old upright yellow-keyed piano piled high with scores. He'd written symphonies and ballets and been a composer for over fifty years. In 1925, when he'd adopted the twelve-tone system — one of the first Americans to do so — he'd been called an enfant terrible. "I felt the need to express new ideas for which the older techniques were inadequate," he'd said. He was the first true artist I'd ever met, and it was an honor to know him. I was glad he was getting some income from my otherwise wasted lessons.

One day I confessed to Mr. Riegger that I knew I could never write any music that would really please me, no matter how hard I worked. I knew this, I said, because of the different feeling I had when I wrote plays or stories — the sense that I could ultimately make something that would be perfect. With music this feeling never came.

"Well, then you should stop," he said — so kindly and matter-of-factly that I was stunned. It had never occurred to me to stop. "Stop now," he said. "What are you waiting for?"

I could only think of one reason not to stop — my mother's disappointment. Yet I knew this reason was one Mr. Riegger would allow me no room to consider. To him it would be an "extra," a side issue. If you knew your real work, you gave yourself up to it without hesitation.

I asked him if it would be all right if I stopped that day. I was sad, though, at the thought of not seeing him again.

He laughed and said "Good!" with that wry gaiety he had, and made me a cup of tea to celebrate my decision, plain A&P tea-bag tea with no lemon or sugar in it.

I quit music so totally that I never again played the piano; for a long time I could hardly listen to a record on a phonograph without extreme uneasiness and distraction, even when it was Alex who chose it for me.

My mother took all the music I had ever written and wrapped it in plastic and put it away in the locked drawer where she kept things that were important to her. It made me feel very old, as if my childhood were locked up with it and now belonged more to her than to me. She seemed to believe that someday I'd ask her to open the drawer, but I knew I never would.

7

A GROUP OF MIDDLE-AGED women, ladies, matrons, stand around a table on a patch of grass outside the Barnard deanery. They have name tags pasted on their bosoms stating their maiden and married names. Sometimes two women approach each other, stare uncertainly at each other's faces, then, reading the tags, will say, "Oh my God! Hello!"

I'm looking for the class of 1955, whom I last saw capped and gowned on this same lawn the day of my nongraduation. A procession of girls filing out of the gym twenty-five years ago to where their parents were waiting with embraces and cameras. In fact, my father rose to this ambiguous occasion and took my picture, once by myself and once with Sheila. Elise was not present. Neither of us were getting our diplomas, but Elise stayed away from the ceremony, sat in the West End Bar all afternoon, got loaded, went back to the Yorkshire Hotel and went to sleep.

I walk up to the table and pour wine into a plastic glass. Time has not been kind to the class of '55, putting wrinkles around the eyes of fresh-faced girls, thickening their bodies, playing its nasty biological tricks wholesale, as I could have foretold.

"What do you do?" one of my classmates greets another.
"I live in Scarsdale."

Well, that's an occupation, I suppose.

"I'm so *excited* to be here," she says.

I'm not excited. What am I? Subversively curious. Time has made my quarrel with Barnard into a comedy. Despite technicalities of status, I seem to be a legitimate alumna. They mail me the bulletin, requests for funds, invitations to this annual get-together.

At nineteen, I told my first full-time employer, "Wait, before you hire me, there's something you should know." She was a literary agent, British — a warm, absolutely straightforward woman; I didn't want to pull the wool over her eyes. "I didn't get my B.A.," I said. "I flunked physical education." She tried to look suitably solemn. "That doesn't worry me, actually," she said.

That was my real graduation from Barnard. I never made up the classes I cut.

I've had a lifelong reluctance to reenter places I've left, a resistance to anniversaries, family holidays, visits to graves or to offices I used to work in. My adult life has been one of discontinuities. To pass a house where I once lived is to feel a magnet pull upon my innards — I feel I could open the door, climb up the steps, take the key out of my pocket, walk into rooms just as they looked before moving day. Thus I avoid certain streets. If I visit my mother in the apartment where she still lives twenty years after my father's death, an enormous drowsiness overtakes me. She has a cat who shreds the furniture. One night it vomited on the piano top, removing its mahogany finish. My music is still in the locked drawer.

My mother is fiercely custodial, like some of my classmates. Alumnae who sit on committees, they concern themselves with keeping in touch. They collect news of marriages, births, deaths, divorces, and promotions. Barnard was evidently their great time. Some made cross-country flights to attend this reunion — with husbands who will escort them to the "21" Club tomorrow night to the gala class dinner.

I've truly forgotten most of these women. If I stare at a face long enough, the young face begins to return and I almost get the name before I glance at the tag. A faint recollection of sitting next to the adolescent ghost of this person in Psychology I, sunlight coming in the window, the dreamy school smell of chalk and old dry wood. A polite smile passes between us — no basis for anything more. We've ceased to exist for each other until this moment, and will fade out again.

I watch the gate through which late arrivals come from Broadway. Any time now Elise will appear, swinging her black handbag, her hair streaked with grey, cut shorter than ever, as she used to threaten she'd wear it after she'd passed her thirtieth birthday — but maybe she changed her mind and let it grow long after all, twisted into a knot. We'll laugh at the folly of finding each other here, the insanity of meeting, all grown up, at this reunion.

"I notice of course you're not wearing your name tag," I say, and I pull off mine and put it in my pocket. "Listen, Elise, there's an apropos line of Eliot's for this gathering —"

Serious but not sad, she peers at me through her glasses and says in her quiet, clipped accents, "Hurry up, please. Its time."

I MOVED OUT OF 116th Street on Independence Day, 1955 — a date I'd chosen not for its symbolism but because it was the first day of a long weekend. I'd taken a tiny maid's room in an apartment on Amsterdam Avenue five blocks away, to which I planned to move all my things, going back and forth with my mother's shopping cart.

I got up early that morning and started putting books into shopping bags. When I thought my parents would be awake, I walked into their room. They were dozing in their twin beds, an oscillating fan whirring between them. I said, "I have something to tell you. I'm moving out today." I felt sick to my stomach, as if I had murdered these two mild people. I could see their blood on the beige summer covers.

Two weeks earlier I'd found the room. With the first paychecks from my new job, I'd bought an unpainted rocking chair, a small desk, two sheets, and a poster of Picasso's *Blue Boy* — the furnishings of my first freedom. I knew children did not own furniture.

All this had been accomplished in secret, like the arrangements for a coup d'état. I wouldn't speak until it was time to leave. There was nothing to discuss. I was terribly afraid of being talked out of it.

"I need to borrow the cart," I said to my mother, "for my clothes and books."

"Don't think —" she said. "Don't think you can just come around here for dinner any time you want."

All day long I dragged the cart back and forth over the hot red brick sidewalks of the Columbia campus. No one shouted. No one stood at the door on 116th Street and tried to bar my way. In the stillness of their house, my parents moved slowly around the rooms as if injured.

I was done by evening. On my way out for the last time, I wrote my address on a piece of paper and left it on the kitchen table. From my new apartment, I called Elise and Sheila, who were sharing a place in Yorkville. "I really did it, I guess," I said.

Everyone knew in the 1950s why a girl from a nice family left home. The meaning of her theft of herself from her parents was clear to all — as well as what she'd be up to in that room of her own.

On 116th Street the superintendent knew it. He'd seen my comings and goings with the cart. He spread the word among the neighbors that the Glassmans' daughter was "bad." His imagination rendered me pregnant. He wrote my parents a note to that effect. My mother called and, weeping over the phone, asked me if this was true.

The crime of sex was like guilt by association — not visible to the eye of the outsider, but an act that could be rather easily conjectured. Consequences would make it manifest.

I, too, knew why I'd left — better than anyone. It was to be with Alex. He was the concrete embodiment of my more abstract desire to be "free." By which I meant — if I'd been pressed to admit it — sexually free. The desire for this kind of freedom subsumed every other. For this I was prepared to make my way in the world at the age of nineteen, incurring all the risks of waifdom on fifty dollars a week. In fact, fifty dollars seemed a lot to me, since I'd never had more than ten dollars in my pocket all at once. I opened a charge account at Lord and Taylor.

I didn't think I'd actually be living in my new room for

very long. It was just until Alex and I got married. All I had to do was prove to him how different I was going to be, now I was no longer under my parents' roof. I would demonstrate how independent I was, how little I really expected from him. In my strange scheme of things, independence seemed the chief prerequisite for marriage. But it was for Alex's sake, not mine, that I was going to be independent.

In the room of my own, on the nights I was there—which became more and more frequent—I'd lie on my bed with my eyes wide open, waiting until it was time to go to sleep. I wouldn't feel homesick so much as uninhabited, like a coat Alex had taken off and hung up on a hook.

In the morning I'd inhabit myself again, getting up to go to the office, plunging into the subway rush hour. Emerging into daylight at Fiftieth Street, I'd feel I'd been swept into an enormous secretarial army advancing inexorably upon Madison Avenue. There was comfort in this, a way of leaving the girl on the bed behind me. As part of this army, I typed, read manuscripts, answered the phone, ate egg-salad sandwiches in the downstairs luncheonette (I'd learned very quickly to locate the cheapest item on a menu).

My boss, Naomi Burton, who'd hired me despite my lack of a B.A., took an interest in me. I was talented, she told me. I could become a literary agent myself if I worked for her for a few more years. She persuaded me to show her a story I'd written at Barnard and published in the college literary magazine. "You're a writer," she said. "You should try your hand at a novel." She rang up a friend of hers, an editor named Hiram Haydn who ran a famous novel workshop at the New School for Social Research, and asked him to let me into the course.

It was thrilling but terrifying—as if I were really in danger of fulfilling the destiny my mother had wanted for me, which I had gone to such lengths to avoid. It seemed to be happening to a person outside the person I really was. I'd hidden from my mother's eyes the story Naomi Burton was sending Hiram Haydn—a story I'd written over and over again in various forms ever since my high-school days—

about a thirteen-year-old girl whose mother confides in her one day her bitter disappointment with her marriage.

Some time that year *Bonjour Tristesse* was published, causing a great furor in the United States. It was about a young French girl's loss of innocence in an affair with an older man married to a woman who had been very kind to her. The author, Françoise Sagan, was only a year older than I was. Her prose was like an elegant shrug of Gallic detachment and sophisticated regret. Sagan's schoolgirl face, knowing and slightly melancholy beneath her *gamin* haircut, appeared in every magazine and newspaper for a while. Her right thumb hovered just at the corner of her mouth, an indecisive gesture half infantile, half provocative. She seemed, however, to have taken possession of her fame with great aplomb, living it up the way young male writers were supposed to. She had a predilection for very fast driving in expensive sports cars; she dashed from literary parties to weekends at chateaux, alighting occasionally at cafés to be photographed with her thumb in its memorable position. Anyhow, that was my envious vision of her. She was a girl F. Scott Fitzgerald could have invented to torment poor Dick Diver. Americans forgave her amorality because she was French.

Sagan came to America for a few weeks, and Alex read every interview with her he could find. There was something in her speed, her coolness, that seemed to him totally new. He kept saying he wished there was some way he could meet her. Fortunately this wasn't likely. I loved Alex so much myself I was positive Sagan would find him irresistible.

Around April, Alex fell in love with a girl named Bobbie Weintraub, who wasn't anything like Sagan. He took her away from his roommate Anton, a graduate student in physics who'd moved in to share expenses and whom Bobbie visited on trumped-up overnight passes from the Barnard dorms. She was small and earnest and neat as a pin and planned to be a social worker; she'd always tidy up the living room on 112th Street much better than I could. She seemed either struck with wonder by everything Alex said or greatly shocked and offended by it, which he also enjoyed. One night she came over when Anton was at the library, and she and Alex went to bed. For weeks Anton threatened suicide.

I couldn't seem to get past my violent anguish. Each morning it would tear through me when I woke up remembering that Alex now wanted Bobbie Weintraub and not me. I knew that since I could never love anyone else, I was going to be alone for the rest of my life. "I want you as a friend," Alex insisted, but he'd only speak to me on the phone, always sounding curt and hurried and making it plain that if he met me anywhere, he'd have to bring Bobbie along as well.

"Try therapy," he'd urge me. "Promise me you'll try therapy."

$\mathcal{7}$

N JUNE I didn't get my period. First it was a little late, and then a lot, but I still thought it would come anyway, and I waited, thinking I felt it sometimes. But finally it didn't come. A tangible, unbelievable fact, like sealed doom.

I was going to have a baby. But it was impossible for me to have a baby.

The father wasn't Alex. The father was a child of my own age — a wrecked boy I'd known from Columbia who already had a drinking problem and lived, doing nothing, with his parents in Connecticut. I didn't love this boy. Sometimes you went to bed with people almost by mistake, at the end of late, shapeless nights when you'd stayed up so long it almost didn't matter — the thing was, not to go home. Such nights lacked premeditation, so you couldn't be very careful; you counted on a stranger's carefulness. The boy promised to pull out before the danger — but he didn't. And although I could have reminded him of his promise in time, I didn't do that either, remembering too late it was the middle of the month in a bedroom on East Ninety-sixth Street that smelled of smoke and soiled clothing, with leftover voices from that night's party outside the closed door.

I'd gotten a therapist by then — a $7.50 man, a rejected boyfriend of the woman whose apartment I was living in.

I told him my problem. "I see," he said, rubbing his large chin, staring out over Central Park West.

There was a box of Kleenex on the small Danish-modern table near my head. He had pointedly placed boxes of tissues in several locations in his office. But I never cried.

I explained to this therapist why I didn't see how I could become a mother. Aside from being twenty years old, I lived on fifty dollars a week and had cut myself off from my family. I said I would rather die. And then I asked him what Elise had told me to: "Could you get me a therapeutic abortion?" (I'd never heard the term before she explained what it meant.)

"Oh, I wouldn't even try," he said.

I hadn't thought he wouldn't try.

Life was considered sacred. But independence could be punishable by death. The punishment for sex was, appropriately, sexual.

There were women in those days who kept slips of paper, like talismans to ward off disaster, on which were written the names of doctors who would perform illegal abortions. Neither Elise nor I knew any of these women. You had to ask around. You asked friends and they asked friends, and the ripples of asking people widened until some person whose face you might never see gave over the secret information that could save you. This could take time, and you only had two months, they said, and you'd lost one month anyway, through not being sure.

The therapist called my roommate, got from her the name of the boy who had made me pregnant. He called the boy and threatened to disclose the whole matter to his parents unless the boy came up with the money for an illegal abortion. The boy called me, drunk and wild with fear. I hadn't expected anything of this boy except one thing — that when I had an abortion he'd go there with me; there had to be someone with you, I felt, that you knew. But as for blaming this boy — I didn't. I knew I had somehow let this happen to me. There had been a moment in that bedroom on Ninety-sixth Street, a moment of blank suspension, of not caring whether I lived or died. It seemed important to continue to see this moment very clearly. I knew the boy wouldn't come with me now.

I went to see the therapist one last time to tell him he had done something terribly wrong.

"Yes," he admitted, looking sheepish. "I've probably made a mistake."

I said, "I'm never coming back. I owe you thirty-seven fifty. Try and get it."

Someone finally came up with a person who knew a certain doctor in Canarsie. If you called this person at the advertising agency where he worked, he wouldn't give you the doctor's name — he'd ask you if you wanted to have a drink with him in the Rainbow Room, and over martinis he might agree to escort you out to see the doctor. This person wasn't a great humanitarian; he was a young man who had a weird hobby — taking girls to get abortions. He'd ask you if you wanted to recuperate afterward at his house on Fire Island. You were advised to say no.

Blind dates were a popular social form of the fifties. As I sat in the cocktail lounge of the Rainbow Room, staring through the glass doors at crew-cutted young men in seersucker suits who came off the elevator lacking the red bow tie I'd been told to watch out for, I realized that despite the moment in the bedroom, I probably didn't want to die, since I seemed to be going to an enormous amount of effort to remain living. If it happened that I died after all, it would be an accident.

He turned up a half-hour late in his blue and white stripes. "Why, you're pretty," he said, pleased. He told me he liked blondes. He made a phone call after we had our drinks, and came back to the table to say the doctor would see us that night. "I hope you don't have anything lined up," he said.

He offered me sticks of Wrigley spearmint chewing gum on the BMT to Canarsie. People in jokes sometimes came from there, but I'd never been to that part of Brooklyn in my life.

Canarsie was rows of small brick houses with cement stoops and yards filled with wash and plaster saints. Boys were playing stickball in the dusk. You could disappear into Canarsie.

The doctor seemed angry that we had come, but he led us into his house after we rang the bell, and switched on a light in his waiting room. He was fat, with a lot of wiry grey hair on his forearms; a white shirt wet and rumpled with perspiration stretched over his belly. The room looked like a room in which only the very poor would ever wait. There were diplomas on the walls, framed behind dusty glass; I tried to read the Latin. He glared at me and said he wanted me to know he did tonsillectomies. To do "the other" — he didn't say *abortions* — disgusted him. I made efforts to nod politely.

My escort spoke up and said, "How about next week?"

"All right. Wednesday."

I felt panic at the thought of Wednesday. What if my mother called the office and found out I was sick, and came running over to the apartment? "No," I said, "Friday. It has to be Friday."

"Friday will cost you extra," the doctor said.

That night I called Alex and asked if he'd please go with me on the day of the abortion.

"Only if you and I and Bobbie can have a drink."

I'd managed to borrow the five hundred dollars from a friend in her late twenties, who'd borrowed it from a wealthy married man who was her lover. With the cash in a sealed envelope in my purse, I stood for an hour that Friday morning in front of a cigar store on Fourteenth Street, waiting for the young advertising executive. I got awfully scared that he wouldn't come. Could I find the doctor's house myself in those rows of nearly identical houses?

There was a haze over Fourteenth Street that made even the heat seem grey. I stared across the street at Klein's Department Store, where my mother had taken me shopping for bargains, and imagined myself dying a few hours later with the sign KLEIN'S the last thing that flashed through my consciousness.

But finally the young man did materialize out of a cab. "Sorry to have kept you waiting." He'd brought some back issues of *The New Yorker*, and planned to catch up on his reading during the operation.

Upstairs in Canarsie, the doctor who did tonsillectomies had a room where he only did abortions. A freshly painted room where every surface was covered with white towels. He himself put on a mask and a white surgeon's gown. It was as if all that white was the color of his fear.

"Leave on the shoes!" he barked as I climbed up on his table almost fully clothed. Was I expected to make a run for it if the police rang his doorbell in the middle of the operation? He yelled at me to do this and do that, and it sent him into a rage that my legs were shaking, so how could he do what he had to do? But if I didn't want him to do it, that was all right with him. I said I wanted him to do it. I was crying. But he wouldn't take the money until after he'd given me the local anesthetic. He gave me one minute to change my mind before he handed me my purse.

The whole thing took two hours, but it seemed much longer through the pain. I had the impression that this doctor in all his fear was being extremely careful, that I was even lucky to have found him. He gave me pills when it was over, and told me I could call him only if anything went wrong. "But don't ever let me catch you back here again, young lady!"

I staggered down the cement steps of his house with my

110

life. It was noon in Canarsie, an ordinary day in July. My escort was saying he thought it would be hard to find a cab, we should walk in the direction of the subway. On a street full of shops, I leaned against the window of a supermarket until he flagged one down. Color seemed to have come back into the world. Housewives passed in floral nylon dresses; diamonds of sunlight glinted off the windshields of cars.

On the cab ride across the Manhattan Bridge, the young man from the ad agency placed his hand on my shoulder. "I have this house out on Fire Island," he began. "I thought that this weekend —"

"No thanks," I said. "I'll be okay in the city."

He removed his hand, and asked if I'd drop him off at his office — "unless you mind going home alone."

I said I'd get there by myself.

THERE IS A MOUNTAIN in the state of Washington called Desolation Peak, although desolation is not something that rises but a force with a downward pull. That same July, Jack Kerouac went there to confront the Void in a fire lookout's cabin on Starvation Ridge. He was thirty-four years old — a Zen pilgrim in Salvation Army clothes and new hiking boots with soles that would be worn to nothing by the end of his sixty-three days of solitude. There were envelopes of Lipton's dried pea soup in his rucksack, and a copy of *The God That Failed*. He was climbing the path that had been described to him by his friend, the poet and Buddhist scholar Gary Snyder, who had spent a previous summer in the same cabin. Alone on the mountain, with the laconic crackling voices that came over the fire lookout's radio as disembodied human contacts, Jack was prepared to grapple once and for all with the sense of mortality that overwhelmed him periodically, the awful knowledge we're-all-gonna-die which could be crowded out by movement or sex or wine or the frantic conviviality of poets and intellectuals in cities or by his own huge efforts to remember, to get it all down lest it vanish without a trace — writing in skid-row hotels in San Francisco, in a bathroom on Orizaba Street in Mexico City, in Neal Cassady's attic, in Gary Snyder's monastic wooden cottage on Hillegass Avenue, in Rocky Mount on his sister's

112

porch, where he had to put the typewriter on a board on his lap in bed because of the phlebitis in the throbbing veins of his legs — sign of his own march toward death.

Not that his knowledge was limited to signs. There'd been the deaths of his brother Gerard, his father Leo Kerouac, Joan Burroughs — whose ghosts he still continued to address. And earlier that year, troubling him more than perhaps he cared to admit, the suicide of Natalie Jackson. She was one of Neal's girls — "redhaired, bony, handsome, a real gone chick and friend of everybody of consequence on the Beach," Jack remembered her in *Dharma Bums*. It seemed that almost overnight Natalie Jackson went crazy, slashing at her arms with a knife, tormented by visions of a giant roundup of all her friends by the police, whose network would stretch as far as Greenwich Village and even Paris. She jumped from a roof just a few hours after Jack had left her, having failed to comfort her by his insistence that life was just an illusion. She was like everyone else he knew — she hadn't understood that neither death nor suffering existed because *nothing* existed. An *X* chalked on the sidewalk in a newspaper photo marked the spot where she had fallen in what was only Jack's dream of her in the swift, unreeling movie of his life.

But on Desolation Peak, there was the great unpeopled silence of nature; the city was behind him. Only wilderness to fill his vision. Mount Hozomeen loomed above Jack's cabin. Black rock, implacable, it was the Void he'd come to find — although he could see it more benignly if he did a handstand as "just a hanging bubble" in space. At times the city melted into another bubble, "the Void upside down." Negative space, all of it, cold and forbidding, canceling him out. Or else a Golden Eternity like "a babe's dream," into which he could blissfully merge. "It's me that's changed and done all this and come and gone and complained and hurt and joyed and yelled, not the Void!" Jack shouted at Mount Hozomeen.

At night in his cabin, as if he were in his mother's kitchen in Lowell, he played a baseball game he'd invented as a boy. Or he'd conjure up Frisco, red brick and neon, the roaring bars of North Beach, a girl with an enticing round white collar on her sweater, a pint of Christian Brothers port drunk in the Chinese movie theater on Broadway in the late afternoon, and walking out into Chinatown afterward, an earthly paradise with golden ducks hanging upside down in windows. But then — "the bottomless horror of Chinatown at dawn when they slam garbage pails and you pass drunk and disgusted and shamed. Bottomless horror everywhere." To which Joan Burroughs, whispering from her grave after "a lifetime of irony," assented that all is "right damnable, right got rid of."

There were no conclusive answers to his questions. Like a prisoner he counted off the days till his descent. Looking into a mirror, he saw the bleary, unshaven face of boredom. A man who desired an ice-cream cone more than love. A murderer, too — drowning an inoffensive mouse in a dishtub of water.

A giant black bear stalked the mountain that summer. He found its signs but never saw it. He called it *Avalokitesvara*, Bodhisattva of mercy and compassion. "I am waiting for him," he wrote.

After sixty-three days it was September, and Jack came down. He passed through Seattle, then took the road to Frisco. It was the autumn of the "San Francisco Renaissance."

After Jack Kerouac became famous, he would often speak of his wish to be a hermit in the mountains.

Celebrated Good Time Poetry Night. Either you go home bugged or completely enlightened. Allen Ginsberg blowing hot; Snyder blowing cool; Phil Whalen puffing the laconic tuba ... One and only final appearance of this apocalypse.

IT'S AN EVENING the previous May, 1956. A small makeshift theater in Berkeley. An audience gathered in response to a post-card invitation. Young people, mostly — poets and students, wives and girlfriends of same. The theater is dark, but there are line drawings tacked on the walls. If you walk up to them and look closely, you will see that they are drawings of two naked men, Allen Ginsberg and Peter Orlovsky, in acts of love.

The audience is unshockable, at one with the thin, intense young man in black raveled sweater who gets up on the tiny stage to read from his as yet unpublished manuscript. "I saw the best minds of my generation destroyed by madness ..." Or if there is shock, it's the shock of recognition popping off in a series of electrical synapses. "... starving hysterical naked / dragging themselves through the negro streets at dawn looking for an angry fix, / angelheaded hipsters ..."

The poet reads in that low, oddly compelling voice he had

even when he was seventeen and first met Jack Kerouac on the Columbia campus — that almost diffident voice with the power hidden in it. "Moloch!" he shouts, the power rising to the surface. "Moloch whose love is endless oil and stone! Moloch whose soul is electricity and banks! Moloch whose poverty is the specter of genius!"

Each indictment of Moloch sets off boos and hisses. Like a prophet of a coming revolution, Allen captures the crowd, finishing in a rainbow razzmadazzle of all the colored stage lights on the board and the forward rush of fellow poets to grip his hands, and the embrace of Kerouac.

Jack, who has given Allen's poem its title, is drunk again, as he was the first time Allen ever read *Howl* publicly — the October night at the Six Gallery when the San Francisco Renaissance was actually born. There, too, Jack had played the buffoon, uproariously good-natured on the sidelines, plying the audience with jugs of wine. Since 1951, he has written eleven books himself. Faithfully, Allen plans to list them in the dedication to the upcoming City Lights edition of *Howl*, with the ironic notation "All these books will be published in heaven."

One curious thing is that despite appearances this reading in May is not a starting point but a reenactment. The same poets, the audience arriving knowing what to expect, and thus part of the performance themselves. The ritual of a movement that's less than a year old but maturing quickly.

Cautiously turned on by what he sees, a visiting poet from the East, Richard Eberhart, writes an article for the *New York Times Book Review*. Something new is stirring in San Francisco, a revolution in consciousness. Neglecting indigenous West Coast poets like Kenneth Rexroth, Robert Duncan, and Michael McClure — and sowing the seeds of rivalry — he devotes most of the article, which will be published early the following September, to Allen Ginsberg.

By the time Jack Kerouac came down from his mountain, a photographer from *Mademoiselle* had flown in and was trying to line up the San Francisco Renaissance poets for a group portrait. Not wishing to be photographed with Allen

Ginsberg and his circle, Michael McClure and Kenneth Rexroth made appointments for separate sessions. "Hand in hand, it's got to be," Allen insisted. He was torn between disappearing and moving the revolution elsewhere.

In the fall of '56, having narrowly survived my twentieth year, I was just turning twenty-one. My crash course in the depths of human experience sometimes made me feel extremely old. This was not entirely an unpleasant feeling but new and strange, like walking around in an exotic garment that suddenly made you impervious to everything but didn't connect you to most of the people you knew in your everyday life. Once you'd touched bottom, what was there to be afraid of anymore? I was continually lonely, but very fearless. Life seemed grey but not impossible.

I found a new job at another literary agency and got a little more money. I moved into a new apartment of my own that happened to be around the corner from Alex's. I worked on the novel about Barnard I'd begun in Hiram Haydn's workshop. Elise and Alex were characters in it. By making Alex into a character, I took away his power to hurt me. Just like me, my heroine would have an affair with the Alex character and end up alone. But in my fictional rearrangement of life, it was she who was going to leave him after their one and only night together. I rewarded her with a trip to Paris. I typed forty letters a day and dreamed of taking off myself.

There was a restlessness in everyone I knew. Journeys seemed imminent. Elise and Sheila actually went to Rockefeller Center one day on their lunch hours and applied for passports, had their pictures taken and everything, even though neither of them had a dime.

The Sunday the article on Allen appeared, Elise called and read it to me over the phone, her voice taut with excitement. With that, our collective travel fantasies switched over to San Francisco, city of poets and accessible by Greyhound bus, whose hilly streets in our imaginations took on a perpetual golden haze. I thought about San Francisco the way I'd thought about the Village when I was thirteen, before I ever went there. Could it possibly be what it was said to be? A vision of community into which I would somehow fit. I didn't seem to fit into the rest of America, although I did it better than Elise. It took great effort and vigilance to report to my job on Madison Avenue, my hair wound into a chignon around a horrible doughnut-shaped thing called a rat. My office identity seemed as precarious as my hair style. Someday they would find me out. I had broken the law, I had slept with men, I had contempt for the books the MCA Literary Agency was attempting to sell to publishers. The lives of my superiors seemed desiccated rather than enviable. Only the publication of my novel would transform my existence into what I wanted it to be.

Elise, although she wouldn't come out and say it, wanted to go to San Francisco for purposes of love. This worried me. What if Allen Ginsberg wouldn't be so glad to see her? It had been three years since that night on East Seventh Street that she still talked about. I myself had come to place value on forgetting as a way of getting through life. Lovers you couldn't forget were dangerous. Allen Ginsberg had somehow always been legendary, even before he became famous in the *New York Times*.

A Barnard friend of mine worked for *Mademoiselle*. I visited her there one day and she showed me proofs of the article they were going to run on the San Francisco Renaissance. There was a photo of Allen with three other men, a cherubic hoodlum named Gregory Corso, a scholarly Philip Whalen, and a writer who had a crucifix around his neck and tangled black hair plastered against his forehead as if he'd just walked out of the rain. He looked wild and sad in a way that didn't seem appropriate to the occasion. This was Jack Kerouac, whose reputation was underground. Like the others, he was said to frequent North Beach, a run-down area where there were suddenly a lot of new coffee shops, jazz joints, and bars, as well as an excellent bookstore called City Lights that was the center of activity for the poets. Thus several thousand young women between fourteen and twenty-five were given a map to a revolution. *Mademoiselle* made it its business to keep up with things.

I remembered the man with the dark, anguished face and the name that was unlike anyone else's, the harsh music of its three syllables. Soon afterward I found it on a book at the office. A battered copy of *The Town and the City* was on a shelf where they put things that weren't active any more. I asked what it was doing at MCA, and was told it was the work of a talented but very terrible person who had briefly been handled by the agency. He had grown more and more enraged and unreasonable as his various novels proved impossible to place. Sometimes he seemed under the influence of alcohol — or worse, probably. Then one day an equally crazy Mr. Ginsberg had turned up without an appointment, demanding the return of the three manuscripts and announcing that *he* was Jack Kerouac's agent. Good riddance!

I asked if I could borrow Kerouac's book. I took it home and never brought it back.

8

O N A BITTER MORNING in November, 1956, a dust-covered car, its roof piled high with a motley collection of baggage, its interior crammed with passengers, like those vehicles you see in the circus, pulls into the Village and makes a stop on a street near Sheridan Square. It's Allen Ginsberg arriving at Finland Station. A door opens and he gets out, stretches his cramped legs; followed by Peter Orlovsky, followed by Peter's fifteen-year-old brother Lafcadio, followed by Jack Kerouac. Rucksacks are taken off the roof. The car pulls off with the two strangers in it with whom they've driven the three thousand miles from Mexico City to New York, a Puerto Rican man and a schoolteacher who had advised Lafcadio to shape up and join the Army.

Destinationless, they stand on the sidewalk in the shock of the cold air, lighting cigarettes, debating where to go. Jack is gloomy, thinner than Allen has ever seen him, coughing over his smoke. Dead broke despite the anticipation of money — the possibility that *The Subterraneans* will be sold to Grove Press for a penny a word. Five hundred dollars would get him to Tangier, where Allen is planning to join Burroughs once he and Jack and Gregory Corso have captured New York, as he's convinced they will. It's their moment. America is waiting for prophetic poets. "Big trembling Oklahomas need poetry and nakedness," Allen had told Jack in Mexico City, trying to rouse him from his lethargy, an exhaustion of spirit that's overtaken him just now when they're finally breaking through, when they're about to become famous. Maybe even internationally, Allen keeps insisting to Jack, knowing his hunger for fame, knowing also his pitiable secret — the worm of envy hidden in his heart.

Obscure on a New York street corner for the moment, Allen's ragged army needs places to stay. Allen goes to a phone booth and starts making calls.

"You stole the Void from me," Jack will say to him four years later.

There was a dark radiance about Elise when she was happy — you could always hear it immediately in her voice, like a light turned on behind the words.

"Allen's back," she said.

He was back, but not for good, of course, he'd be going away in a couple of months. Peter was with him, Peter was so beautiful. They'd be moving in that night. Sheila didn't mind.

I asked her who Peter was.

"Oh, Allen's lover."

I went up to see them later that week. It was sometime early in December.

The apartment shone, as if every inch had been mopped and swept. Peter loved to clean, Sheila told me. He'd been a hospital orderly, which was how he'd learned to do it so well. "I adore him," she said, and showed me how they'd rearranged the furniture. In one of the rooms, the two mattresses she and Elise had bought from the Salvation Army and carried up the six flights of stairs when they first took the place were lying on the floor side by side.

I remember feeling very shy.

I lost my shyness after a few more visits. It all seemed strangely normal, like being with a new kind of family. I saw that what you learned to consider normal did not necessarily have to remain constant; "normalcy" in fact might be an artificial idea.

The truth was that to me, those four small tenement rooms in Yorkville seemed the most exciting place in the world that winter. Allen's energy was like a magical force, sweeping up people, ideas, manuscripts, bringing them together in new combinations that would last for an afternoon or a lifetime. He excluded no one from the warm, steady beam of his attention, talking as earnestly to a kid who'd come up on the subway with a notebook of doggerel in his pocket as he would to Randall Jarrell.

Howl had just been published. You could find the small, square, black and white books in only two places in the city — Elise's kitchen and the Eighth Street Bookshop. Like a guerrilla general, Allen ambushed the world of the established literati — presenting himself to be interviewed at the *New York Times*, *Time*, *Life*, and the *Village Voice*; turning up at publishing houses and cocktail parties to convert agents, editors, critics into supporters of his revolution. He exhorted, charmed, raged, stripping himself naked on occasion to prove his point, as he'd done at a reading in Los Angeles in response to a heckler. Like a young blond apostle or a little brother, Peter Orlovsky was always at his side, sweet and tireless, providing a balance.

In the apartment in Yorkville, Elise waited, ironing, making soup, taking messages, lying down on a mattress to smoke a cigarette and stare out at the vista of rooftops where pigeons circled in the winter sky. She spent a lot of time with Lafcadio Orlovsky, who was staying alone in a rooming house. A weird silent boy whose adolescence flamed across his face in pimples, who'd spend hours hunched in a corner drawing tiny science-fiction pictures everyone passed around and who, if he spoke, would ask you what you dreamed. His inertness troubled her. She lured him into going for long walks, took him to the Frick Museum to look at Fra Angelicos. She'd promised to look out for Lafcadio after Allen and Peter went to Tangier, when she knew her waiting for Allen would again be vast and unpeopled.

*

Sheila thought Elise was disappearing into Allen. "Whose idea is that — Allen's or yours?" she'd yell, banging pots into the sink. She confided to Leo Skir that she was losing all respect for Elise. Peter was the best of the lot, in her opinion, the only one who considered other people's feelings. Leo came to visit, and disapproved of the whole setup. "I went to Columbia," he told Allen, "after you." Allen took a long look at Leo and said reflectively, "Columbia ruined a lot of people." They all went to the movies on Forty-second Street that night and saw *Il Vitteloni,* a film about a gang of rootless young men in Rome. Lafcadio, according to Leo, thought it was about New York.

The Orlovskys disconcerted people. You almost believed they were true Karamazovian angels, as Allen said they were, because you didn't know what else to think. There was a rawness about Peter's innocence. He seemed shockingly brand new, a person suddenly launched into a world for which he totally lacked a frame of reference. Peter was only a year older than I was. He'd grown into adolescence nearly illiterate, with four other neglected, frightened children, in a converted chicken coop in Northport, Long Island. His Russian immigrant parents were alcoholics; his father, a painter of designs on silk neckties, was perpetually out of work. Northport was a middle-class town; the Orlovsky boys were outcasts there. Julius, the eldest, went mad and was institutionalized; Peter escaped into the army and ended up in San Francisco. He modeled there for a painter, and became his lover. Visiting Robert LaVigne's studio one afternoon in 1955, Allen was overwhelmed by a portrait of a blond, naked boy with onions at his feet. A little later Peter had walked in. They'd been together ever since. With Allen's help, Peter had rescued Lafcadio and brought him back to the Coast.

In the late spring of 1956, six months before they came to New York, a telegram had arrived informing Allen that his mother Naomi had just died in a state mental hospital. Around that time Allen had panicked. For a while he thought Peter and he should break up and see girls. Perhaps Naomi's death finally freed Allen to be himself. He apparently no longer felt torn by the need to make such choices. Peter and he could share women or love them separately or love other men. It seemed to make no difference — they possessed each other's souls. They would always love each other.

If this pained Elise, it was something she couldn't admit and I couldn't bring myself to ask her. The question seemed to indicate a possible narrowness of spirit, something I'd have to work on in my own life.

I read *The Town and the City*. Sometimes I tried to imagine the man whose face I'd seen in the photo in *Mademoiselle*. Allen and Peter introduced me to Gregory Corso, but I always went to the apartment in Yorkville with the secret hope that this time Jack Kerouac would appear. He had a girl, of course, so he wouldn't be interested in me.

Their first day in New York, Allen had found Jack a place to stay in the Village with two women he knew, both of whom were named Virginia. "Jack's with the two Virginias," he would tell people with satisfaction, as if the Virginias were big, fierce Amazonian guardians, when they were only two girls from the Midwest who happened to resemble each other a little, being tall and boyish and sloe-eyed and under analysis. They were girls who liked to enjoy themselves. Their refrigerator was always full of beer and they had little parties and propped their feet up on things, showing off their long legs, and turned on the radio and made people dance with them to the songs of Sinatra and Presley. One Virginia had been madly in love with Lucien Carr for years; understandably, Jack was now crazy about the other.

As a lover he seemed extremely disorganized, though. Night after night he'd call Allen from successive phone booths in Fugazi's, the San Remo, and the Riviera Bar, as he moved around the Village with noisy groups of drinkers while the two Virginias fumed at home. Jack's Virginia berated him for his irregular habits, accused him of taking advantage of her, broke out in a rash, and inflicted the ultimate punishment of announcing he could no longer sleep with her, on the orders of her psychiatrist. Over Christmas, Jack escaped her wrath and hitchhiked down to North Carolina, to take melancholy refuge with his mother and sister.

On New Year's Eve, Allen, Elise, Peter, Sheila, and I piled into a Checker cab and went to a party at Lucien Carr's apartment on Grove Street. I remember what I was wearing that night — a sleeveless black velvet dress with a long satin sash that I'd recklessly charged to my unpaid account at Lord and Taylor. It was my last attempt at such bourgeois elegance for about the next fifteen years.

Of course I knew the famous story told around Columbia about Lucien Carr's gratuitous act, and it was odd to think I was actually going to see him. The Lucien I met was a thirty-one-year-old man (although he seemed to me much older) who got up every morning and went to an editing job and had an awfully nice wife and two towheaded little boys in blue pajamas who came and said good-night to everyone at the party. He had his hair cut in a funny, uneven way and wore horn-rimmed glasses and a brown tweed suit in which he didn't look at all like Rimbaud. He put logs on the fire and dropped ice in people's drinks. He took a fancy to Elise — her name seemed to give him great amusement. Ellipse, he called her. Or Eclipse. "Well now, Eclipse, what'll you have?" he'd shout across the room, and his wife Cessa would redden and say, "Oh, *Lucien!*"

That was the extent of the wildness of the evening, which probably would have been much less subdued, everyone agreed, if Jack had been there. Mostly Lucien talked on and on with Allen about the past, events that had happened twelve years ago. Stories about the West End, and an apartment on 115th Street, and a girl called Edie Parker, and Joan Burroughs, the woman who had died. It was as if part of Lucien had gotten stuck back there and eternally lost, and he'd ended up becoming what he was not supposed to be.

At midnight some people down in the street blew whistles. It was 1957.

*A*s of 1982, there is the Jack Kerouac Society for Disembodied Poetics, founded in Boulder, Colorado, in 1976. There is *Jack's Book*, as well as *Desolation Angel: Jack Kerouac, the Beat Generation and America* and *Kerouac: A Biography* and — the one I like best — *Kerouac: A Chicken Essay*, by a French-Canadian surrealist poet; as well as proliferating pamphlets, theses, articles, chapters in books. A journal published annually celebrates the Beats and the "Unspeakable Visions of the Individual." It's hagiography in the making. Jack, now delivered into the Void, would be amazed to know there's even a literary fan magazine devoted entirely to him, called *Moody Street Irregulars* (after the street in Lowell where he lived as a child). For a back issue, a graduate student somewhere put together a rather randomly chosen chronology of Jack Kerouac's life. In a column labeled *1957*, there's a cryptic entry: *Meets Joyce Glassman.*

"Hello. I'm Jack. Allen tells me you're very nice. Would you like to come down to Howard Johnson's on Eighth Street? I'll be sitting at the counter. I have black hair and I'll be wearing a red and black checked shirt."

I'm standing in Elise's kitchen, holding the phone Allen

has just handed me. It's a Saturday night shortly after New Year's.

"Sure," I say.

I put on a lot of eye shadow and my coat and take the subway down to Astor Place and begin walking westward, cross-town, passing under the bridge between the two buildings of Wanamaker's Department Store and the eye of the giant illuminated clock. It's a dark, bitter January night with ice all over the pavements, so you have to be careful, but I'm flying along, it's an adventure as opposed to a misadventure — under which category so far I've had to put most of the risky occurrences in my life.

The windows of Howard Johnson's are running with steam so you can't see in. I push open the heavy glass door, and there is, sure enough, a black-haired man at the counter in a flannel lumberjack shirt slightly the worse for wear. He looks up and stares at me hard with blue eyes, amazingly blue. And the skin of his face is so brown. He's the only person in Howard Johnson's in color. I feel a little scared as I walk up to him. "Jack?" I say.

There's an empty stool next to his. I sit down on it and he asks me whether I want anything. "Just coffee." He's awfully quiet. We both lack conversation, but then we don't know each other, so what can we say? He asks after Allen, Lafcadio, that kind of thing. I'd like to tell him I've read his book, if that wouldn't sound gauche, obvious and uncool.

When the coffee arrives, Jack looks glum. He can't pay for it. He has no money, none at all. That morning he'd handed his last ten dollars to a cashier in a grocery store and received change for a five. He's waiting for a check from a publisher, he says angrily.

I say, "Look, that's all right. I have money. Do you want me to buy you something to eat?"

"Yeah," he says. "Frankfurters. I'll pay you back. I always pay people back, you know."

I've never bought a man dinner before. It makes me feel very competent and womanly.

He has frankfurters, home fries, and baked beans with Heinz ketchup on them. I keep stealing looks at him because he's beautiful. You're not supposed to say a man is beautiful, but he is. He catches me at it and grins, then mugs it up, putting on one goofy face after another; a whole succession of old-time ridiculous movie-comedian faces flashes before me until I'm laughing too at the absurdity of this blind date Allen has arranged. (The notion of Allen Ginsberg arranging blind dates will crack people up years later when they ask me how on earth I met Kerouac.)

As for what he saw in me that night, I'm not sure at all. A very young woman in a red coat, round-faced and blonde. "An interesting young person," he wrote in *Desolation Angels*. "A Jewess, elegant middleclass sad and looking for something — she looked Polish as hell . . ." Where am I in all those funny categories?

As our paths converge in Howard Johnson's, we're looking for different things. At thirty-four, Jack's worn down, the energy that had moved him to so many different places gone. He's suddenly waited too long. The check for *The Subterraneans* will never arrive; *On the Road* will never be published. Why not let Allen rescue him? He can't go back to the two Virginias.

I see the blue, bruised eye of Kerouac and construe his melancholy as the look of a man needing love because I'm, among other things, twenty-one years old. I believe in the curative powers of love as the English believe in tea or Catholics believe in the Miracle of Lourdes.

He tells me he's spent sixty-three days on a mountaintop without anyone. He made pea soup and wrote in his journal and sang Sinatra songs to keep himself company.

Some warning to me in all this. "You really liked being alone like that?" I ask.

"I wish I was there now. I should've stayed up there."

He could somehow cancel you out and make you feel sad for him at the same time. But I'm sure any mountaintop would be preferable to where he's staying — the Marlton

Hotel on Eighth Street, with the dirty shades over the windows and the winos lounging on the steps.

"And where do you live?" Jack asks. He likes it that it's up near Columbia and the West End Bar where he used to hang out. Was Johnny the bartender still there? Johnny the bartender would remember him from the days he was a football hero at Columbia but he broke his leg in his sophomore year and stayed in his room reading Céline and Shakespeare and never went back to football again — thus losing his scholarship at Columbia, but he's always had affection for the neighborhood. "Why don't you let me stay at your place?" he says.

"If you wish," I say in *Desolation Angels*, deciding fast. And I know how I said it, too. As if it was of no great moment, as if I had no wishes of my own — in keeping with my current philosophy of nothing-to-lose, try anything.

We stood up and put on our coats, we went down into the subway. And there on the IRT, on a signboard I'd never seen before that night, was an ad for an airline with a brand-new slogan: FLY NOW. PAY LATER.

"That's a good title for a novel," I said, and finally told Jack I was writing one, I wasn't just a secretary. He said *Pay Me the Penny After* would be a better title. "You should call your novel that." He asked me who my favorite writer was. I said Henry James, and he made a face, and said he figured I had all the wrong models, but maybe I could be a great writer anyway. He asked me if I rewrote a lot, and said you should never revise, never change anything, not even a word. He regretted all the rewriting he'd done on *The Town and the City*. No one could make him do that again, which was why he always got nowhere with publishers. He was going to look at my work and show me that what you wrote first was always best. I said okay, feeling guilty for all that I'd rewritten, but I still loved Henry James.

All through this literary conversation, Jack stood swaying above me on the subway, hanging on to the strap. Just before we got off, he leaned down. Our foreheads scraped, our eyeballs loomed up on each other — a funny game where I knew you weren't supposed to blink, no matter what.

That was the start of *Meets Joyce Glassman*.

The apartment I lived in at the time was dark and cavernous, on the first floor of a brownstone halfway down the block from the Yorkshire Hotel. Two furnished rooms — the furnishings being the uselessly massive, weak-jointed kind found in the lobbies of antediluvian apartment buildings. A small refrigerator and a two-burner stove stood behind a screen in one corner of the living room, but you had to wash your dishes in the bathroom sink. The windows looked out on a rank back yard where a large tree of heaven battened on bedsprings and broken bottles. I always felt very small in that apartment. One night outside the house a huge grey tomcat with a chewed ear had rubbed against my legs. I'd hauled him inside under the impression I was rescuing him, but he spent his days on the windowsill longing for the street, trying to pry the window open with his paw, or he lurked in the closet vengefully spraying shoes. Jack was the only person I'd brought home so far who saw the beauty of this animal, whom I'd unimaginatively named Smoke. He said he was going to call it Ti Gris, after a cat he once had in Lowell. He seemed to like to rename things. On the walk from the subway I'd become Joycey, which no one had called me since I was little, and he'd put his arm around me, leaning on me playfully and letting his hand dangle down over my breast — that was how men walked with their women in Mexico, he said. "Someday when you go there, you'll see that for yourself."

When we got in the door, he didn't ask to see my manuscript. He pulled me against him and kissed me before I even turned on the light. I kissed him back, and he acted surprised. He said I was even quieter than he was, he had no idea quiet girls liked kissing so much, and he undid the buttons of my coat and put both his hands up my back under my sweater. "The trouble is," Jack said with his voice against my ear, "I don't . . . like . . . blondes."

I remember laughing and saying, "Well, in that case I'll just dye my hair" — wondering all the same if it was true.

In the morning Jack left to get his stuff out of the Marlton. He returned with a sleeping bag and a knapsack in which there were jeans and a few old shirts like the one he was already wearing and some notebooks he'd bought in Mexico City. That was all he owned. Not even a typewriter — he'd been borrowing other people's typewriters, he said. I'd never seen such foreign-looking notebooks, long and narrow with shiny black covers and thin, bluish paper on which Jack's slanted penciled printing sped across page after page, interrupted here and there by little sketches. One notebook was just for dreams. He wrote in it every morning.

There was something heartbreakingly attractive in these few essentials to which Jack had reduced his needs. He reminded me of a sailor — not that I knew any sailors — something too about the way he looked coming out of the shower, gleaming and vigorous and ruddy with a white towel around his neck.

Very quickly it didn't seem strange to have him with me, we were somehow like very old friends — "buddies," Jack said, squeezing me affectionately, making me feel both proud and a little disappointed. Crazy as it was, I sometimes really wished I was dark — like this Virginia I felt jealous of for making him so wild. Or the girl named Esmeralda who lived in Mexico City and whom he'd loved tragically for a long time and written an entire novel about in one of his notebooks, calling her Tristessa. But he'd slept with her only once. She was a whore and a saint, so beautiful and lost — one of his mysterious *fellaheen* women, primeval and of the earth.

I was unprimeval and distinctly of the city. I was everydayness, bacon and eggs in the morning or the middle of the night, which I learned to cook just the way he liked —

sunny-side up in the black iron frying pan. I'd buy slab bacon in the grocery store, like he'd always had in Lowell — not the skinny kind in packages — and add canned applesauce (a refinement I'd learned from Bickford's Cafeteria), which Jack had never thought of as anything that might enhance eggs. He took extraordinary pleasure in small things like that.

As a lover he wasn't fierce but oddly brotherly and somewhat reticent. I'd listen in amazement to his stories of Berkeley parties where everyone was naked and men and women engaged in some exotic Japanese practice called *yabyum* (but Jack, fully clothed, had sat apart brooding over his bottle of port, something he didn't tell me). In my memories of Jack in the good times we had together, I'm lying with my head on his chest, his heart pulsing against my ear. His smooth hard powerful arms are around me and I'm burying my face into them because I like them so much, making him laugh, "What are you doing there, Joycey?" And there's always music on the radio. Symphony Sid, whom he taught me to find on the dial, who always comes on at the stroke of midnight, bringing you the sounds of Charlie Parker, Lester Young, Miles Davis, and Stan Getz, and who, according to Jack, is a subterranean himself — you can hear it in his gravel voice smoked down to a rasp by innumerable weird cigarettes. "And now — after a few words about that fan-tastic Mo-gen David wine — the great Lady Day . . ." In the darkness of the room we drift together as Billie Holiday bewails lost loves . . .

But then Jack leaves me. He goes into the small back bedroom where I never sleep because there's no radiator there. He pulls the window all the way up, closes the door, and lies down on the floor in his sleeping bag alone. This is the cure for the cough he brought with him from Mexico City. In the morning he'll do headstands with his feet against the wall, to reverse the flow of blood in his body. He tells me a frightening thing about himself. He's known for eight years that a blood clot could finish him off at any minute.

How can you bear living, I wonder, knowing death could

132

be so close? Little by little I'm letting go of what I learned on the abortionist's table in the white upstairs room in Canarsie.

I'm good for him, Jack tells me. I don't mind anything he does. I don't mind about the sleeping bag, do I?

I didn't really mind, that was the strange part. Everything seemed so odd, so charmed, so transformed. At night when the cold air came with a rush into the little room where Jack was sleeping, and seeped under the edges of the closed door, I could imagine myself in a place without walls, an immense campground where, lying wrapped in blankets, I could feel in my own warmth absolute proof of my existence.

> I'm a regular fool in pale houses enslaved to lust
> for women who hate me, they lay their bartering
> flesh all over the divans, it's one fleshpot — in-
> sanity all of it, I should forswear and chew em all
> out and go hit the clean rail — I wake up glad to
> find myself saved in the wilderness mountains —
> For that lumpy roll flesh with the juicy hole I'd
> sit through eternities of horror in gray rooms il-
> luminated by a gray sun, with cops and alimoners
> at the door and the jail beyond? — It's a bleeding
> comedy — The Great Wise Stages of pathetic un-
> derstanding elude me when it comes to harems —
> Harem-scarem, it's all in heaven now — bless their
> all their bleating-hearts — Some lambs are female,
> some angels have womanwings, it's all mothers in
> the end and forgive me for my sardony — excuse
> me for my rut.
> (Hor hor hor)

Not for Joyce Glassman to read, this bleak passage later written in *Desolation Angels*, this awful metaphysical linking of sex, birth, the grave. I hate Jack's woman-hatred, hate it, mourn it, understand, and finally forgive.

ONE NIGHT HE almost went back to Virginia. He called me from the Village. He was with her, so I shouldn't sit up anymore and wait for him. He'd been drinking in a bar called the White Horse, around the corner from her house, when she'd happened to walk in with the other Virginia's dog, and they'd had a big reunion. She'd begged him to come home with her despite what her analyst had said. So there he was.

He seemed very drunk, a little regretful, and peculiarly unresistant — like someone who'd boarded the wrong train and couldn't get off and figured he might as well take in the passing view.

I hardly got out one word on the phone. All my not-minding had turned into a giant knot of hurt. How could he go back to this Virginia who'd kicked him out? I put down the receiver, grabbed my coat, and rushed blindly out the door and into the street. On Broadway I hailed a cab. It was one o'clock in the morning, I was on my way to the White Horse. I had some thought I'd find Jack there, although it was a place he'd already left, and that seeing me, he'd be reminded of his forgotten destination.

But when I walked into the White Horse and didn't see him, I marched to the phone booth in the rear. I knew her last name and got the number. Quaking, I put the nickel in and made the call. "I want to speak to Jack Kerouac," I said. When he got on, I told him where I was and said we had to talk, that I'd sit and wait for him in the bar for fifteen minutes, and that if he didn't come, it would be good-by for good. Tears came to my eyes when I made this ultimatum, and I didn't even know whether I meant it or not.

He sounded amazed. "How'd you get downtown so fast?" He said I should wait, he'd be right there. I dried my tears and sat at an empty table by the window, and finally, as I stared at the street, he came around the corner.

I thought he'd be very angry, but he wasn't at all. He just couldn't get over the fact that I'd come to get him back. It was as if I'd pulled off some daring exploit and he was most impressed to be kidnapped by me back to the West Side, singing "I'm a Fool" in the cab we took uptown.

As he sang in the cab with his head heavy on my shoulder, he looked out the window — *Desolation Angels* tells me — at the "oceangoing vessels docked at the North River piers," reminding him that anyway, he was about to move on.

In 1957, Jack was still traveling on the basis of pure, naive faith that always seemed to renew itself for his next embarkation despite any previous disappointments. He would leave me very soon and go to Tangier. In his mind he often seemed already there, walking Arabian Nights streets under a brilliant blue sky with his friend Bill Burroughs, narrow streets of bone-white houses, with the sweetish odors of hashish and honey and decay, veiled women beckoning him into the mysteries of the Casbah. Then, on to Paris — as softly, anciently grey as the stones of Notre Dame. Speaking the patois of his childhood, he, Jean Lebris Kerouac, would instantly penetrate its soul when he returned to reclaim his ancestral heritage after many previous lifetimes. In the Bibliothèque Nationale he would search the records and there find *Kerouac*, the fierce name of vanished Breton nobility that had emigrated to Canada and mixed its blood with the Indians.

I'd listen to him with delight and pain, seeing all the pictures he painted so well for me, wanting to go with him. Could he ever include a woman in his journeys? I didn't altogether see why not. Whenever I tried to raise the question, he'd stop me by saying that what I really wanted were babies. That was what all women wanted and what I wanted too, even though I said I didn't. Even more than I wanted to be a great woman writer, I wanted to bring life into the world, become a link in the long chain of suffering and death. I said of course I wanted babies someday, but not for a long time, not now. Wisely, sadly, Jack shook his head.

He never told me the whole story of his relationship with Edie Parker, about the baby she had aborted through forced labor at five months, when he'd shipped out to Greenland on the *Dorchester* in 1942.

One day, though, he showed me a picture he had in his wallet. It was a snapshot of a beautiful little girl of about five with dark braided hair, standing solemnly holding the handlebars of a tricycle. "Who do you think that is?" he asked. I had no idea. Was the little girl a niece? You could see the family resemblance. "Jack, she looks just like you," I said.

He grabbed the snapshot away and went and stood by the window and stared at it in the light. "Well, she's not my daughter, I don't care who she looks like. I know who's her father." That was the first time I heard about a woman named Joan Haverty, to whom he'd been married in 1951 for only six months. But it had all been a huge mistake. She'd laughed at his writing, wanted him to quit and support her, she'd treated him like a fool and made it with other men. There was no way the child could be his, no matter what any blood test said, despite any accidental resemblance. As a matter of fact, he knew his wife's lover had been dark — Puerto Rican, he thought. But he put the photo back carefully in his wallet. I wonder if it stayed in there for years.

Sometimes I'd think of this little girl and how she'd never get to know Jack, probably never see him, not even once, yet go through life carrying his face, her eyes blue as his. I'd think of my father and our walks down Broadway, and how he still loved me even though I hadn't turned out the way he wanted, and of the child scraped out of me, too, the boy I could have had and been forced to give away. How could you live not knowing your child?

Could I blame Jack more than I blamed myself? Perhaps it was not a question of wrong and blame but of terrible loss and sorrow. For me, too, freedom and life seemed equivalent.

Six weeks after I met him, Jack packed his rucksack, rolled up his sleeping bag, and was ready to take off. He was leaving America just as there were concrete indications that his days of obscurity would soon be ending. After years of rejection slips, two novels, *On the Road* and *The Subterraneans*, would be published within weeks of each other the following fall. *On the Road*, which Jack had written in fourteen days on a scroll of teletype paper while he was married to Joan Haverty, had been held by Viking Press for three years, while debate went on among the editors as to whether or not it was the right time to bring out such a daring book. Suddenly it was Jack's moment. The "bottled eagerness" of the fifties was about to be uncorked. The "looking for something" Jack had seen in me was the psychic hunger of my generation. Thousands were waiting for a prophet to liberate them from the cautious middle-class lives they had been reared to inherit. *On the Road* would bring them the voice of a supreme outlaw validated by his art, visions of a life lived at dizzying speed beyond all safety barriers, pure exhilarating energy.

The *Mademoiselle* piece on the San Francisco Renaissance hit the stands that February. A few days before Jack sailed for North Africa on the Yugoslavian freighter *Slovenia*, he, Allen, and Gregory Corso were interviewed by a reporter for a recently founded newspaper, the *Village Voice*. The article, when it ran, was entitled "Three 'Witless Madcaps' Come Home to Roost." A hip putdown of three poetic stooges, it was a foretaste of some of the later publicity given the Beat Generation. Jack got very drunk on his way to meet the reporter, and was quoted as saying, with alcoholic profundity: "Pity dogs and forgive men."

The *Slovenia* sailed on Sunday, February 15. On Saturday morning Jack and I went down to Lucien's, and he drove us out to the Brooklyn Navy Yard with Cessa and their two kids. Lucien had bought two bottles of champagne. We sipped it out of paper cups in Jack's cabin, then took the little boys up on deck. Their voices piping like excited birds, they went climbing all over the place; you had to keep grabbing their wrists to prevent them from ducking under railings and falling into the water. Jack put on dark glasses, as befitting a mysterious, lonely transatlantic voyager. I was going to stay on board all night and leave in the morning before the *Slovenia* went on to Perth Amboy to take in fuel. It all seemed romantic, like those grey French movies with Jean Gabin wandering along the dockyards in the fog; the melancholy of departure was part of it, too.

Early in the evening, Lucien and his family left. I lay down with Jack in his bunk. Boats passed slowly on the East River, and I thought I could feel its currents moving beneath us, reverberating in the steel floor.

I really did want to stay the night, but around eleven Jack woke up in a strange panic. Most of the crew had gone ashore and it was all too quiet for him. He wanted us to go back to the city and find a bar where there were lots of people drinking beer, he'd sleep one last night on land. We put on our clothes, walked down the gangplank, and wandered for blocks along the waterfront. The dark had come down over the river like thick black velvet. Here and there at the ends of dead-end streets were dim taverns all brown inside, with dock workers and sailors steadily drinking under yellow lights. There were no women in this nighttime world. Steam was coming out of the stacks of motionless freighters. It rose in startling whiteness against the black sky. I'd never seen anything like it before. It was strange to think that because of my sex I'd probably never see any of this again,

138

and would probably never have seen it at all if it hadn't been for Jack.

We took the subway back to the city. At Ninety-sixth Street the train stalled abruptly as it pulled out of the station. A few minutes later the conductor came around and told everyone to get off. Someone had jumped onto the tracks and been killed. Jack turned white and grim. He yanked me after him up the stairs and out onto Broadway. We walked in silence to the West End Bar, where Jack thought Johnny the bartender looked at him oddly, as if he saw death in his face. "It's only because you've been drinking," I said, but I felt scared for him suddenly. To me as well, the suicide in the tunnel had seemed an omen of some horror waiting in the future.

After many beers, I made Jack come home with me. He slept tossing and sweating, muttering through clenched teeth. At dawn he sat up in bed and said he'd had a terrible dream — "an endless train pulling into an endless graveyard, the passengers not monsters but geek faces of friends." When I put my arms around him, he was shaking.

He said he had to get up, had to leave, his boat might sail without him. I tried to convince him to stay a little longer, but he wouldn't change his mind.

At the door he kissed me and told me to go back to sleep. "We'll meet again," he said.

9

EIGHT MILES OFF the African coast in the midst of a fiery tropical sunset, Jack wrote to me for the first time. He expected to reach port by dusk. In case I was still feeling disappointed by his abrupt departure, he pointed out it was a good thing I hadn't gone back with him to the *Slovenia* — from Brooklyn it had only gone on to big gas-tank barges off Perth Amboy.

Ten days at sea studying history and Kierkegaard had opened "new cracks" in his mind. He'd slept a lot, walked on deck in the sun, breathed the fresh sea air, and "now I'm my old self again (the healthy Jack you never saw)." He spoke of Tangier as the City of Vice, the Blue Pearl of the Hesperides. He was raring to go.

All through the voyage he'd dined in silence with the only other passenger, a mysterious Yugoslavian Mata Hari. The *Slovenia* had almost foundered five hundred miles out in a fearsome storm. In all his years as a seaman, he'd never seen such mountainous waves. The ship had gone plunging up and down in them like a rowboat. But during this ordeal had come a moment of luminous calm when Jack had heard the words —

EVERYTHING IS GOD

NOTHING EVER HAPPENED EXCEPT GOD

He had believed, and still did.

140

I could believe too, if I tried. Jack urged me to read Kierke-gaard. *Fear and Trembling* was the right book, he thought, not *Sickness Unto Death,* which was too abstract a discussion of despair. *Fear and Trembling* was about Abraham and Isaac and had made him cry.

There was a line he wrote right after that which said, "At moments I was sad remembering your tears." "We'll meet again," he promised.

The postscript was scribbled in Tangier, where Burroughs had immediately taken him to the Casbah to see the veiled women pass and Jack had been so high he thought he'd seen it all before. You could smoke marijuana legally and publicly right in the cafés. He was very excited in this ancient, wild town. He'd get himself a room of his own to write in. It was morning and there was bright sunshine and the cries of Arab peddlers. "Tonight again the mysterious Casbah and that whanging music." Write soon, he signed off. He wanted to hear the latest from New York.

The blue air letter had gone off on its journey to America without postage. Coming home from work, I'd found a no-tice of undelivered mail. I ran to the post office early the next morning, paid the twenty cents that was due, and stand-ing there tore Jack's letter open and read it over several times. Until then I somehow hadn't believed he would ever return to me. "At moments I was sad," he'd written, "remem-bering your tears . . ." It was a wonderful letter, tender and distant.

I wrote back immediately, giving him the news he wanted, enclosing copies of the *Village Voice* article and another written in a similar spirit that had just appeared in the *Nation.* I called Allen and told him I'd heard from Jack. In *my* letter I said, "I miss you, think of you all the time." And I did. It was as if my self were strangely extended, walking around those bright streets on the other side of the world. But I told Jack I had nothing to say about his vision of God, I couldn't believe in God myself.

141

In his next letter he lectured me a little: "When I said 'God' in my vision in the sea I didn't mean a bearded man in Heaven, I meant THAT WHICH PASSES THROUGH ALL." And added, "Which if you said it to the college crowd would pass through one ear and out the other, as is proper and fitting."

But I didn't believe in this Buddhist God, either — my mind came up against a wall in these matters. The here and now was all I saw. I wanted to be happy in the here and now, to someday pull Jack into it with me if I could.

My mailbox has on it the design of a perforated star. I can see through the small holes the white of commonplace envelopes, the mustard of telephone bills. Blue is the color of air letters. Opening the heavy front door at the end of each day, coming into the dusty hall, I look for that little glimpse of blue, having played all the way from the subway the game of Will there be, won't there be blue this time. Sometimes my sureness there's a letter actually produces one. Other times my system fails me; there's a break in the invisible connection between Jack and me, and I lose him to the Void he's always talking about. It's as if I have to be a juggler, suspending him in air through sheer concentration.

I'm friendly with a man at work who always asks me about Jack. "And what do you hear of Mr. Kerouac?" It's ironic to call an outlaw "Mr." He hates MCA as much as I do, it's irony that keeps us going. We joke to each other about the wood paneling and old English hunting prints in the elevators, and the leather-bound sets of *The Decline and Fall of the Roman Empire* and other classics in each reception room that are only bindings minus books, and the dress codes requiring women to wear nylons and high-necked dresses all summer and permitting men to wear sports jackets only on Fridays. All this respectability, he assures me, is only a front. "And what does your friend Jack say about Tangier?" There's something avid, melancholy, about his interest. He's read all the articles, wants me to promise to arrange a meeting between himself and Jack when Jack comes back to the States.

Every day he asks me to come into his office, and shuts the door and talks to me for hours about his disappointing life, staring at me intensely as if maybe I have the key to everything and it's going to come to me any minute and I'll give it to him. He wears ugly, shiny brown suits and white shirts and has the sallow look of being unloved. Sometimes on his way home to his wife and kids he says he'll drop me off in his cab. He tells the driver to wait, then kisses me good-night at my door — I can taste the sallowness in his kisses.

He'd been a war hero in the Pacific, then had his wild period — quite similar to Jack's — in the Village before he got married, when he was writing his novel about the war that a famous critic read parts of in manuscript and praised. One day he says he's decided to tell me the very worst, most shameful thing about himself, he wants me to have no illusions about him. Turns out he's none other than the king of the True Confessions writers; he does it on the side every night after work. Under various pseudonyms he writes those humiliating stories so effortlessly that — the greatest irony of all — he suspects they're natural to him, he's really come to think he can't do anything else. "That can't possibly be true," I say. But he looks at me so sadly, askingly, across his desk — the key . . . the key — that I feel bewilderingly guilty, as if I'm meanly denying him some Dostoevskian absolution, and I end up going out for drinks with him and then to bed for a quick half-hour before he goes home to his wife. I have the strange feeling that if I ever told Jack about this lapse, he would somehow understand and not be troubled by it.

By the end of March, Jack was sounding restless. He hadn't found what he'd expected. "Not too many good vibrations in Tangier and the Arabs very quiet, send out no vibrations at all," he wrote.

In a few days Allen and Peter would be landing and he and

143

Burroughs would row out to meet their ship. Rowing in the bay was one of their principal occupations. Jack was also typing a manuscript for Burroughs called *Naked Lunch*. Most of the time he took long walks, thus avoiding the dull expatriate characters in the cafés. He'd watch the slow dance of the ancient fishermen pulling in their nets, or muse alone in his hotel room. Everything was a little too slow, even the mail — he'd just gotten a letter from me that was four weeks old. Somehow in Tangier he couldn't write, but that could wait. "What I'm actually doing is thinking nostalgic thoughts of Frisco."

He'd go off to Paris early in April — the others could join him later. He'd find a cheap garret, then on to Brittany, London, Dublin — after which he'd work his way back on a freighter. Probably he shouldn't have come at all. This Old World scene didn't interest him. He had more important things to do in America, where it was likely he'd be seeing me in New York in July. He admitted he looked forward to that. None of the girls he'd met spoke English, and he was weary of whores. "Mostly fags abound in this sinister international hive of queens."

With Burroughs as his guide, he'd sampled all the vices of Tangier, smoked opium, eaten hashish. Now he was musing in the darkness of his room, where he knew he was better off. The moon, the sea, the liquid lights of ships at anchor in the bay, were enough.

They should have been — but weren't. He felt abashed remembering the vigor of older American traveler/writers like Twain and Muir, as though he'd never written a line himself. Bitterly Jack compared his "newfound utter listless dispiritedness and no-care of where I am, what I do" to their enthusiasm.

It turned out, though, that he and Burroughs had been poisoned by some hashish that had been sprayed with arsenic. "So that explains my so-far dispirited visit in Tangier and feeling of no vibrations . . ."

HERE'S A RECORD in *Desolation Angels* of the day Jack bought his passage to Tangier. First, Allen Ginsberg had walked him downtown to the passport office in Rockefeller Center. There, coming toward them in the vast lobby, waving, was Elise. I'm sure she was embarrassed to run into them, flushed with pleasure and mortification, her eyes filling with the unexpected sight of Allen — a gift snatched from the impending emptiness of time, when he'd no longer be with her. She stopped, said a few forgotten words, went out through the revolving glass door onto Fifth Avenue.

As a matter of fact, they had just been discussing her. "I don't want no big Jewish wives yelling at me over the dishes," Allen had said, and quickly changed the subject, pointing at a strange woman: "Look at that sickened face just went by ... Got the expression of sneers and hopelessness, gone forever, ugh." "Doesn't God love her?" Jack had asked.

Elise is a bit player in Jack's fiction. On the next page she makes a last unaccounted-for appearance, waving at them again that same afternoon from a street corner down on Twelfth Street. This time Allen and she stand laughing, actually giggling together like children, over some obscurely ridiculous joke Jack doesn't understand — some "yiddishe controversy," he calls it, taking rapid-fire note of the comical alikeness of this pair, these "lazy ladies of Manhattan."

I didn't see much of Elise once Allen and Peter had left. She moved out of the apartment in Yorkville and got a place without a phone in the distant reaches of the Lower East Side. She took a night job and slept during the day. There was some deep rift between Elise and Sheila. Sheila's version of it was that she was sick of watching Elise throw herself at Allen. You invested love — you got a return, right? If you didn't, you gave up your investment. So what was so complicated about that? She herself wasn't going to waste much more time in New York waiting for Elise to come to her senses; she began looking for a secretarial job overseas. Leo Skir moved in with her for a while.

Elise said only that Sheila didn't understand that she needed to be alone. The night job suited her — straight typing for an outfit that made copies of television scripts. She found she could dull the boredom by drinking wine or smoking marijuana before she went there, and still manage to type; she'd walk away from her typewriter and drink more wine in the ladies' room, despite the risk of being caught.

What she liked was leaving there at dawn. Sometimes she'd walk almost all the way home, watching the cold pale light take color over the black rooftops. There was an all-night bakery on her block that made bagels; she'd stop off and buy herself one still hot from the oven ... Well, it was a life.

Now and then we'd arrange to meet in a coffee shop before she went to her job, but Leo would usually show up too, so it would be hard to talk. He always gave me the feeling he was standing off at a distance observing Elise, Sheila, and me, as if we were specimens of something — *types* of girls who might crop up handily in his later writings. He seemed almost gleefully proprietary about Elise, as if she were his own invention. Even her mistakes were exactly what he would have attributed to her character. Sheila sent him into raptures of delight by being so bourgeois. Me he wrote off — I could tell — as "the ambitious one." Allen Ginsberg's ambition was decidedly questionable, but it was a worse trait in a woman. Leo was watching as I typed my way up the Madison Avenue ladder of success, already compromised by my $60-a-week job at the MCA Literary Agency.

A large publishing company across the street from MCA advertised an opening that spring for an editorial secretary. Out of sheer restlessness I went over to apply. A woman with upswept white hair and the operatic bosom of a Helen Hokinson dowager came out into the waiting room, sized me up with tightened lips, and led me back into her office. "What are you doing here?" she asked.

I'd seen the ad, I said, and handed her my résumé. She glanced at it and handed it back.

"Miss Glassman, you are mistaken. There is no opening here at present." I stared at her, somewhat baffled. "Nor," she intoned coldly, "is there ever likely to be one suitable. And I think you will find that to be the case elsewhere. In fact, I'd advise you to get out of publishing altogether. Try other fields," she said with the heartiness of a guidance counselor, as she led me out.

For days I brooded over this mystifying encounter, wondering what I'd done or what I'd said to offend this connoisseur of girls. Had there been a spot on the white gloves I wore only to job interviews? Had my chignon started to slip? I concluded the problem lay with my appearance, since I'd managed to say so little. What had she seen in me that made me so unacceptable that she was sure no publisher would ever have me? Had she detected with her trained eye something at variance with the demure surface I thought I presented to her? Something possibly not ladylike? I'd recently come to realize that in the world of work, gentility strangely counted more than brilliance, and young women were judged by prospective employers the way they'd be judged as candidates for marriage to the kinds of young men who didn't interest me one bit.

It did not occur to me until much later that I had probably

been disqualified because of my name. My mother would have figured this out immediately, but she had educated me too well into forgetfulness of being Jewish. As for the pursuit of gentility, all that seemed quite ridiculous now, and even pitiable. I saw it only as a necessary mask.

Office life and real life had to be kept separate. On weekday mornings, you locked the door on your unacceptable self; you let it out again after five. This was the arrangement by which I knew I had to live. But only for the time being. Holding my breath, I was waiting for much more. Someday the publishers that would not have me as a secretary would have me as a writer. As a writer, I would live life to the hilt as my unacceptable self, just as Jack and Allen had done. I would make it my business to write about young women quite different from the ones portrayed weekly in the pages of *The New Yorker*. I would write about furnished rooms and sex. Sex had to be approached critically, I thought. I would not succumb to the ladylike stratagem of shimmering my way toward discreet fadeouts. I'd decided this even before meeting Jack or reading *Howl*. The writing itself seemed to lead me into it. Sometimes I'd stop and feel scared and think "Can I really say this?"; then I'd think "Yes I can" and go on. I'd call Elise late at night at her job and read her the new pages of my novel, or bring them with me to Hiram Haydn's class, where people actually seemed to like them as much as Elise did. Intoxicated by these bits of approval, I'd stay up several nights in a row and write more, reporting groggily to MCA in unironed dresses and making a million typing mistakes on their letters, but who cared? Even though, despite Jack's advice, I still wrote each paragraph over and over, the sheets of paper I kept in the green typewriter-paper box swelled to fifty. No longer could anyone mistake my novel in progress for a mere short story.

One windy day at the end of March I put extra pins in my hair and applied for a job at another publishing company, Farrar, Straus and Cudahy, where a friend of mine from Hiram Haydn's class was already working. This time I was

148

hired right away. I was secretary to John Farrar. My friend's boss was the editor-in-chief, Robert Giroux.

I'd heard a lot about Mr. Giroux even before I came to Farrar, Straus. He was the editor who had discovered Jack, published *The Town and the City* at Harcourt Brace, and even convinced him to revise and cut it. He was someone Jack always spoke about with admiration. "A great French gentleman," Jack said, who ate only in the best restaurants. Once when Jack was a little drunk, he'd described Giroux cryptically as "a great white panda." The two of them had a terrible misunderstanding that went back six years, to the day Jack had finished *On the Road.* After typing it nonstop for two weeks in a great burst of spontaneous energy onto the huge scroll of teletype paper Lucien had given him, Jack had rolled it all up, stuck it under his arm, and taken it immediately to Giroux's office. There, he'd triumphantly unfurled the whole thing. "Here's your novel!" But Giroux had evidently not responded in the proper joyous spirit. Staring in astonishment and dismay at the river of words flooding his office, he'd wondered aloud how it would ever be possible to rework it. Affronted, Jack had shouted that not one word would ever be changed. He rolled his manuscript up, took it away, and never returned.

Although I did reluctantly see Giroux's side, my twenty-one-year-old sympathies were with Jack. The exuberant, outrageous Jack whom I'd only seen traces of now and then. Mad Jack, impossible Jack. The dark young man rushing out with his manuscript, rage in his blue eyes, walking dazed on the midtown sidewalks where ordinary people were going about their business. Jack Kerouac was his own worst enemy, anyone reasonable would have said. He should have retyped the thing properly, double-spaced on fine white bond, *then* taken it to his editor, having made an appointment in advance, having taken into account editorial weariness and bleariness of eye, the torpor that comes after lunch in the offices of publishers . . .

He paid for that mistaken afternoon with six years of rejection from editors much less imaginative than Giroux, and in his hurt pride counted Giroux among those others who had rejected *On the Road*. But by 1957, the quarrel had become enfolded into the benevolence of the past — a mock-heroic encounter between the artist/savage and the gentleman. When I wrote Jack about my new job, and mentioned meeting his former editor, he sent friendly messages to Giroux in the letter he wrote back to me, just as if the two of them had never been out of touch.

It was the last of Jack's air letters. He mailed it on April 3, just before he took the packet to Marseille, cutting short his visit to Tangier by months. "April in Paris is all I keep singing (AT LAST)." He threw cold water on any romantic images I might still be harboring about his North African adventure: "The Medina is full of narrow damp alleys, robed Arabs, vegetable stands, smoke of frying fish, & Allen Ginsberg wandering around looking for asparagus."

"Be seeing you in New York before 4th of July," he ended down at the bottom of the blue page just before he wrote "love."

Suddenly time contracted like a concertina. "Before 4th of July." In June, then? I tried to decode the hidden meaning of "be seeing you," which somehow seemed a wave of the hand rather than a promise. I assumed it meant we'd be together again — but for how long? Would he stay with me in New York or go off somewhere else? And would he take me with him this time? I was sure I was quite ready to be taken away. Without a qualm I'd walk out on my New York life-without-Jack, carrying only the manuscript of my novel with me.

All those first spring weeks, as red, sticky buds appeared on the tree of heaven, as florists' windows on Broadway filled up with daffodils, as I typed letters to scores of unfortunate writers, declining manuscripts with courtly eloquence, or sneaked bits of my novel into the typewriter on slow afternoons in the office, or had sandwiches in Schrafft's with girls I'd known at Barnard, or spent more time in the Village than I had since I was sixteen, wanting to be out at night in

the world, the focus of which had shifted downtown again
— the Village was making a comeback, everyone said, waking up into some new phase as yet undefined; the streets
those limpid evenings were filled with more people than I
ever remembered seeing, young people like me, subway
riders, wandering, looking, jamming the Square on Sundays
where the singers still came — all that spring, I was counting
off days, one less and one less, and soon it would be June.

"Write to me at American Express," he said, and I did but
never got a reply. April in Paris had captured him, or American Express had lost all my letters, or he'd found another
girl in Montmartre, tough and cool, dark as Tristessa — that
was the most likely thing, I had to admit.

April dissolved into May. I came home late from the Vil-
lage one night and found a telegram shoved under my door.
SAILING TODAY ON NIEUW AMSTERDAM. OK TO STAY
WITH YOU? JACK.

I ran to the phone, called up Western Union. Could you
cable someone on a ship? Would it get there right away? I
remember the message I gave the clerk: DOOR WIDE OPEN.

*H*E CAME BACK not because of me but because he was profoundly homesick. He wanted America, a bowl of Wheaties by a kitchen window; he wanted Lowell, not New York.

Across the Atlantic he hadn't found the Old World but a new one he was inadvertently helping to create. Through a perpetual haze of marijuana he'd viewed the international scene like a dismayed elder, noting a cool that was colder and deader than any hipster's earned fatalism, a pose conveying nothing. He saw himself imitated, and hated what he saw. Was that bored indifference his? These new young people with their cultivated inertia, their laconic language (consisting mainly, he observed derisively, of the word *like*), seemed to have the uniformity of an army. They'd invaded Tangier, swarming around Burroughs; when Jack went to Paris, he found them there, too. He left and went to London, but stayed less than a week. Just before he'd sailed, he'd found his family's genealogy in the British Museum and read for the first time the emblematic motto of the Kerouacs: *Aimer, travailler, souffrir.*

Five days after I sent the cable, he knocked on my door. He stood out in the hall, smiling rather shyly, the rucksack at his feet. Since early that morning I'd been waiting, calling the office to say I was sick, wanting to go down to the dock and actually see the ship come in, but what if I missed him

152

there? Now he was here, and in that first moment I thought Who is he? But I kissed him in the doorway and he followed me inside. He left his rucksack on the floor and we lay down on the couch. The cat walked all over our bodies with utter disdain. "Ti Gris, Ti Gris," Jack called to it coaxingly, and then I knew he was back.

But it turned out he wasn't. He'd only be passing through for a few days — three or four at most — to pick up some money the publisher owed him. Then he'd be taking the bus down to Orlando, Florida, where his mother was now. Maybe he'd be back in the fall when Viking was publishing *On the Road.* He seemed a little embarrassed. "You have to let me go and be a hermit," he said, as if he was counting on me to understand.

I remember I went into the bathroom and cried and splashed a lot of cold water on my face before I came out. I got up my courage and said brightly, "How about staying a week?" But he shook his head and said he couldn't.

Hadn't I been the one, he reminded me, to say that what he needed was a home? Hadn't I said exactly that to him before he went off on this trip he never would have taken if he'd had any sense? Well, now he was going to have a home at last — in California. Ah, Berkeley was the place . . . A beautiful little wooden house with trees and flowering bushes in the yard, where he could lie on the grass and write haikus like Li Po and where Neal Cassady and Gary Snyder would come visiting, but most of the time he'd be alone. There was no room for me in this house, because his aloneness would include his mother, stirring her big pots in the kitchen, watching her game shows on the television set he was going to buy her, with a glass of red wine in her hand. It had always been his dream to do what he'd promised his father — settle down in a house with Memere, who'd worked in shoe factories so he could stay home and write his books, who didn't understand but always forgave her no-good, lazy son, who didn't like Allen, hadn't liked either of his wives; she'd been right about them, too. Memere was the woman he was going to now. "I really like you, though, Joycey," he said.

153

For the first time, I asked Jack, "Would Memere like me?"

He said, "Maybe. Yeah, she might. She doesn't approve of sex, though, between unmarried people."

Of course not. Neither did my parents. Suddenly the problem seemed clarified.

He was going to Memere the way he'd gone to Tangier, dreaming the whole thing before he ever got there. It was as if the power of Jack's imagination always left him defenseless. He forgot things anyone else would have remembered. Like how lonely and bored he was quickly going to be in Memere's house. Or that maybe Memere didn't even want to move. I was sure old ladies liked to stay in one place, not be trundled around with all their stuff in boxes, back and forth across the country on Greyhound buses.

But somehow I knew I couldn't say any of this — even though he always told me how practical I was and treated me like a worldly person, an authority on publishing, for example. No matter how skeptical you were, you couldn't strike at someone's deepest vision. Why, I was very hard-boiled, really, I thought, compared to Jack.

"You should get yourself a little husband," he said to me with sad generosity.

I said I didn't want that.

"Well, then finish your book, travel with Elise."

I said, "What if I came to San Francisco?"

With a flash of exhilaration I saw that I could do it. I didn't need Jack to take me, only to be at the other end of my destination. I started talking about how I'd begin saving money immediately, how I'd collect Unemployment out there until I found another job, how I'd get my own place in the city where he could come. I was sick of New York anyway, I said. I'd spent my entire twenty-one years in one place, and he was right, that was too long.

Somehow this solution to our relationship never had occurred to Jack. Once again I'd surprised him.

"Well, do what you want, Joycey," he said. "Always do what you want."

It was disconcerting, though, to be left so free. Men were

supposed to ask, to take, not leave you in place. I wanted to be wanted. Unlike Alex, Jack took what you gave him, asked no more. For Jack you didn't have to be anything but what you were — just as Ti Gris the cat was only Ti Gris, to be admired in all his hopeless Ti Grisness. Sometimes it was Jack who fed Ti Gris. Crouching motionless at a respectful distance from the plastic bowl, he'd watch with tender attentiveness each tiny ingestion of food. Could leaving in place be a kind of loving?

All I knew two days later when Jack left for Florida was that when I got off the bus in San Francisco at the end of the summer, I'd find him waiting for me in the Greyhound terminal, ready to carry my suitcase through the streets of North Beach until he found me a beautiful cheap room in some hotel where Allen Ginsberg had once lived, where we'd make love on the new bed. And he'd take me out to all the jazz joints that very night, and introduce me to everyone — Neal Cassady, in particular, was going to be crazy about me, because I'd remind him right away of his first wife, a sixteen-year-old blonde runaway named Luanne.

Interestingly enough, the only woman Jack Kerouac ever actually took with him on the road wasn't me or Edie Parker or Carolyn Cassady or any of the dark *fellaheen* beauties of his longings, but Gabrielle L'Evesque Kerouac, age sixty-two, with her bun of iron-grey hair and her round spectacles and her rosary beads in her old black purse.

As Jack laments the dreariness of bus stations, the awful unendingness of transcontinental highways, the nights of upright, jolted sleep to which he's subjecting his mother, Memere cheerfully looks out the window at the Texas plains, the Rio Grande Valley, the Mojave Desert, keeping the two of them going with the aspirins she's sensibly brought with her, alternated with Cokes. She buys souvenirs and, in a restaurant where she orders oysters, flirts with an old man and writes her address for him on a menu. Memere's thrilled by the small adventure of an overnight stop in a run-down hotel that humiliates Jack by its cheapness. It's all luxury and gaiety, not hardship. With her boy Jackie beside her, she's seeing the world at last. What had she known but work and poverty and Sunday masses? As a child of fourteen she'd gone into the shoe factories, married at seventeen, had three babies — a lifetime of sewing and mending, soapsuds and thrift. In thrift, she'd surpassed even my mother, saving the last inches of thread on a spool, half a potato, a quarter of an onion, a packet of needles from 1910. The boxes Jack packed for Memere to bring to California were full of what the affluent would consider mere debris. Perhaps to her those few days on the Greyhound bus seemed the bridal journey she'd never had.

But no house awaited Memere and Jack after all. Only a three-room apartment without enough furniture and they had to watch every penny at the supermarket. Memere hated Berkeley, hated the hills and the morning fog that kept the clothes from drying on the line, hated the crazy strangers that kept dropping in to lure Jack away from her, hated the sound of his typewriter behind his shut door. She missed her daughter and her neighbors and the beautiful Orlando sunshine. Why couldn't Jackie just live with her in some nice place there? What was the good of all this foolish moving around? she asked her son.

"Anxiously awaiting your coming out here now," Jack wrote me in his letter of June 11, adding that not only he but Neal was pleading with me to hurry up and to bring Elise and Sheila with me, so that we'd all be ready for a great new season. Berkeley was quiet and flowery; San Francisco wilder than before. The papers every day were full of news and editorials about *Howl*, which had been banned for obscenity and removed from bookstores by the local police.

The main North Beach hangout, The Place, had clippings about *Howl* on the bulletin board as well as paintings by local artists and phone messages and letters that the bartender held for his customers. "You will love this mad joint,"

Jack wrote. "Nothing like it in New York." One night he'd gotten into a ridiculous fight there, which he described with relish. A small bespectacled man had been hitting his wife. When Jack intervened, he took a swing at him. Holding his assailant by the arms, Jack had simply "dumped him sitting" to the floor.

But the letter ended bewilderingly and sadly: "It's the end of the land, babe, it gives you that lonely feeling — I KNOW that I'll eventually return to NY to live. Mad Jack."

I wanted to get my bus ticket the minute I read that letter, but I was scared to arrive there penniless. Somehow I had to save two hundred dollars. I gave up my apartment and moved in for the time being with my friend Connie who had worked for Robert Giroux. The change was too much for Ti Gris, who found a way to slide open a window screen and make his getaway from my life at long last. "Well I guess Ti Gris's on his way to China, where he will become an immortal and ride away on a dragon," Jack wrote.

Meanwhile I'd talked Elise into going to California with me. Hadn't we always planned to go adventuring together? She had nothing to lose but her awful typing job. From Tangier, Allen had gone on to Paris with Peter and wouldn't be back till next spring. It was dangerous to wait for him anyway. In Berkeley, Elise could go to graduate school — it would be easy for her to do that, according to Jack. Everything was easy in California, land of blue skies and leafy streets and a million new interesting scenes and people.

"I hope, when you get here," Jack worried, "you'll allow me to be a little bugged in general, I just can't imagine what to do or think anymore. Incidentally, tho, I'd like to draw you or paint you, at leisure . . ."

10

*J*UST WHEN I WAS so eager to abandon New York, it seemed to turn before my eyes into a kind of Paris. The new cultural wave that had crested in San Francisco was rolling full force into Manhattan, bringing with it all kinds of newcomers — poets, painters, photographers, jazz musicians, dancers — genuine artists and hordes of would-be's, some submerging almost instantly, others quickly bobbing to the surface and remaining visible. Young and broke, they converged upon the easternmost edges of the Village, peeling off into the nondescript district of warehouses and factory lofts, and Fourth Avenue with its used bookstores, and the broken-wine-bottle streets of the Bowery. An area with an industrial rawness about it, proletarian, unpretty — quite illegal to live in, but landlords were prepared to look the other way. An outlaw zone that silently absorbed people who'd sneak their incriminating domestic garbage out in the dead of night or hide a bed behind a rack of paintings, always listening for the knock of the housing inspector.

An older group of painters had survived here since the late 1940s. In lofts deserted by the garment industry, where sewing-machine needles could still be found in the crevices of floorboards, they'd dispensed with the confinements of the easel. Possessing space if little else, they'd tacked their canvases across larger and larger stretches of crumbling plaster,

158

or nailed them to the floor. They threw away palettes and used the metal tops of discarded kitchen tables. Paint would rain down on the sized white surfaces — house paint, if there was no money for oils — colors running in rivulets, merging, splashing, coagulating richly in glistening thickness, bearing witness to the gesture of the painter's arm in a split second of time, like the record of a mad, solitary dance. Or like music, some said, like bop, like a riff by Charlie Parker, incorrigible junky and genius, annihilated by excess in 1955, posthumous hero of the coming moment. Or like Jack's "spontaneous prose," another dance in the flow of time. For the final issue of *Black Mountain Review*, he'd jotted down his own manifesto, which many of the New York painters soon would read: "Time being of the essence in the purity of speech, sketching language is undisturbed flow from the mind of personal secret idea-words *blowing* (as per jazz musician) on subject of image."

Substitute *painting, color, stroke,* and it was close in spirit to the way the painters defined themselves in their heated discussions at "The Club," a loft on Eighth Street where they met regularly, or over beers at the Cedar Bar, continuing on into dawn over coffee at Riker's. Blearily they'd stagger back to their studios, switching on the light to stare at the new canvas up on the wall, matching it to the words still spinning in the brain, feeling exhausted or depressed or dangerously exalted — with the rent due, after all, and not enough money for the tube of cadmium red, and no gallery another goddam year.

But Jackson Pollock had broken the ice, they said, broken it for all of them, and then died — in classic American style — in his Oldsmobile, in his new affluence and fame that seemed to mean so little to him by the time he got it that he veered off the road into a tree by the side of Montauk Highway on his way to a party with his teen-age mistress and her girlfriend. Suicide by alcohol, this accident they all still talked about obsessively even a year later. Endless Jackson stories they told, and they journeyed out to Amagansett to the grave marked by a granite boulder that had been outside

Pollock's house, with his signature on it in bronze as if he'd signed his death — the name of the artist at the very end completing the painting.

Legend adheres to artists whose deaths seem the corollaries of their works. There's a perversely compelling satisfaction for the public in such perfect correspondences — like the satisfaction the artist feels upon completing an image. It was fitting that Jackson Pollock, whose paintings were explosions of furious vitality, dizzying webs of paint squeezed raw from the tube, who ground cigarette butts into his canvases with seeming brutal disrespect for the refinements of Art, would smash through a windshield at eighty miles an hour. Thirteen years later, Kerouac's quiet death in St. Petersburg would be viewed as improper, slightly embarrassing — at best, supremely ironic. Better to have died like Pollock or James Dean, or like Neal Cassady had — of exposure on the railroad tracks.

Artists are nourished by each other more than by fame or by the public, I've always thought. To give one's work to the world is an experience of peculiar emptiness. The work goes away from the artist into a void, like a message stuck into a bottle and flung into the sea. Criticism is crushing and humiliating. Pollock was hailed as a genius by the time he died, but could he have forgotten the widely repeated witticism that his paintings could have been done by a chimpanzee? As for praise, somehow it falls short, empty superlatives. The true artist knows the pitfalls of vanity. Dangerous to let go of one's anxiety. But did you *understand*? must always be the question. To like and admire is not enough: did you *understand*? And will you understand the next thing I do — the wet canvas in my studio, the page I left in my typewriter? Unreasonably, the artist would like to know this, too. Praise has to do with the past, the finished thing; the unfinished is the artist's preoccupation.

> Follow roughly outlines in outfanning movement
> over subject, as river rock, so mindflow over jewel-
> center need (run your mind over it, *once*) arriving

at pivot, where what was dim formed "beginning"
becomes sharp-necessitating "ending" and language
shortens in race to wire of time-race of work, following law of Deep Form, to conclusion, last
words, last trickle —Night is The End.
— Jack Kerouac

It's with a fire that the summer of 1957 comes in, in my
memory, a giant conflagration on Eighth Street and Broadway. I remember the night sky filling with smoke and flame
and the fire engines clamoring, and that it was a Friday and,
being at loose ends, I'd stayed downtown after work. Wanamaker's Department Store was burning — the massive old
landmark that had stood for so long like a boundary wall between the Village and the East Side. That Friday night it
burned to the ground. The famous clock I'd walked under in
January on my way to meet Jack melted like one of Salvador
Dali's watches.

What a strange night it was. The summer restlessness, the
mobs watching the fire, the smell of ashes everywhere. On
East Tenth Street a half-dozen galleries were opening that
night for the first time, according to fliers pasted up around
the Village. Owned and run by artists, they seemed to have
come into being all at once in deserted storefronts. Gradually, the shabby block between Fourth Avenue and the Bowery had become a little country of painters. Franz Kline and
Willem de Kooning, men whose names had just become
familiar to me, lived on that street, as did many of the totally
unknown artists whose works I was about to see in the small
new galleries. For me Tenth Street had the charm of foreign
territory — to enter it that fiery night was like finding Washington Square all over again.

Under the strange dusky orange glare, as passing sirens
wailed, groups of people moved from storefront to storefront,
talking intensely, laughing, congratulating each other, gulp-
ing wine from paper cups, calling out to friends: "Have you
seen the stuff at the March yet?" ... "Hey, I'll meet you at

the Camino!" ... "Is Franz here? Anyone seen Franz?" To get into a gallery you'd first stand back from the narrow doorway to let a rush of others out, and, once inside, you'd be drawn into a slow circular progression from painting to painting and have to look at everything for at least a few moments, whether you liked what you saw or not. That seemed the unspoken rule — everyone's work must be given attention.

I didn't really know what to make of the paintings. What was I supposed to see? Where were the images? My college teachers had taught me always to look for images; but I found very few as recognizable as those in even the most difficult Picassos at the Museum of Modern Art. There was just all this paint. Sometimes you had the impression of tremendous energy or an emotion you couldn't quite put into words; sometimes nothing came to you from the canvas at all. Was this how you decided which ones were good or bad?

But goodness and badness didn't even seem important that night. It was the *occasion* that was important. What I'd wandered into wasn't the beginning of something, but the coming into light of what had been stirring for years among all these artists who'd been known only to each other.

Major or minor, they all seemed possessed by the same impulse — to break out into forms that were unrestricted and new.

7

I T WAS NEAR the end of June. One Friday night, Elise, leaving work, found a notice in her pay envelope. She was fired; there was no explanation.

On Monday night she went back. She walked to her typing machine and sat down at it. All the people she'd worked with stared, as if there was something frightening in this behavior. She'd known all of them for months, but no one acknowledged that. She took a piece of paper from the drawer and put it in the machine. She typed her name over and over again, and when that began to weary her, "The quick brown fox jumped over the lazy dog."

One of the men came over and said, discreetly, "Miss Cowen, you know you're through here. Why don't you leave like a good girl?"

"I want to know why I've been fired."

"Just go," he said. "Okay?"

She'd typed all the way down the page, so she removed it from the machine and reached for a fresh sheet.

"*Hey!* What are you *doing!*"

"I want to know the reason."

"Get the boss," someone said.

"Yes," she said. "Get the boss."

She waited for him, ready to hear whatever he'd tell her. She'd be the first to agree she wasn't a particularly good worker. She made mistakes, she often came late. Let him also say, "Elise, you are a drunk and a stinking dyke." She was a human being like he was. Human beings addressed each other directly.

She sat typing, her pocketbook in her lap. Around her people were gathering to gawk as they would at a street accident, and this distracted her from her work. She stopped and put her arms around the machine, feeling anchored by its heaviness. Speaking out clearly, she said, "I want a reason or explanation" — and felt like Bartleby the Scrivener sitting in his corner of the law office endlessly saying, "I would prefer not to."

It was the police who came, three of them. They asked her to go with them. And when she refused, they began pulling at her arms, prying at her fingers, since she still held the machine in her embrace. Her glasses fell on the floor. Everything blurred as the three of them tore her away, dragging her out of the place in a rush, her feet scraping the ground.

"I want to know the reason!" she cried one last time — and got punched in the stomach going down in the elevator.

She called her father from the station house. "This will kill your mother," he said.

Leo Skir had a call from Elise early Tuesday morning. Her father and her uncle had come and she'd been released without charges. She needed to see someone. Leo said they could meet on his lunch hour. A little while later she called me and said she was leaving for California. At noon Leo waited in a pizza joint on the Lower East Side, but Elise didn't show up. She was selling her books on Fourth Avenue. She returned to her apartment, packed one suitcase, and slipped past her super's door with it, skipping out on the rent.

That night I saw her off. In silence we ate chop-suey specials in the maroon gloom of a Chinese restaurant, then sat together till midnight in the waiting room at the Greyhound terminal, drinking bitter coffee out of cardboard containers, watching the flotsam and jetsam of America arriving and leaving.

She'd saved me a book. A tattered Modern Library edition of *The Idiot.* "It's time for you to read it," she said gravely.

Everyone looked like a fugitive that night. I didn't feel Elise was going to San Francisco but somehow simply disappearing, merging into some appalling anonymity. I kept saying I'd be seeing her by the end of August. We were going to get an apartment together, weren't we? Meanwhile she should get in touch with Jack. But it was still like someone going away forever.

The phone rang late one night. It was Jack, calling from a bar in Berkeley. All day he'd been pacing in his yard thinking about what to say to me. "Joycey, I don't know how to say this, so I'll just say it honestly. I don't want you being disappointed by San Francisco. But this town is really nowhere. I wish I hadn't painted such glowing pictures and made you decide to throw up everything. I'm just warning you against a possible mistake that I myself started, damn it."

When I asked him what was wrong, he said he'd been stopped by cops four times for walking in the street after midnight. One had even fined him two dollars for going through a red light. Because of the *Howl* obscenity trial, there was all kinds of cop trouble. People's poetry books were being impounded. What would happen to Gregory's *Gasoline,* or *Evergreen Review* Number Two which had *Howl* in it? "This is a mad silly stupid place!" His coins ran out and he said he'd write me. He just wanted me to think hard about what I was doing. "Seeing you is all right with me anytime," he said. "I really like you. You're a real kid, a real true heart. But I just foresee being driven out of America."

The letter he sent that week described a California fallen captive to what Jack called the Total Police Authority. It was now a culture for old people on retirement, where cops prowled the streets all night to keep anyone else from having any fun. The "wild, end-of-the-landish" California he'd loved so much was gone. "Imagine one woman writing in that if Jesus Christ was alive, he would have led the police to the bookstore to impound *Howl*, and all that kind of negative oldwoman attitude all over the place with all these new dreary neat cottages and clean streets with white lines and signs that say WALK, STOP, DON'T WALK."

He knew he couldn't stand much more of it. "I admit I'm flipping and am bugged everywhere I go but I can't make it here." Even "glorious wild Neal" had been deprived of his freedom of movement. His license had been taken by the elderly police because he drove "like a human being instead of an old man." It was possible the Total Police Authority might eventually clamp down on the East, although New York might prove too vast and ungovernable.

Mexico was where he thought he'd have to settle. Maybe if I was still determined to get to San Francisco, we could go to Mexico together when he was ready to leave. But he'd rather start out with me from New York after Christmas. "But you decide and you do what you *want*," he ended.

It was much harder to do what you *wanted*, I was discovering, than to do what you had to, quite apart from what made practical sense. I wished I'd gotten on the bus that night with Elise, which would have decided everything. "I'm only going to be around for a little while longer," I kept telling people. "I'm going to San Francisco." Then I'd go home and read Jack's letter again and not be sure, and wonder if his mood had shifted back to liking California or if it was really as terrible there as he said. Or was he saying that because it was *me* he wanted to escape? That was the doubt I kept coming back to.

Somehow I missed in that letter what I see in it today so plainly — the strange pervasive elderliness of the Total Police Authority with its "negative oldwoman attitude," the neatness of retirement that it enforced. Which I now connect with Memere, whom I didn't see yet as my overwhelming adversary; she was just an old woman who complicated things somehow.

I wrote back that I was still leaving New York as I'd planned. Would he still be in San Francisco when I got there? Had he heard from Elise or run into her anywhere? But there were no more letters from Jack for weeks. From Elise I got only a post card of Lombard Street, "the crookedest street in the world." Most San Francisco houses were white, she informed me — "style emphasized, extremes norm." She'd gone to The Place, but no one had seen Jack there for a while. "A little Eastside-sick," she wrote. But what was her *life*?

Standing in a phone booth in the Cedar Bar one Saturday night in July, supplied with many quarters, I get the number of The Place — "A very-well-known bar in North Beach, operator" — then make a call to Miss Elise Cowen, listening to the phone as it rings on the other side of America. It's a busy Saturday night out there, too, although three hours earlier — I have to remember that. When the bartender answers, there's a beery undersea roar behind him that anyone would also hear if they tried to call the Cedar. The operator asks for Elise, and I hear the bartender bellow out her name: "E-lise Cowen! E-lise Cowen!...Sorry, not here," he says. "You're sure?" I say. "A dark girl with glasses, new on the scene." "Nope. Sorry." I debate asking for Jack, but feel too embarrassed by his fame out there: "Kerouac? Everyone wants to speak to *him*."

I step out of the booth back into New York time, where the night game at Yankee Stadium is on the radio and a lot of men in shirt sleeves are listening to the familiar summer drone of it, speculating loudly on the next batter coming up, like the patrons of any ordinary neighborhood bar.

Setting up for the next round, which may be free if the spirit moves him, the owner wipes the bar down with his cloth. He likes his customers, they're all right, steady, big drinkers. Beer and wine mostly, some go in for boilermakers.

167

He never planned to have an artists' bar — they came to him, what the hell. His customers have some running joke about the Currier and Ives prints on the walls. What's so funny about Currier and Ives? If you have walls, you put something on 'em. One thing's as good as another.

One week, the following story goes around the Cedar: A well-known collector is morally outraged by an abstract painting he's seen on Tenth Street. "What kind of painting is that?" he demands. "Call that a painting?" An artist asks the furious man to describe what he's seen. "Well, it's about four by six and white with an eight-inch stripe of black down the middle." "What more do you want?" the artist says triumphantly. A Zen-like rejoinder attributed to Franz Kline, who has the drooping, sharply pointed mustache of an Oriental warrior, but brown eyes of sad and glinting kindness. At the end of the bar nearest the door, he sits and greets his cronies: "Have one on me, come on..." Fifty years old and the money has just started to come in. He's like an amazed child — he'll get a bigger studio, buy a house on the Cape, maybe, hire some of these ragged kids fresh out of Black Mountain College to build his stretchers. Just today he bought a brush, the best brush he ever had in his life — this wide! — for twenty-five dollars...

The Cedar is like the Waldorf reborn, and in fact has some of the same patrons, but now I'm no longer an unconscious fourteen-year-old. One night I walked in, knowing no one. In less than a week I have not only a frame of reference but an enthusiastic Black Mountain boyfriend, sort of, named Fielding Dawson, whom everyone calls Fee. About this last development I have some guilt. "I'm not going to be around long," I inform Fee. "As soon as I hear from Jack, I'm splitting for the Coast."

But since I don't hear from Jack, this plan of departure seems less and less real. Perhaps I'll never hear from Jack again. Perhaps the best way to have a love affair is to be the one leaving, not the one left. Meanwhile I've moved out of Connie's apartment into a room at the Yorkshire Hotel, where I once swore I'd never live. And indeed the Yorkshire is only a place to store yourself; you can only be there when you're sleeping. I share a bathroom with an unseen stranger. It's between our two rooms — you unlock your own door to get in, lock his door from inside, then vice versa when exiting. If I live anywhere, I suppose it's at the Cedar. I even walk down there sometimes on lunch hours, coming into its sudden brown twilight from the bright, busy street. I sit at a table in the back and write in my notebook and order Manhattan clam chowder. To Hiram Haydn, who's asked to consider my novel for publication at Random House, I send my Yorkshire Hotel address on a post card. He calls me up at work sounding disapproving and fatherly as he sighs, "You've had so many addresses!" Three in one summer is kind of a lot.

Sometimes I go home with Fee to his little studio just off the Bowery, which is the worst place I've ever seen, worse than the Yorkshire or Elise's old room on 108th Street. The building seems about to fall down. There are holes in the floorboards, chasms in the ceiling, no heat (but fortunately it's not winter), a rusty trickle of water from one 1907 faucet; papers, beer bottles, squeezed-out paint tubes, accumulating laundry on the floor. I sit on the cot bed and Fee draws my picture on a large newsprint pad with lightning strokes of his charcoal pencil.

Kline himself taught him to do it that way one summer at Black Mountain. Fee had been only eighteen, a dazzled kid fresh from the proud humiliation of high-school oddball status in St. Louis. He had talked his mother into sending him to the green hills of North Carolina to meet America's avant-garde — not only Kline but Buckminster Fuller, Paul Goodman, Willem de Kooning, John Cage, Merce Cunningham, Edward Dahlberg, Robert Creeley, and Charles Olson. It was an extraordinary collection of visionary, eccentric, overpowering individuals. Life in that experimental and incestuous community was so highly pitched that Fee, like other Black Mountain alumni I met, never quite got over it.

Even Black Mountain's decline had been drastic. Schisms divided the faculty. The school ran out of money in 1954.

That winter there was no coal and nothing to eat. One small group held out, chopping down trees for firewood, stealing food if necessary from the A&P, fighting over possession of the few available women, and drinking large quantities of the local moonshine. But by the last year the entire faculty was gone except for the poet Charles Olson and the painter Joseph Fiore, and there were only a dozen ragged students remaining. One day in the fall of 1956, they all got into cars and drove sadly away, some heading west to San Francisco, others to New York and the Village.

Seven years after he first met Kline, Fee still has the look of a boy, the lanky grace of someone who dedicated his adolescence to sandlot baseball as he now dedicates himself to art, intoxication, and the intensities of the Cedar — always ready to be wowed. "That kid Fee," the older painters say, with the rueful affection of elders watching the young sow wild oats. Kline buys him beer and sandwiches — "If you drink, Fee, you have to eat."

If I weren't in love with Jack and maybe going away, I might be tempted to become Fee's "old lady," straighten him out a little, clean up the studio, contribute to the rent, have a baby or two, become one of those weary, quiet, self-sacrificing, widely respected women brought by their men to the Cedar on occasional Saturday nights in their limp thrift-shop dresses made interesting with beads. Even a very young woman can achieve old-ladyhood, become the mainstay of someone else's self-destructive genius. It might almost be enough to live on Fee Dawson's stories: *The night Jackson Pollock's pleading bloodshot eyes appeared in the little window in the Cedar's door and John the bartender said, "You've been a bad boy, Jackson. You can't come in." . . . The night that Franz . . . The night Bill de Kooning walked in and said . . .*

In fact, it's the storyteller in Fee that I can't resist — the memorialist of a hundred small occasions when in the ripening atmosphere of some midnight or endless beery afternoon came the moment when the absolutely right and perfect, irreducibly masculine thing was said or demonstrated unfor-

170

gettably — an illumination worth waiting hours for, "you *see*, don't you?" Exhausted, he sways on his bar stool as he tries to convey it, nearly tearful, brown cowlicks falling over his forehead.

In Fee there are echoes of Jack and Allen that I'm responsive to in men. Some pursuit of the heightened moment, intensity for its own sake, something they apparently find only when they're with each other.

ONE AFTERNOON IN mid-July I had to ask permission to leave work an hour early. I said I had a doctor's appointment, and took the bus uptown to Random House to see Hiram Haydn. When I was shown into his office, he said, "Well, we want to be your publishers. What do you think of that?"

What did I think? I couldn't think at all. The blue folder with my fifty pages in it was on his desk; behind him were shelves of all the books he'd edited. Like a schoolgirl I said "It's wonderful," but knew a real author would say something with far more resonance than that. He pressed a buzzer, and an editorial secretary, a very young woman like me, came in with coffee. "I want you to meet Joyce Glassman," Hiram Haydn said. "And see if Bennett Cerf is in his office."

Afterward, leaving Random House, which in those days of Bennett Cerf's reign as publisher was an actual red stone mansion, Joyce Glassman the author paused dizzily on Madison Avenue and wondered if the hour that had just passed was the best one of her life, but still had the distinct feeling of not quite possessing it or coming by it entirely honestly; of merely having fallen into luck in acquiring a publisher at the age of twenty-one, not to mention the extraordinary sum of five hundred dollars. It felt as if a whole necessary sequence had somehow been omitted — the genteel indifference and scorn of editors, years of near-starvation and struggle like Jack's, during which only the comradeship of fellow

172

writers also doomed to obscurity would be sustaining. Instead, Bennett Cerf had shaken my hand. "Your commercial book," Fee called it when I told him.

But it continued to be my lucky week. The following day at work, Robert Giroux called me in and told me I was going to be promoted from secretary to editorial assistant. It was an honor to get such a promotion. I knew it was possible to remain a secretary your entire working life. Perhaps someday I could even become an editor myself, although very few women got that far and the ones who had were all ladies of at least forty. You didn't turn down luck like this unless you were crazy or rich or engaged to be married. I accepted the job in a daze, realizing afterward it meant I'd given up on California. Then I went home to my room at the Yorkshire and finally found a letter from Jack.

He'd mailed it from Orlando, where he'd just moved Memere into an apartment around the corner from where she used to live — everyone down there thought it was an enormous joke. They all came around to laugh at him. He had thirty-three dollars left, the review copy of *On the Road* lay ignored on the shelf, "and now beyond the bugging stage," he was becoming enraged, so tomorrow he was off to Mexico. Maybe Viking Press would feed him.

I could join him if I wanted, unless I was still set on going to Frisco. A Greyhound bus — southbound this time — would take me to him, baggage and all; there were "lush apartments" for twenty dollars a month. We could be two writers in Mexico together. Meanwhile he would live in an eleven-dollar hovel, writing by candlelight in his solitary room. "So, sweet Joycey, decide what you wanta do."

I decided — casting my ballot on the side of art and love.

The next morning I told Mr. Giroux I'd be leaving Farrar, Straus in August. I was going off to Mexico to finish my novel and to be with Jack Kerouac. He looked a little startled, but he didn't try to talk me out of it.

Good-by New York. In Mexico you could live practically forever on five hundred dollars. I told my parents I was going there for a vacation. I told Hiram Haydn he'd have the rest of the novel in six months. I bought a Spanish phrase book and got addresses of Mexican Bohemians to look up from artists in the Cedar. "I'm sick, crazy," Jack had confessed in his letter, but I knew he'd be all right once he was with me.

In California there had been a mad neon night when Jack, breaking free of his solitude enforced by the elderly Prison Authority, tore off for San Francisco with Neal Cassady and other drunken accomplices who'd come to get him, passing around joints and a jug in the car, whooping across the Golden Gate Bridge — "Whooee!" Fiercely singing, Jack gulps California red with head thrown back, drowning Memere left behind grim-lipped in front of the television set's flickering inanities. Off and gone with his boy gang, he collects in the various drinking places visited in North Beach an army of roisterers, poets, chicks, out-of-work musicians, amiably strung-out deadbeats: "Where you *been*, man? Haven't seen y'around, y'know." As the mad night gets madder, the slurred exchanges become cosmic though impossible to repeat afterward, the juke box music soul-piercingly profound.

Lost in wine, Jack's no longer the leader of this reveling mob but its wild, blind child, legs buckling like a baby's — "Hold him up, somebody!" — as Memere's round face reproaches him, *What are you doing, pauvre Ti-Jean?* Guilty tears fill his eyes, although in the Void where nothing exists there are no tears, no Jack, not even Memere the sainted criminal, expelling babies between her legs into the suffering graveyard of the world. Only Jack's awful disembodied consciousness persistently remains.

In The Place he sees a strange girl, dark and troubled, standing frozen in the crowd around the bar. A lost girl who knows no one, no one speaks to her. She's come down into the streets from some room in a hotel that she hasn't left for a week, and wandered here. A face last seen on a street corner in the Village with Allen. A name is rendered up by the memory that never fails him.

Elise.

174

"I was too much for her with drinking gangs behind me," he wrote cryptically in the letter that invited me to join him in Mexico. "Everything exploded . . . I was afraid to write to you . . . But here's your enraged bum."

In my imagination Mexico is like one of those fruits you're warned not to eat — sweet and mango-colored. Bite into its pink and orange flesh in the wrong place and an invisible poison will invade your system. Peasants in white garments mass with guns as in an Orozco painting. Doves circle the gilded dome of a cathedral. Gringos gone spectacularly to seed, like Malcolm Lowry's Consul, sit on balconies sipping liquid fire. There's a white room with an iron bedstead where Jack and I sleep late in damp, tangled sheets, light slanting in through the broken slats of shutters, shadows of palm trees outside, flies abuzz on the cracked ceiling. The day waits, bright and treacherous — unknown adventure to be shared.

"What great happy fears and excitements you must be feeling now," Elise writes me about a week before I'm to leave New York in the state of happy fear she somehow is able to name so accurately even three thousand miles away. "Well, Rejoyce, have a beautiful celebration & lovetime of it in Mex. Give my embarrassed hello to Jack."

Calling The Place over and over three nights in a row after reading Jack's letter, I'd managed to find her. I had no idea what I was going to say, but when I finally got her, I told her the truth: that I knew and that it didn't matter and how was she anyway? — that was the important thing. She was broke, she said, but otherwise fine, the scene was weird, no job yet; eating one meal a day gave you an interesting high feeling, sharpened the senses, so maybe she'd keep it up. "If my father happens to call you, tell him I'm working as a waitress or something."

I'd wired her twenty-five dollars the next morning. She sent back a post card with basking seals on it. "You are my sunshine."

175

N Mexico City, Jack got off the Greyhound bus and walked to Orizaba Street, to the house where he'd stayed on other trips — first with Bill Burroughs after Joan's death; then alone four years later in an adobe cell on the roof — a summer that floated in his memory like a marijuana dream, a desolation that seemed peaceful now. In his padlocked room he had read all the sutras by candlelight; chastely, tormentedly, he'd loved Esmeralda Villaneuva, the Mexican woman with enormous sad eyes who supplied him with morphine. On the first floor lived the old man Bill Garver, an aging junkie who seldom left his tiny apartment, a withered shaman from Manhattan who quoted Mallarmé and spoke of lost civilizations and had once made his living stealing overcoats. Nine months ago, the last time Jack saw him, Garver had said, "You'll never see me alive again."

He'd always rapped on Garver's window when he wanted to visit him. Now as he approached the house, he saw that a pane of glass that had been broken for years had finally been replaced. He ask the landlady where Mr. Garver was. "Señor Garver se murio." He went inside and climbed the stairs to the rooftop room he still thought of as his, where he'd written *Tristessa* and the poems called *Mexico City Blues.* The door was open, and inside it had all been freshly

176

whitewashed; a young Spanish woman in a lace blouse lived there now.

It was the last visit Jack ever made to Mexico. He went downtown and found a room in a "sinister marble hotel."

Three days later he awoke there in a rocking, shuddering darkness that made him think at first he was at sea in the fury of an Atlantic tempest. He could hear walls crashing, sirens, women wailing. The living and dying world was ending inside the Diamond Sutra of Paradise, where he lay in terror with the hush of silence in his ears.

But when the great tremors of the earthquake subsided, his vision of Apocalypse left him and he was alone and mortal, exiled from all other human flesh, from warmth, from touch, ice around the heart.

He got up and tore pages out of his notebook, scribbled frantic sentences in a letter to be air-mailed to New York. "Come on down, I'm waiting for you. Don't go to silly Frisco . . ."

What could I see in Frisco that would be new and foreign and strange? Instead I was to hop a plane to Mexico City (the bus took too long), take a cab straight to Jack's hotel, knock on his door.

In case I was hesitating for any reason, such as his inconsistency, which he couldn't help, or the "irresponsibility" Elise had sadly reproved him for, he even described his cloistral room, which he already hated as "Arabic magic." We would sleep in its tiled splendor on a big clean double bed surrounded by huge oval "sex-orgy" mirrors. Our private bath would have twenty-foot ceilings and "Mohammedan windows." When we tired of this sultan's room and living the downtown life to the hilt, we'd rent a cottage out in the country with flowerpots in the windows. "We'll do our writing & cash our checks in big American banks & eat hot soup at market stalls & float on rafts of flowers & dance the rumba in mad joints with 10¢ beers."

Perhaps *after* Mexico I could go to Frisco to see Elise and finish up what Jack called my educational tour. "But I am lonesome for yr friendship & love." There were a hundred reasons for me to come down. We'd eat and drink and make love in that enormous bed and wander arm-in-arm visiting Aztec pyramids and pink cathedrals, "& wait till you drink big water glasses of fresh orange juice every morning for 7¢."

Three days before, I'd already written Jack, care of his mother, that I was coming to Mexico; but that letter never reached him. I would have come to him without any inducements at all. No Arabic magic room, no pyramids, no orange juice. It seemed so strange he didn't know this. Instead, he thought of me as some free spirit who didn't altogether match my image of myself. A girl capable of coolly pondering alternatives. Mexico or Frisco? Which would be more interesting? He even generously recognized the hungry writer in me that I hadn't learned to put first. He was going to show me things most Americans never saw. "And you can write a big book," he promised.

In 1975, crossing the border for an afternoon, I did see Tijuana once. Tijuana was all baked mud and frayed tawdriness, dispirited vendors of pottery pigs hustling cars in the heat. It wasn't Jack's Mexico. I never saw that country of words or penetrated its mysteries, never took the cab from the airport, bumping through the fissured streets where the debris of the great earthquake was being cleared away, hanging out the window until I saw the number of the marble hotel and called to the driver to stop, dizzily counting out pesos and running in so eagerly to ask for Señor Kerouac — whom I find miraculously in the exact state of wanting in which he wrote his letter and erase forever with my presence his sadness, the gnawing restlessness that makes no place right, poisons every destination.

Jack was gone from Mexico City a week before the date on my plane ticket, struck by a fever that seemed the final sign that the place itself was turning on him, driving him out. "I don't want you to be confused," he wrote just before he left. "This latest change of mind I can't help." He was on his way to his mother's house in Orlando. He'd see me in New York in my green room in the Yorkshire Hotel around the time *On the Road* came out in September. After all, the publisher might want him to make personal appearances. "Someday you'll see Mexico, right now I just couldn't sweat it out sick and alone." He even thought Mexico might very well have removed me so much from the concerns of my present novel as to have demoralized me altogether. But San Francisco would have been a waste of money. "Save your money for writing-time, then when rich go to Paris."

11

*O*n the Road was published on September 5, 1957. I have the distinct recollection of spending much of September 4 sitting in one of the tall narrow windows of the apartment I'd moved into just two days before. I remember the view of the opposite brownstones, unrenovated then and tatty, and the high stoops where supers stood smoking and which old ladies slowly climbed with their wheezing dogs. Positioning myself to face west, I could see all the way to Columbus Avenue and Donnelly's Irish Bar, and beyond that to Broadway, where Jack might come around the corner walking with rucksack from the subway any time that afternoon, turning up Sixty-eighth Street with a thirsty glance at Donnelly's on his way to what he'd called in his last letter from Orlando "our apartment" — so happy that I'd found it, although he swore he would have been content to stay with me in the Yorkshire. Anything was better than gloomy Mexico.

I'd mailed him thirty dollars from my writing-time money for the bus ticket to New York, where tomorrow he was going to be interviewed by *Time* magazine, which was also sending a reporter to talk to Allen Ginsberg in Paris. By noon the phone had started ringing with messages from Viking Press. Was Jack Kerouac there yet? Would he call as soon as he arrived? Would I tell him they had a lot of things lined up for him? Would I *make sure* he called? The publicity director seemed on the edge of being distraught. "Who am I speaking to, by the way?" she asked cautiously. Was she entrusting important matters to one of those abandoned young women the author of *On the Road* wrote about? I said I was a friend of Jack's, and added in my best Barnard voice that I'd worked in publishing until recently myself. Between calls I'd run back to the window.

It was the time of year, not quite fall, when usually nothing important happened, when the city, lulled by the last fierce heat, took a breath before what Jack still called with boyish fervency "the great new season." Even the Cedar had emptied — the painters had all gone swimming, like people who took vacations from more ordinary trades. The only excitement there lately had been provided by a visit from the poet Robert Creeley, whom Fee had described to me as a somewhat notorious personage, black-cloaked, one-eyed and bearded like a pirate, who had a fatal aura that caused vicious fights to break out wherever he went. Creeley would escape unscathed, but those unfortunate enough to accompany him to the working-man's bars he frequented were likely to have chairs broken over their heads. Legions of women were said to have fallen under Creeley's spell and to have been stolen by him briefly from their husbands and boyfriends. *"For love* — I would/split open your head and put/a candle in/behind the eyes," he wrote in "The Warning." Even Jack was impressed by Creeley's reputation. "Oh please write and tell me in detail," he had implored me from Florida, "how and where you met Bob Creeley and what happened and what he said and what he's going to do. You know, he's a mysterious figure and everyone was wondering where he was." But all I'd had to report was an uneventful evening around a table in the Cedar, where Creeley, Fee, and a couple of other Black Mountain poets too impoverished to leave town had discussed Charles Olson's theory of projective verse and rehashed Black Mountain softball games until two o'clock in the morning.

Somewhere on the Cape or on the Sound, Orville Prescott, the conservative middle-aged daily reviewer for the *New York Times*, was taking his annual vacation. In the August doldrums, the task of reviewing *On the Road* had fallen to a younger man named Gilbert Millstein, who had quietly been keeping track of Kerouac for years — ever since he'd come upon the phrase "Beat Generation" in John Clellon Holmes's novel *Go* and, pursuing the definition further, asked Holmes to write a piece about it.

Apparently it was sheer luck, this matter of timing — much as it later seemed like brilliant strategy on Viking's part.

In the late afternoon of September 4, the Greyhound bus slipped in toward the back door of Manhattan. It crossed the Jersey flatlands, the cattail marshes — oil-ravaged now — where industrial chimneys spout eternal flame and where, suddenly, the Pulaski bridge rusts against the sky, a Kline painting too vast for any gallery. It's just beyond there that the towers of the city first appear, silver ghosts rising above the rank wastes, the asbestos rooftops of mean towns, marking the journey's final lap.

It was a return route Jack knew by heart. New York was the bitter testing ground of promises, never giving you what you bargained for, always holding something back. With his first book no one could have made him believe that. But by now he believed he was ready to settle for much less than he'd wanted then: enough money to tide him over for a while, a few good times to remember later, some acknowledgment wrested from the critics that at least in the music of his prose he'd broken ground (little chance they'd look kindly on his subject matter).

He had mixed feelings about *On the Road*. It had been written six years ago, the work of a very young man, about his adventures with Neal. When he'd given Neal one of the first bound copies in California, he'd felt a coldness in the way Neal had looked at him. The Viking editors had violated its spontaneity anyway. Now, when it was too late, he regretted every revision they'd talked him into. As for *Dr. Sax* and *Visions of Cody*, the two books he considered his great, wild, important works, no publisher wanted any part of them.

Still he imagined celebrity with total naiveté — the longing of a shy man to become less tenuously connected to the world. Through your book you could become known without giving yourself away. When he'd had enough of all the literary parties, the mad Manhattan nights, he'd pick up his earnings, say good-by to his New York friends, head out again freer than ever.

Standing at the window as the afternoon of September 4 shifted into evening, my own mind was on nonliterary matters. In fact, the old-fashioned sentence I was thinking of wouldn't have sounded at all like Kerouac to any of his million future readers — "I can hardly wait to hold you in my arms" — written in pencil at the end of the letter he'd sent five days ago.

I saw a man come down Sixty-eighth Street. He had gleaming black hair, a Hawaiian shirt in a loud blue pattern — blue as his eyes . . . It took me a moment to be sure. Then I ran down the stairs.

On the Road is the second novel by Jack Kerouac, and its publication is a historic occasion insofar as the exposure of an authentic work of art is of any great moment in an age in which the attention is fragmented and the sensibilities are blunted by the superlatives of fashion (multiplied a millionfold by the spirit and power of communication).

> — Gilbert Millstein, *New York Times*, September 5, 1957

THERE WAS A newsstand at Sixty-sixth Street and Broadway right at the entrance to the subway. Just before midnight we woke up and threw on our clothes in the dark and walked down there still groggy with the heaviness, the blacked-out sleep, that comes after making love. According to Viking, there was going to be a review. "Maybe it'll be terrific. Who knows?" I said. Jack said he was doubtful. Still, we could stop at Donnelly's on the way back and have a beer.

We saw the papers come off the truck. The old man at the stand cut the brown cord with a knife and we bought the one on the top of the pile and stood under a streetlamp turning pages until we found "Books of the Times." I felt dizzy reading Millstein's first paragraph — like going up on a Ferris wheel too quickly and dangling out over space, laughing and gasping at the same time. Jack was silent. After he'd read the whole thing, he said, "It's good, isn't it?" "Yes," I said. "It's very, very good."

We walked to Donnelly's and spread the paper out on the bar and read the review together, line by line, two or three more times, like students poring over a difficult text for which they sense they're going to be held responsible.

> ... the most beautifully executed, the clearest and most important utterance yet made by the generation Kerouac himself named years ago as "beat," and whose principal avatar he is.
>
> Just as, more than any other novel of the Twenties, *The Sun Also Rises* came to be regarded as the testament of the Lost Generation, so it seems certain that *On the Road* will come to be known as that of the Beat Generation.

It was all very thrilling — but frightening, too. I'd read lots of reviews in my two years in publishing: None of them made pronouncements like this about history. What would history demand of Jack? What would a generation expect of its avatar? I remember wishing Allen was around to make sense of all this, instead of being in Paris.

Jack kept shaking his head. He didn't look happy, exactly, but strangely puzzled, as if he couldn't figure out why he wasn't happier than he was.

We returned to the apartment to go back to sleep. Jack lay down obscure for the last time in his life. The ringing phone woke him the next morning and he was famous.

The call was from Keith Jennison, one of Jack's editors at Viking, who was rushing up to the apartment with half a case of champagne. He carried it up the four flights of stairs and we drank it with orange juice, which seemed more Lost Generationish than Beat, as the phone kept on ringing with news of reporters who wanted to interview Jack, and excited

185

old friends, and invitations to various gatherings, and my mother, who wanted to know when I was coming to dinner and what was all that talking going on in the apartment. It was the radio, I said. But it was Jack, who'd downed a lot of champagne rather quickly and finally gotten smashed and broken the quiet that might have seemed gloomy to Keith Jennison, achieving the boisterous high spirits appropriate to the occasion. Jack had his own extravagant ideas of courtesy — in some way he felt honor-bound to meet other people's expectations. Three bottles of champagne were emptied with a rapidity that astonished Keith Jennison. When he left to go to his office, quite mellow by then himself, he took me aside for a moment. Squeezing both my hands in his, he looked urgently into my eyes. "Take care of this man," he said.

The first of many interviewers of the author of *On the Road* arrived a few hours later to get the inside story on the Beat Generation and its avatar. What was it really like to be Beat? he wanted to know. "Tell me all about it, Jack." When did you first become aware of this generation? And how many people are involved in it, in your estimation? Is America going to go Beat? Are you telling us to now turn our backs on our families and our country and look for kicks? What kind of society will we have in two years?"

"Hey," Jack said. "Have some champagne. My publisher came up with all this champagne this morning."

"Thank you, no. I'll stick to coffee." The interviewer made a note on his pad and explained that he did not want to cloud his impressions. Jack advised him to try writing when he was high. The interviewer said maybe he'd do it sometime, but it didn't go along with journalism when you were dealing with fact. Expansively Jack revealed he'd wanted to be a journalist himself, a great sportswriter, and his father Leo Kerouac had always hung out with newspapermen in the days when he was a printer in Lowell. The interviewer wasn't too interested in that. "Let's get back to the Beat Generation for a minute. Jack, why do you consider yourself and your friends 'beaten'?"

Eavesdropping from the kitchen, where I'm boiling water for coffee, I don't think much of this reporter, who seems to have swallowed Millstein's review without understanding it at all. Millstein had spoken of excesses and kicks and "violent derangements," but had also insisted Jack was expressing the need for affirmation — " 'even though it is upon a background in which belief is impossible,' " he'd written, quoting the Lost Generation critic John Aldridge. Was that so hard to understand?

Beaten? Bewilderedly Jack laughs and shakes his head, then with weirdly courteous patience launches into the derivation of the epithet — first uttered on a Times Square street corner in 1947 by the hipster-angel Herbert Huncke in some evanescent moment of exalted exhaustion, but resonating later in Jack's mind, living on to accrue new meaning, connecting finally with the Catholic, Latin *beatific.* "*Beat* is really saying *beatific.* See?" Jack so earnest in making his point so the interviewer can get it right, respecting the journalistic search for accuracy although he knows accuracy is not the same as truth.

Again and again in the coming months he will go through this derivation with increasing weariness — for other journalists, in labored articles he himself will write. Blinking into the glare of hot white lights he will repeat it before television cameras and deliver it into microphones on the stages of auditoriums, the words slurring progressively, emptying; wine will make them flow disconnectedly from the shamed fool on stage.

No one had much patience for derivations by 1957. People wanted the quick thing, language reduced to slogans, ideas flashed like advertisements, never quite sinking in before the next one came along. "Beat Generation" sold books, sold black turtleneck sweaters and bongos, berets and dark glasses, sold a way of life that seemed like dangerous fun — thus to be either condemned or imitated. Suburban couples could have beatnik parties on Saturday nights and drink too much

187

and fondle each other's wives. I forget when it was that *beatnik* entered the vernacular — could it have been as soon as October? The San Francisco columnist Herb Caen gets the credit for inventing it. How deftly it got the whole thing down to one word. The Russian-sounding suffix (the ascent of Sputnik was in the public consciousness at the time) hinted at free love and a little communism (not enough to be threatening), as well as a general oafishness. "Beat Generation" had implied history, some process of development. But with the right accessories, "beatniks" could be created on the spot.

I went downstairs every morning and found the mailbox jammed with letters forwarded by Viking. "Dear Jack," they invariably began. He'd start reading one thinking an old friend of his had perhaps turned up, and discover the yearnings or fantasies of a stranger.

> Dear Jack, I am dying in this little hick town. If I could only meet you, touch you . . .

> Dear Jack, I don't know what you're driving at and I've put down your book half a dozen times because it made me dizzy & sick & thrilled & confused, and I said the hell with it. But when I get home at night, fed up with working and all the corny doings of the one-minded people who always know where they are going to sleep at night and where the next meal is going to be, I pick the damn thing up, and wow! Good luck to you. If you ever get sick of New York and don't mind masses of collies and cats, give me a ring and come out for a weekend. I'm so ancient you won't have to be embarrassed . . .

> Dear Jack, Jefferson said — Yessir he did — "I have sworn on the altar of GOD ETERNAL hostility to every form of tyranny over the MIND OF MAN," hostility which THE AMERICAN PEOPLE make their own!! Hostility too, of course, to the obscene

tryanny of Vaticanism & its evil cabal of celi-
bates . . .

"Fuffnik's fan mail," Jack said sadly.

The mad letters were less alarming than the other kind
— the lonely communications from people so starved that
they demanded that the page become flesh. "If you will only
give me ten minutes of your time, you will see how very
much we have in common."

A letter from Jack's first wife, Edie Parker, turned up one
day in the pile. He read it over a couple of times, then sat
brooding and told me the story again of how Edie had come
and bailed him out and how they'd gotten married in City
Hall with the cops as witnesses. Edie had always been after
him to get married, wild as she was. "But not you," he said.
"We're just gonna go on being friends. That's better." "What
happened to Edie?" I said. He pushed the letter in front of
me. I felt it was wrong to read it, but I had to see what she
would say after so many years. Edie Parker was a heroine in
Jack's legend, and in fiction her daring would have been rewarded; she'd have won him forever. Instead she'd gotten
married to a midwestern businessman for a while and now
was looking to feel alive again. It was thirteen years since
Jack had told her, "We can't live on mayonnaise sandwiches,"
and now she was dreaming of going with him on the world
tour she thought he was surely going to make.

I didn't want Jack or anyone ever to make me feel that
way. I wanted always to feel alive and never to become old
like my parents had or like Edie sounded at thirty-five. But
Edie's letter was like a telescope through which I could
glimpse some point in the future in which there would be
no Jack but only me and some different life I could not imagine. For just a minute I saw this clearly and painfully.

Meanwhile Jack filled the present. Fame was as foreign a
country as Mexico, and I was his sole companion in its unknown territories. He'd quickly learned it was a country with
sealed borders. You couldn't leave it when you'd had enough
of it, though it could cast you out when it had had enough

of you. It feted you and stoned you, flattered you and mocked you — sometimes all in the same day. It demanded your secrets and whispered insulting innuendos behind your back. It corrupted your life with its temporary excitements; it invaded your dreams. The night he read Millstein's review, Jack dreamt of being followed by a parade of children chanting his name. With a wound in his forehead, he escaped with his army into Mongolia. But inside the Victory Theatre, the fame police had nearly caught him.

I often wished I could just swoop down like Edie Parker and bail him out of his awful success. Mostly I found myself waiting around to get him out of places where he'd stayed too long and drunk too much and where men would be wanting to take him on in a fight and terrifyingly avid women would be hanging around his neck. "You're only twenty-one," one of them said to me. "I'm twenty-nine. I've got to fuck him now."

"C'mon, Jack," I'd say, pulling at his sleeve. "Time to go. It really is." Sometimes he'd be mad, but he'd be grateful in the morning.

At WOR-TV I sat in a glass booth with the publicity director of Viking, watching Jack in black and white on a monitor. It was the new John Wingate show, fortuitously entitled *Nightbeat*. Talk shows had just recently been introduced on television, and they were all the rage. People could sit securely in their living rooms and watch the latest celebrities being shown up. It was great democratic entertainment. Jack sat on a swivel stool with a spotlight on him like a suspect awaiting the third degree, his hair tangled and wet, his face gone slack. I knew exactly how much wine he'd had to drink to get himself there, and I felt scared for him.

"Tell me, Jack, just exactly what you're looking for," John Wingate asked in his smoothly supercilious announcer's voice.

"I'm waiting for God to show me His face."

It was the truth, but somehow not the right kind of truth for television. Much as your host seemed to prod you toward a striptease, you were not supposed to show yourself naked.

That night Jack knew he'd crossed some dangerous line. He'd failed to protect that deep visionary part of himself that had to remain in darkness, that could only reveal itself in dreams or books. For the next two days he stayed in the apartment and hardly spoke at all, even to me.

I remember trying to turn my twenty-one-year-old self into an instant expert on fame. Someone had to put it into the right perspective for Jack. I lectured him about taking it all too seriously. "What you do is all wrong. You think that anyone who comes to interview you is going to be your friend, and then you're hurt when everything you say comes out twisted in their rotten stories." Looking very embarrassed, Jack admitted this was so. "Why don't you say no to things you don't want to do?" I advised him.

That seemed to him the best idea I'd come up with. He would remain in hiding with me and stop drinking and eat a lot of bacon and eggs and Lipton's pea soup and read the Diamond Sutra. For a few days he said no to everything. Then he said yes to doing articles for *Esquire*, *Playboy*, and *Pageant*, and speaking to a few more reporters, and appearing on more television shows, and doing a nightclub act at the Village Vanguard in December.

But the night Gilbert Millstein gave a party in his honor, Jack couldn't bring himself to go. He lay in bed shaking, and I had to phone and say he couldn't make it; he wasn't feeling too well, I explained.

John Clellon Holmes had come all the way down from Connecticut for the occasion. Jack wouldn't speak to Millstein but only to him. He couldn't bear the thought of seeing anyone that night but a very old friend. He asked Holmes if he could leave the party for a while.

Holmes came uptown and sat with Jack, and he calmed down a little. He spoke to Holmes of not knowing who he was anymore.

Outside the Victory Theatre the critics stood waiting to hurl bricks at the hoodlum, Neanderthal, "slob running a temperature," whose freakish manifesto seemed to threaten all that they held sacred, who spoiled the view from the mullioned windows of the ivory tower by throwing garbage all over the Prufrockian lawn — entrails of cars and broken bottles of the cheapest wines, discarded old shoes and ominous white powders. Soon madmen would roam the marble corridors of culture, and what about common decency? As for those who considered themselves truly hip, they detected something decidedly uncool in *On the Road* and dismissed Jack as a sentimentalist. Grammarians were also offended, by the unstructured prose that they declared mere incomprehensible drivel. The fans stood waiting at the stage door for someone who resembled Neal Cassady to come out — and got Jack Kerouac instead. "Your boyfriend's a homo, isn't he?" said a young actress who'd flirted with Jack unsuccessfully all evening. "Too bad he's an alcoholic," said a host who had plied Jack with drinks at a literary party on Park Avenue. For a few weeks there were rumors in Hollywood that *On the Road* would go for $100,000 in a movie deal negotiated by Sterling Lord. ("The Lord is my agent, I shall not want," Jack quipped, and in his mind blew the whole bundle on a house for Memere much grander than anything she'd ever imagined, to which her son Baron Jean Louis Lebris Kerouac would return after a triumphal flight to the West Coast where he would hobnob with Frank Sinatra — they would join their masculine voices in song, astonishing the bored blonde starlets in the cocktail lounges of Beverly Hills.) In Jack's old haunts on Bleecker Street and MacDougal, in the San Remo and the Kettle of Fish, the subterraneans whispered to each other that Jack Kerouac had sold out, would never write another word worth reading.

I was making sporadic attempts to keep a journal. One day I wrote in it:

> At five o'clock in the morning of these endless nights a kind of panic comes over me ... I do not

know why this is. When I was younger and had to be home on time to find my father getting out of bed to peer at his watch with a flashlight, I wanted to stay up forever and see the dawn and have 6 A.M. coffee in cafeterias with lean, sharp-faced boys in corduroy jackets and walk back through all the streets of the city and collapse exhausted on someone's couch in a room where six people lay on the rug as if slain . . . but now I insist in tones of outrage that *it is time to go home* even though I do not really want to go there and will probably not be able to sleep — but have only chosen sounds to make, which mean, "Look at me. Let me know that you know I'm here."

$\mathcal{T}$HERE WAS ONE glorious weekend, though, when we got away from it all. It was late September by then, and the sky had that thin, bright gilding over blue that comes with the first fall weather. We were driving upstate with Lucien and Cessa to their country house in Cherry Valley. For weeks I'd seen nothing but the smoky insides of rooms and bars. All time had come to seem nocturnal, greyly hazed over by Jack's hangover glooms. I remember looking with astonishment at the trees massed along the highway, so many of them in all their varied colors, turning different reds already, oranges and yellows.

Lucien was at the wheel, shirt sleeves rolled back from his fine blond arms, looking boyish that day — you could see his fatal, mischievous beauty. He drove with deliberate wildness, wickedly flouting all speed limits, saving us from each brush with death with tensile brilliance. Cessa was furious in the back seat, clutching her little boys. Only Jack was completely unflinching — Lucien the bold would never have an accident, he assured Cessa and me. The radio played "A Foggy Day in London Town," and he scat-sang along, riffing à la Charlie Parker around the slow notes. Somewhere up in Rensselaer County an announcer broke in with the news that the Russians had successfully launched Sputnik. Lucien whistled through his teeth. "They beat us to it, Jack, those

194

crafty sons of bitches!" Jack said anyway it was all vanity, a drop in eternity's ocean.

We turned off a dirt road into an apple orchard and came to a stop in front of an old frame farmhouse. Jack and Lucien carried the sleeping children inside. It was close to four, and the air had chilled already. "Lucien, we're going to need a fire tonight," Cessa said, running upstairs to the children with her arms full of blankets. Jack told her there was nothing he liked better than the red glow of a potbellied stove, and went off with Lucien to chop wood.

I could hear the strokes of the ax as I wandered around for a while among the apple trees. Their boughs had been loaded with fruit, but a storm had blown a lot of it down. I was quite excited to find apples lying everywhere, for the taking, in the long wet grass. I ran into the kitchen, got a bucket and proceeded to fill it quickly, inspecting each apple in the fading light and tossing away the ones that had softened and gone brown. The ground smelled as if it had been drenched in wine. I'd done many things in my short life, but I'd never gathered apples before. I proudly showed Jack my full bucket. "What the hell are you going to do with those wormy things?" Lucien teased me. I said I was going to make a pie.

I was a novice cook with no experience at all in pie making, but I wasn't going to let that stop me. I'd watched my mother make crusts out of graham crackers. I decided on that. All I needed were the crackers. I asked Lucien how far away the store was. "About two country miles," he answered cryptically. When I inquired how long a country mile was, he said only a farmer could tell me.

"I'll walk you there, Joycey," Jack offered.

"Walk! For Christ's sake, take the car, Jack!" Lucien said.

Jack kept trying to refuse it, but Lucien kept insisting. Finally we both got into it, and very slowly Jack backed out of the orchard and we crept along the dirt road until it turned onto the highway just out of sight of Lucien's house. There Jack stopped and said we should get out. I was astonished when he told me he'd always been a passenger rather than a driver. But he didn't want to hurt Lucien's feelings. He could drive a little, but it would be a much better idea for us to walk to the store and enjoy the sunset.

We walked the rest of the way at a pretty fast clip as the sky turned pink and the sun went down over the Berkshires. We arrived at the store just as the owner was locking up. Jack bought not only the crackers I needed but vanilla ice cream for the little boys, a bottle of bourbon for Lucien, and a can of Reddi-Wip — he said this pie I was making absolutely had to have whipped cream. We hitched a ride from the owner most of the way back, picked up the car and crawled up the road into Lucien's orchard. Jack got out from behind the wheel and gave the door a loud slam. He grinned at me because he knew I wouldn't say a word, and we went inside the house.

Blind intuition guided me that night as I went through Cessa's spice shelves, smelling the contents of the small glass-stoppered jars, sprinkling a little of this and reckless amounts of that on my sliced apples. "How about cloves, Cessa?" She'd laugh and say, "Why not?"

I liked her enormously. She was a tall, beautiful, capable woman; her long delicate face was slightly worn around the eyes, which somehow made her all the more lovely. She'd already bathed her little boys and put them in pajamas and made stuffing for roast chicken and picked squash from her garden. Even when she was furious with Lucien, you knew she was crazy about him. Because of her, Lucien had the most settled life of any of Jack's friends — a life that resembled that of ordinary people and was almost the real thing, despite the edge to it that you always felt, the shadows gathered in the corners.

To Jack, Cessa was a goddess of domesticity, second only to Memere. It meant a lot to me to have her acceptance. Now that I'd launched myself into what I'd once childishly considered "real life," ordinary life was coming to seem exotic, like the trees I saw on the highway.

I've never tasted pie as good as the one I made that night. "Ecstasy pie!" Jack shouted. He put down his fork and ran out to the kitchen for the Reddi-Wip I'd forgotten. He and Lucien squeezed great swirling drifts of it over everybody's portion, which only made everything that much more ecstatic.

In one biography it was later said, "Lucien called Joyce 'Ecstasy Pie' and her affair with Jack would endure for an erratic year and a half," which, aside from obliterating the historic actual pie, allows for no nuances whatsoever.

There was an early-morning walk with Jack on the Sunday of that weekend, which was also, as it happened, my twenty-second birthday. Wet September woods that smelled as if we were inside a mushroom, jack-o'-lanterns hanging on dried stalks, scarlet-berried bushes, a mistiness around us like a web. Under pines we discovered moss like a constellation of tiny milky-green stars. We came out finally into a meadow where the sun had already warmed the grass. We lay down on it together. I put my head on Jack's chest, and his heart beat into my ear like a slow clock. After a long time he said into the silence, "Well, I know we should just stay up here and get married and never go back." Feeling the saddest happiness, I said that was what I knew, too.

But my next thought had to do with being twenty-two, which, although it was older than I had ever been, was also, I suddenly realized, quite young after all; and, as if I were floating above Jack and me, looking down, I thought, I can do this now, be here with him like this. It's all right. I have all the time in the world.

We went back to the city that afternoon, and Jack's fame. Since the measurements of its ingredients were unrecorded, ecstasy pie turned out to be unduplicatable — or could only be made with apples from Lucien's orchard, on a day when they'd achieved a precise state of ripeness.

We did return to Cherry Valley once more, in October. This time Jack had a plan: The Carrs and I would drive home on

Sunday, leaving him by himself with a week's supply of groceries. He'd walk in the woods, chop logs for the fire, cook simple meals, speak to no one. When we came to get him the following weekend, we'd find him fully restored. Solitude had always worked for him. And a week alone in Lucien's old house was nothing, compared to the sixty-three days he'd spent in the fire lookout's cabin on Desolation Peak. This vacation from him was something I needed, too, he told me. Lately he'd been unable to go anywhere without a pint of Thunderbird in his pocket. He could see how all the drinking scared me. He said he felt bad about wearing me out. And I wasn't writing my book. How would I explain that to Hiram Haydn?

He stood on the porch on Sunday night, waving and grinning as the car pulled out, looking like a woodsman in his red flannel shirt.

My writing-time money was almost gone, so I'd taken a temporary typing job that week. When I came home from work on Tuesday evening, lights were on in the apartment and water was running in the bathroom. I was so sure Jack was still up at Lucien's that I was terrified, until he called out to me to come and talk to him. I found him lying in a hot bath with his pint of wine.

It had taken him the whole day to hitchhike back. He'd waited for hours by the side of the highway for a ride. But he'd known as soon as he woke up that morning that he couldn't stick it out. He didn't want to say much about it. Only that it had been too cold, too much trouble to keep the wood fire going. He'd probably have come down with bronchitis in another day or two. "Sorry to ruin your vacation, Joycey." Looking bewildered and afraid, he lay there naked in the steaming water with some terrible coldness inside him.

He said it was time for him to go back to Florida.

A few days later I saw him off. Seven weeks ago he hadn't even been able to afford a bus ticket. Now that he'd come up in the world and was a relatively famous author, he was taking the train. On the way to Penn Station, we stopped at a hamburger joint called the White Tower. There Jack ordered eight hamburgers to go, medium rare with ketchup. He stuffed the bag of them into his rucksack. They'd last him all the way to Orlando, he told me.

12

ELISE HAD DISAPPEARED again, atomized into the windy blue spaces between New York and San Francisco. The last time she'd written me from the Coast — still thinking I was on my way to Mexico — she'd ended, "N.Y. is going to be that old tree falling in the empty forest now." The letters I sent to her rooming house afterward came back in the mail. From Florida, Jack wrote to the poet Michael McClure and asked if anyone at The Place knew of her or had seen her lately. No one had. "I know," Jack consoled me, "I'll send a big false report to my agents in Frisco announcing that Allen has actually returned to NY and Elise'll hear it and come back home. Okay?" But Allen was still in Paris with Peter Orlovsky, and would remain there until the following summer.

All I could do was write a poem, which I did in my own adaptation of Beat style:

> Elise
> got on the Greyhound Bus.
>
> Having sabotaged
> a few of the clocks
> in the city —
> she left me the rest,

and a destiny
of endless chop suey,
a beat-up copy of *The Idiot*.
She didn't own much.

When the electrical doors closed
and the air conditioning began,
the black leather roads
took her.

Her friends
celebrate her departure
with beer and a fist fight.
Her parents
in their impenetrable living room
have drawn the blinds.

Very shyly I sent it off to Jack, who was more enthusiastic
about it than about anything I'd shown him, and even urged
me to send it to a new jazz magazine in New Orleans. But
somehow I felt embarrassed and never did.

A twenty-four-year-old girl was murdered in North Beach
that fall. Even in the East the newspapers had a field day.
BEATNIK SLAYING, the headlines proclaimed. Her raped,
battered body had been found in an alleyway lying among
trashcans. She was identified as a "drifter," one of those girls
who moved in and out of the cheap hotels in the area, co-
habiting carelessly, drunkenly, with various men until one
of them put an end to her short, confused life. Bartenders
and janitors remembered her. She got what she asked for.
"Poor thing," they added as an afterthought.

Her name was Connie, but I read *Elise* into her story. For
a strange moment I even thought the two of them were the
same person, that Elise, intent on losing herself, had taken
on the identity of this girl who had been killed. And then I
became sure that Elise and Connie had known each other.
I could see the two of them in old bathrobes sitting on the
edge of a bed drinking wine in the fluorescent glare of a room

like the ones in the Yorkshire. I knew Elise would have tried to look out for Connie, just as Allen embraced the outcast, the mad.

I go on a rescue mission myself one night in November. In Paris, Peter has gotten disturbing news of his brother Lafcadio. Lafcadio, who's been back on Long Island in Northport since Peter and Allen left, is having difficulties with his mother, who claims the boy's crazy. He hits her, she says. She in turn threw a beer-can-opener at him that pierced his arm almost to the bone. Peter's afraid Lafcadio will end up in a state hospital like his brother Julius, and is ready to rush home. Meanwhile someone has to convince Lafcadio to cool it.

I seriously doubt my ability to do this. Lafcadio never said a word to me those months he was around, never looked up from those drawings of his, maybe won't remember who I am. It was Elise who took him to museums and talked to him — I wish I knew about what. His mother will think I'm some social worker anyway, and won't open the door.

Still I get a Columbia friend of Elise's, Howard Shulman — the one person I know who has a car — to drive me out to Northport. Howard Shulman's given to recurrent attacks of schizophrenia, but in between is manically lucid if not brilliant. Jack, who met him that fall, says he has "luminous, good eyes."

He drives the Chevy his wealthy parents have given him for his twenty-first birthday with a ferocity that surpasses Lucien's as I use a flashlight to study the scrawled map Peter Orlovsky has sent from Paris. We're looking for a dirt road going up a hill that, when we find it, is so overgrown and treacherous that I have to get out and walk in front of the car with my flashlight, yelling directions to Howard, who drives hanging out the window, giggling that we're probably going to meet our deaths. Near the top of this hill is supposed to be the chicken-coop house — "small red cube," Peter wrote on his map — where Lafcadio Orlovsky has been living

for the past five months. "Let's just kidnap the kid!" Howard
shouts, even though to make our getaway he'd have to drive
backward while I did the flashlight routine again.

Finally my light catches a red wall, but the house is so
dark it looks as if no one's home. We walk up to it and I
start knocking on the door, nervously calling, "Lafcadio!
Lafcadio!"

The door opens and Lafcadio stands there, much bigger
than I remember him — he's grown a lot, there are even a
few delicate hairs on his cheeks. He stares at us, startled,
wary. There *is* a light inside the house; like a thin, blue gas
it comes from the television set. Someone — Mrs. Orlovsky?
— moves heavily behind the boy into another room.

"I'm Elise's friend whom you met in New York, and this
is Howard Shulman, Lafcadio." He nods after a moment and
murmurs hello. I wish I'd brought him some drawing paper
or something. "Peter's worried because you don't write him
anymore. He wants you to know he's trying to get money to
come home. You've just got to wait a little and he'll be back.
But he wants you to stay out of trouble. I know Elise is thinking about you, too, and Jack sends his regards."

"Elise sends me post cards," Lafcadio says.

And I think, with enormous relief, *Then she's alive.*

"You want to go for a ride?" Howard asks. "How about it,
Lafcadio?"

Lafcadio shakes his head. "Tell Petey I'll be all right,"
he whispers, and closes the door.

On the way back, Howard and I drove around Northport
looking for a place to get hamburgers. In the dark the town
had a romantic look — despite the sufferings of the Orlovskys. There were lots of elm trees and piles of dead leaves
heaped up in yards and roomy old wooden houses with deep
porches and sheaves of Indian corn tacked to the doors. The
main street led right down to the waters of a bay, which
lapped black and shining against a pier where a few boats

of summer were still tied up. There was a park down there, too, with an old-fashioned bandstand; some teen-agers were necking on its steps.

In fact, it was so achingly all-American that it made me feel awfully lonely for Jack. Maybe this was where he could live and I could be with him — though I only got at that very obliquely when I wrote him later in the week: "It seemed like New England. It seemed like a place where you could be someday. And you could still come to NY whenever you wanted and see the people at Viking and all your friends."

It seemed that down in Florida with Memere, Jack's exuberance had returned to him. Hearing that *On the Road* was number eleven on the *Times* best-seller list, he predicted it would be number one by Christmas. From New York, Lillian Hellman had proposed that he write a play. Borrowing his brother-in-law's typewriter, he wrote all three acts in twenty-four hours: "Couldn't sleep till it was finished. I find that writing plays for me is like rolling off a log. I could do a million of 'em like Lope de Vega." He intended to call it *Beat Generation*, "utilizing all that publicity."

He rented a new typewriter on which he thought he could "swing and swing and swing" at ninety-five words a minute, and bought a scroll of white teletype paper "that reaches from Orlanda Fla. to NYCity . . . huge, a dollar forty," on which he was all set to write *Memory Babe*, a new novel about his childhood. On a smaller scroll he planned to type his final translation of the Vajracheddikaprajanparamita, which he'd read like the Torah every morning. And he kept tossing off poems ("perms"), which he'd sometimes type out for me on the backs of his letters. "Perms" tended to be exuberantly outrageous. One rudely addressed "Sweet Emily Dickinson." Sweet Emily Dickinson had disregarded "natural phenomena in hairy men," but perhaps death had humbled her. "Meet you in the churchyard," said the poet.

Like a shameful snail in comparison, I was trying to inch

along again on my novel, wishing I could just follow Jack's advice and get it all done, not worrying whether it was good or bad: "It's written in the stars, you have no power over the Stars any moren I do. The Already Stars." To cheer myself up, I'd write Hiram Haydn reassuring letters about my progress ("As you see, I haven't absconded or anything. I'm afraid I was rather demoralized for a while, but here I am"). I'd promise him an entire first draft in three months, and stuff the letter in a drawer.

Now I was about to send this long-suffering man my fifth address in six months. I'd just moved into my latest cheap apartment — this one downtown, finally, on East Thirteenth Street, the farthest I'd succeeded in getting from my parental home. Even Sheila had taken off for Paris — the only one of us to actually get there. According to Peter Orlovsky, she was working for Berlitz and had a sinister Arab boyfriend.

Having run completely through Random House's five hundred dollars, I was a full-time secretary again. Employment agencies had warned me my record was spotty. My new boss, an irascible man who'd had nine secretaries in one year and had been in the automobile salvage business before he became a publisher, filled his office with oppressed intellectuals who had Ph.D.'s in esoteric subjects, and boasted to me he'd hire "pinkos, fairies," whoever did an honest day's work. "Beatniks," he added, apparently not fooled by my attempts at a respectable appearance.

"My little secretary," Jack kept calling me in his letters. "With the long black stockings." How Beat could I actually be, holding down a steady office job and writing a novel about an ivy-league college girl on the verge of parting with her virginity? "If I had to go and apply for jobs like you, they'd have to drag me into Bellevue in two days," he wrote. "That's why I am and will always be a bum, a dharma bum, a rucksack wanderer." Maybe Professor X hadn't been wrong when he said real writers would be out hopping freight trains.

But I didn't last long at my new place of employment. One Friday in December it was payday, the sun was shining brightly, I hadn't succeeded in balancing my boss's checkbook, and he'd be back to yell at me after lunch. I ate my 35¢ cream-cheese sandwich at Chock Full o' Nuts, then phoned the office manager to say I had just quit. That weekend I composed a letter of resignation, enumerating my boss's flaws of character and ending with: "I know you don't care what happens to your employees after five o'clock, but I found that I felt so dead and dispirited after a day in your office that I couldn't even read a newspaper, much less work on my novel — and I've come to the conclusion that even if you paid me $100 a week, it couldn't compensate for that."

To my delight, this letter came back to me two days later with my boss's reply scribbled on the back of it (his favorite method of conserving stationery). He said he was sorry for having caused me "discomfort" and had never suspected he was hurting me so deeply. High on my moral victory, I looked in my purse and I saw I had enough money for exactly one more week of freedom from offices. At last I'd joined the ranks of the scufflers.

$\mathcal{S}$CUFFLING WAS WHAT you did in my new neighborhood, soon to be called the East Village. The original poor of the Lower East Side had scuffled without hope, of course, selling their labor for low wages. Their children grew up and fled to Queens or Jersey, leaving room in the tenements for middle-class children loosely defined as "artists," who believed for a while, under the influence of all the new philosophy and rejecting the values of their own parents, that they had no use for money. Nomads without rucksacks, they joyfully camped out among the gloomy Ukrainians, the suspicious Poles, the Italian fruit vendors, the retired Jewish garment workers dying in their fourth-floor walkups. The newcomers to the neighborhood regarded jobs the way jazz musicians regarded gigs — brief engagements. A steady gig (really a contradiction in terms) was valued chiefly as a means of getting unemployment insurance. The great accomplishment was to avoid actual employment for as long as possible and by whatever means. But it was all right for women to go out and earn wages, since they had no important creative endeavors to be distracted from. The women didn't mind, or, if they did, they never said — not until years later.

Meanwhile rents were low, you could eat for next to nothing, toilets were in the hallway, bathtubs were in the kitchen, and you never let the meter man in if you could help it. Con Ed trucks appeared on the streets on Friday mornings to turn delinquent payers off for the weekend, plunging them into penal darkness even if they could have paid up that very afternoon. Yahrzeit candles, or the Puerto Rican kind with rainbow-colored wax, were hoarded for such emergencies. Poems were written about roaches who lived in the stove, the woodwork, the innards of portable radios and shoes, and copulated in the chocolate-smelling gas heat of winter. Wives swapped recipes for chicken-back stew or lentil soup with gizzards; tofu had not yet been discovered in the West.

Bachelor poets, I soon noticed, seemed to live by an aesthetic of grime. Moving into a ruin, a poet would faithfully maintain it as such, filling the air behind the permanently filmed windows with nicotine, and accumulating beer bottles so prodigiously that a monument to Miss Rheingold was created, too sacred for any trashcan.

Another approach to tenement life involved denial of the tenement as a tenement and insistence upon it as "a charming place" once it had been stripped to its core, taken back virtually to its prehistory as a dwelling. Plaster was laboriously scraped off brick that had always been plastered; windowsills and lintels were sanded raw; decades of linoleum were ripped up to reveal floorboards underneath, even parquet, sometimes, perfectly preserved by generations of housewives who, like my mother and Jack's, always put a covering on anything "good."

My mother couldn't understand why I'd returned to the streets my grandparents had struggled so hard to stay out of: "At least we never lived on the Lower East Side. We lived near Bronx Park when it was a beautiful area. At least we never lived in the slums."

I loved the slums, my slums, the sweet slums of Bohemia and beatnikdom, where sunflowers and morning glories would bloom on fire escapes in the summer and old ladies weighed down by breasts leaned on goosedown pillows in windows, self-appointed guardians of the street, and Tompkins Square with its onion-topped church had the greyness of photos of Moscow. Who would not wish to be a scuffler on Second Avenue? I bought seven-cent bagels and ten-cent half-sour pickles and sat up till dawn in Rappaport's, where they gave you a whole basket of rolls free, drinking coffee with a jazz trombonist from St. Louis and a poet just arrived from Chicago.

Thirty years before, Yiddish culture had flowered on Second Avenue. All that was left were some dairy restaurants. Around the corner from my apartment was a bar called Slugger Anne's — once the Café Royal, the legendary gathering place of Jewish artists and intelligentsia. In his years of exile, Trotsky had published *Novy Mir* in the basement of a house on St. Marks Place, the much-traveled thoroughfare to the West Village. Now you could see W. H. Auden come down his stoop in his bedroom slippers on his way to the A&P, and you could hardly take a walk there without running into someone you'd just met two nights before and might remain friends with for the rest of your life. The East Side was flowering again. If you couldn't live on Gay Street you lived on East Thirteenth, and knew you'd never never go home again to the Upper West Side.

My new apartment was small and had no light. Plants grew pale and died in the air-shaft window. The Pullman kitchen had been painted black by a previous occupant. Since I didn't have much to put in the two rooms, I decorated according to the principle explained to me by a painter in the Cedar, that space between objects created a field of tension around them. Next door to me lived Mike the alcoholic super, who terrified me now and then by pounding on my door at 3 A.M., demanding to come in and "fix the plumbing," while his wife in robe and curlers screamed "Kurva! Kurva!" on the landing. "What's *kurva*?" I asked a sympathetic neighbor, a married ballet dancer whom the super never bothered at all. "I'm not sure," she said, "but I think it's Polish for *whore*." On the other side of me lived a woman in a black wig who was the super's wife's best friend. As I came up the stairs, she'd always open her door

209

to see who was with me, and once I caught her sprinkling perfume on my doorstep — "Because you cook the cabbage all night and you drive me crazy!" she yelled.

I didn't spend a great deal of time at home anyway. To this day I have a triangular scar on my left thumb reminding me of the night I rushed to my apartment after a day of being a temporary typist for an insurance company, determined to rush out again after the boring necessity of making dinner. Two pork chops frozen together threatened to hold me up. I hacked away at them, cut some flesh off my thumb in the process, wrapped a dish towel around the wound, and went out anyway, bleeding all the way crosstown to the Cedar.

Franz Kline asked to examine my thumb, and lectured me. "If I were your father, I'd take you to get stitches."

"Well, I didn't want to miss anything," I told him.

"No. Of course not." Still holding my wrist, he shook his head with a gleam of mischievous understanding in his eyes.

Affluence was spreading among the painters that fall. They'd turn up self-consciously in stiff new brown corduroy suits purchased at Hudson's on the Bowery, on their way to gallery openings all the way uptown. Socialites too would appear at the Cedar, fairy godmothers in extraordinary furs — potential collectors of artists as well as art. Some painters' old ladies were retaliating by picking up the wilder stuff in thrift shops — Spanish combs and beaded dresses from the twenties that ripped under the arms if danced in too energetically. They draped themselves in embroidered piano shawls, put on purple mesh stockings, and called themselves Beat Pre-Raphaelites.

Every Saturday night now there were parties. The word would spread through the Cedar like wildfire that a certain up-and-coming abstract expressionist was inviting over a few close friends, some collectors, and some important gallery people, and shortly the astonished host would find himself confronting hordes of crashers who'd trudged up five flights of stairs with six-packs and bottles of Gallo — as well as grass, which was smoked with discreet ceremoniousness at these gatherings, in intense little circles of people. Occasionally would-be guests were turned away and fistfights broke out, but most of the time everyone got in. These parties were like giant vibrating rush-hour trains filled with swaying passengers, all being borne along to some further destination — the next love affair, the next party, the next hangover, the next 5 A.M. bowl of wonton soup on Mott Street.

The best place to end up was the Five Spot, which during the summer had materialized like an overnight miracle in a bar on Second Street and the Bowery formerly frequented by bums. The new owners had cleaned it up a little, hauled in a piano, and hung posters on the walls advertising Tenth Street gallery openings. The connection with "the scene" was clear from the beginning. Here for the price of a beer you could hear Coltrane or Thelonius Monk, or an occasional painter/musician like Larry Rivers sitting in and blowing hard and a little self-consciously. Kenneth Rexroth flew in from San Francisco and did a weekend of poetry-and-jazz, staking out his claim on that territory in the East before Jack or Allen or Gregory Corso came back to town and stole his thunder.

But most of all, I remember one night when a middle-aged, sad-faced black woman stood up beside the table where she'd been sitting and sang so beautifully in a cracked, heartbroken voice I was sure I'd heard before. There was silence when she finished, then everyone rose and began clapping. It was the great Lady Day, who had been deprived of her cabaret card by the New York police and was soon to die under arrest in a hospital bed — subject of the famous poem by Frank O'Hara, who also heard Billie Holiday sing that night:

leaning on the john door in the 5 Spot
while she whispered a song along the keyboard
to Mal Waldron and everyone and I stopped breathing

𝄢'M WALKING EAST in a winter twilight some twenty-five years ago, about to pass Cooper Union, where I'll run into a young woman I'll someday think of as my oldest friend. For an hour already she's been standing out there, braced against the freezing wind that blows through the empty spaces around Astor Place. A very small person in an old tweed coat left over from college days, and several knitted scarves, she's handing out mimeographed leaflets — or trying to — about some poetry reading taking place that night that everyone's too cold to be interested in. Extracting one with a numbed hand while clutching the rest with the other, she holds it out to me. "*Take* one!" There's such laughing desperation in her voice that I have to stop (I think I recognize her anyway), and I end up staying there and helping her until snow starts falling on us — which is too much, we agree, even for poetry. So we walk to the B&H deli and thaw our fingers out against thick brown mugs of coffee as a snowstorm thuds against the window and Second Avenue's sparse neon turns to water color.

"Oh, come to the reading!" she urges when I reluctantly say I really should go home. Her husband is one of the poets, and she's a woman in love. For him she would stand on innumerable freezing street corners. She writes poetry herself, but has never stood up with it at a reading of her

212

own — makes no particular mention of it, in fact — telling herself it isn't good enough ("Some of it *was* good enough," she'll admit fiercely, years later).

Two months ago I'd seen and heard her husband the poet; privately I wonder if his stuff is really so great. He'd been reading in a new Bleecker Street coffee shop Jack took me to one night, a tiny place that had opened in the basement of a flophouse. Every head had turned as we walked in. "That's Kerouac," people whispered. The poet, a young black man, short and graceful with a neat professorial beard, glanced up from his page nervously; the poem was academic, with a few deliberately hip touches. He came up to us afterward and introduced himself as LeRoi Jones. "And this woman over here is Hettie," he'd said proudly. So that was where I knew her from. She'd smiled at us, but the protective passion in her eyes was for him. Despite the complications of race, they'd seemed more coupled than most people. Even their smallness somehow made them fit together.

A few months before I met her, the former Hettie Cohen had been pronounced dead in Laurelton, Long Island. That day she'd announced to her parents her intention to marry Roi, and driven off weeping, in a car full of boxes from the room she'd grown up in, never to spend a night under the roof of that house again, or be invited to dinners on the Jewish holidays, not even to speak with her own sister for years. I'd never known anyone who'd orphaned herself so drastically.

Billie Holiday never sang in Laurelton. Even by 1957, you wouldn't have found black people on its streets. It was unthinkable that anyone's daughter would marry a Negro. A girl like Hettie, a nice girl from a Jewish family who got good marks in school and whose father sent her to college, was expected to marry from there into a more affluent suburb and produce pink-cheeked grandchildren who could be brought home on visits. Education would give such a girl a taste for what was respectfully considered Culture — *Swan*

Lake, My Fair Lady, a yearly membership in the Book-of-the-Month Club.

The well-kept home Hettie grew up in was as devoid of books and music as it was of dust. She was left to make up her own interior world. There was the public library, and the Laurelton Jewish Center. At thirteen, Hettie embarrassed her parents by entering an intensely religious period. They were relieved when her fervor mysteriously subsided.

There was an explanation for this mystery. Religion had been superseded by boys. Explorations conducted in the back seats of cars parked in darkened driveways could transform even Laurelton into a thrilling wilderness — although you could lose Laurelton in other ways as well, if you hadn't grown up enough to leave it. On the stage of the high-school auditorium, Hettie threw herself into the roles she played. She was told she had a gift for comedy, which was almost consolation for not being conventionally pretty enough for ingénue.

In an all-girls' college in Virginia, which she'd chosen because of its distance from everything that was familiar, Hettie prepared herself for the theater. For some young girls, the desire to be on stage is really the desire to be in life, to escape from the everyday into something larger, more demanding.

An NYU law student Hettie nearly became engaged to after graduation told her she was bound to end up in Scarsdale despite herself, just like Marjorie Morningstar, who'd also had her Bohemian fling before she settled down. Ambitious young men of the fifties, struggling to reconcile the clamoring of their libidos with their search for appropriate wives, often invoked the wayward Jewish princess of Herman Wouk's best seller. If you had certain unorthodox interests, such a young man might employ his full range of debating skills to argue you out of them, prove they were inauthentic. Hettie's new passion at that moment was jazz, and jazz might lead to God knows what.

First it was Dixieland that intrigued Hettie. She even knew a group of white part-time musicians, Columbia graduate students and the like, who called themselves the Red Onions and played their anachronistic "Saints Go Marching In" at parties and occasional clubs, latter-day Bix Beiderbeckes a couple of Saturday nights each month. But there was the real thing, too, she learned soon enough; the real thing was black. And for Hettie, black came to seem the color of a great deal more that was realer than what she'd known, some purer definition of experience, some essential knowledge that the white suburbs denied their children.

Nineteen fifty-seven found her living on Morton Street in the Village and working as a secretary for a struggling jazz magazine called *The Record Changer*, which would shortly go out of business. LeRoi Jones — late of "the narrow, grey working-class streets of Newark, the brown superfluities of Howard University, and the hopeless sickness of the Air Force" — was working in the mailroom. Although he'd grown up on proletarian streets, his family was middle-class — schoolteachers and civil servants. He'd been christened Everett LeRoi Jones but had discarded the Everett along the way. Perhaps the LeRoi spoke unconsciously to far-reaching aspirations. In the schismatic late sixties, he would rechristen himself once more — as Amiri Baraka.

When Roi got out of the Air Force and arrived in the Village, everyone was reading *Howl*. Today he still acknowledges *Howl* as the "single most important poetic influence of the period," because it exposed "the spiritual desolation of contemporary America." He wrote a letter on a piece of toilet paper to Allen in Paris, asking "Are you sincere?" Allen replied that he was tired of being Allen Ginsberg.

At twenty-four, LeRoi Jones was warm, funny, unassuming. Hettie also saw the brilliance and fire in him. They became friends very swiftly in the everyday camaraderie of the office. At night they troubled each other's sleep. LeRoi Jones remembers Hettie as one of the first New York women he ever talked to — but of course she was more than that. Some rare, deep understanding drew them inexorably together. One lonely Saturday afternoon they ran into each other on Greenwich Avenue, and became lovers. The next day, alone in her apartment after he left, Hettie foresaw that they would marry — and knew the risks, the costs. It was a moment of strange clarity. The following summer at the Newport Jazz Festival, she'd see the children of other interracial couples and think Yes, she and Roi would have children; all that was possible, too.

"We both took up marriage," LeRoi Jones writes, "like hesitant explorers on the shore of some unknown country. Yet we were unprepared for the inner conflicts that such a union portends in America, and only slightly better prepared — though shielded to some extent by residence in the Village — for the traditional outer ones."

His 1980 essay on this period of his life, "Confessions of a Former Anti-Semite," is an oddly reasoned apologia for his vitriolic abandonment of the post-Beat cultural scene in 1965, and for the bad faith he demonstrated in public denunciations of his wife Hettie and of white friends who had been close to him and intensely loyal.

But in 1957 all this lay in the unsuspected future. In the excitement and hope of that moment — in what was real and strongly believed and truly lived out, as distinct from fad — there seemed the possibility of enormous transformations. It seemed entirely possible the newness and openness expressed in the poems, the paintings, the music, would ripple out far beyond St. Marks Place and the tables in the Cedar, swamping the old barriers of class and race, healing the tragic divisions in the American soul. Children of the late and silent fifties, we knew little of political realities. We had the illusion our own passions were enough. We felt, as Hettie Cohen Jones once put it, that you could change everything just by being loud enough. And if her union with Roi was unprepared and "hesitant," and if such a marriage later fell out of political fashion among militant blacks and became subject to that ostracism, too, besides the accumulated hostility in the glances of whites, it should also be seen — even by LeRoi Jones at this remove — as an act of singular courage.

*

I did go to that reading with Hettie, where to my surprise
the poems Roi read were so much better than the ones I'd
heard with Jack, you could hardly believe they were by the
same poet. He seemed to have passed into an entirely new
stage within a few weeks, learning and absorbing with astonishing speed. He'd obviously been reading Allen, and
paid his homage in lines like

> (O, generation revered
> above all others.
> O, generation of fictitious
> Ofays
>   I revere you. . .
> You are all so beautiful).

But the acid in the voice was his own.

In a poem he wrote the following year, I see Hettie as she
was then — and still is — as sharply as if Roi had taken her
picture:

> My wife is left-handed
> which implies a fierce de-
> termination. A complete other
> worldliness. IT'S WIERD, BABY.
> The way some folks
> are always trying to be
> different. A sin & a shame.
>
> But then, she's been a bohemian
> all of her life . . . black stockings
> refusing to take orders. I sit
> patiently, trying to tell her
> whats right. TAKE THAT DAMM
> PENCIL OUTTA THAT HAND. YOU'RE
> RITING BACKWARDS. & such. But
> to no avail. & it shows
> in her work. Left-handed coffee,
> Left-handed eggs; when she comes
> in at night . . . it's her left hand
> offered for me to kiss. Damm.

217

& now her belly droops over the seat.
They say it's a child. But
I ain't quite so sure.

And bearing that same triumphant first child of hers and Roi's, Hettie crosses Greenwich Avenue one spring afternoon with me, her belly out to there in a red-flowered shift dress she's just run up on her sewing machine, and laughs as a truck driver leans all the way out of his window to hoot, "Hey, little momma!"

13

WHENEVER I LOOKED at young Bohemian couples like Roi and Hettie, I'd wish I too were anchored to someone. This was a longing that did me no good at all, since, despite my better judgment, the only person I wanted to be anchored to was Jack. I concealed this shameful thought from him as best I could, filling up my letters with lively accounts of how I'd gone here and there in the East Village, and who I'd seen. "Write as often as you want," he'd urge me, "and I'll answer every letter double." But he seemed to read between the lines. His affection would be accompanied by warnings. He and I were friends, "like two fingers intertwined," but he wanted me to know he was postponing all thoughts of love for the next five years, during which he was only going to be busy writing and publishing. *Then* he'd relax and go cruising around the world on his trust fund in search of l'amour, and "really write my greatest secret personal magic idea works (for myself) ... so don't be sad about brunettes and blondes..."

There were no brunettes and blondes in Orlando, Florida, where he was guarded by Memere, and couldn't even get a copy of the *New York Times* to find out how his book was doing. "Nothing down here but scorpions, lizards, vast spiders, mosquitoes, vast cockroaches & thorns in the grass." Somewhere in every letter he said he was lonely.

"Why don't I come down and see you?" I offered. A young off-Broadway director we knew had told me he was planning to drive to Orlando to read Jack's new play; there'd be room for me in his car. If Leo Garen could visit Jack, why couldn't I?

It took him nearly a month to say no, pointing out among other things that there'd be no place for me to sleep except for "an Army cot next to my mother's couch in the kitchen-livingroom-bedroom and the only other room is my small one which, when you want to go to the toilet, you have to close the door of." Besides, he was working on *Memory Babe* day and night, planning to have it finished before Christmas, when he'd come to New York and see me anyway. And since he was still broke, he didn't want to squander any food money. He typed all the way down to the bottom of the page as usual, but the rest of the letter was just as cold, and he signed his French-Canadian name, Jean Louis. Jean Louis is someone you will never be permitted to know, he seemed to be saying.

I'd evidently gone much too far, daring to suggest Memere and I and Jack could be under the same roof. I heard nothing more from Jack until he was ready to come to New York, and then he made it clear it was not to be with me.

This time he was only coming because Gilbert Millstein had arranged for him to read his work over the microphone at the Village Vanguard and he couldn't turn down the money. He was going to live in the apartment of his old friend Henri Cru, sleep all day, then get up at dusk to type his novel, which wasn't *Memory Babe* any longer but a new book called *The Dharma Bums*, "greater than *On the Road*," and he hated this interruption of his "starry night ecstacies." But he'd just have to be a "cool sound musician" for a while. He'd dress up every night and "sally forth" with Henri Cru to his two performances. Naturally, all his friends would be in the audience. "If this doesn't kill me, nothing will." In the spring, he'd buy a station wagon with all the money and disappear with his rucksack into the West.

220

He wanted to live with Henri now and be in the Village and watch Henri's TV. "Lissen Joyce . . . I don't want to importune you any further because as I told you I'm an Armenian and I don't wanta get married till I'm 69 and have 69 gentle grandninnies. Please don't be mad at me, I wanta be alone, Greta Garbo." He could already predict this Village Vanguard appearance was going to be an enormous fiasco.

The following week posters went up all around the Village advertising Kerouac at the Vanguard. I tried not to notice them. I didn't go to Jack's opening night or read the reviews of it in the papers. I didn't call him at Henri Cru's. I told myself it was over and tried not to cry on Second Avenue and wished at least he wasn't famous so I wouldn't be hearing about him all the time. I tried to be as cold as he'd decided to be and not to think of him with any sympathy. People said he was making a fool of himself at the Vanguard, acting like a drunken clown. Wasn't that what he'd predicted? "Harden your heart," Hettie advised me, although neither of us was good at that.

He called me up one day. "Wanna come and hear me? I'll leave your name at the door tonight." I went there alone and sat at a dark table in the back, surrounded by college couples holding hands. Radcliffe Cinderellas and crew-cutted boys in cable-knit sweaters down to see their hero during Christmas vacation. The lights dimmed, there was a kind of vaudevillian fanfare, a prolonged roll on the drum, and Jack stumbled out on the platform, nearly falling into the piano. He was clutching a pint of Thunderbird for dear life and had that wild-eyed, glassy look that used to come over him in TV studios. He seemed to have forgotten where he was or what he was there for. All he knew was that the musicians were his friends, perhaps his only friends in the world at that moment, and he proceeded to bop along with them approvingly, well away from the microphone, waving his pint at them and turning his back on his audience.

Those nice young people were confused, then restive, then

221

resentful. When some of the crew-cutted boys began whistling and clapping, one of the musicians said kindly, "Hey, man, time to do your gig."

He actually did manage to find the microphone and to read a section or two of *On the Road* into it, to the accompaniment of Zoot Sims, but the audience was paying up and going; the place had emptied out before he was done. Then even the musicians seemed in a hurry to pack up their instruments, leaving Jack slumped on the piano stool, asking forlornly, "Hey, where you going?" "Gotta split, Jack. Tomorrow's tomorrow."

He hadn't seen me at my back table. I started walking forward. I was going to thank him for inviting me and use all my strength to walk to the exit and go home by myself. Maybe he'd be too drunk to ask me what I thought and I wouldn't have to lie to him. I loved him, but it didn't mean a thing to him, really.

I noticed that naturally a girl had appeared — a nocturnal wraith with sharp, pale features and that hipster cool I could never approximate. Slowly buttoning up her coat, she stood waiting with the air of having waited successfully before.

"Well, good-night Jack," I said quickly.

"Joycey!"

He called out my name in such a sorrowful voice that I forgot all Hettie's advice about maintaining a heart of stone. I walked all the way up to him and kissed him on the mouth. He grabbed my arms and ground his forehead against mine and wouldn't let go. "Can you get us out of here? I want to go somewhere with you, but I'm too tired to do anything, you understand. Too tired, too drunk. You don't care, do you? Can you get us out of here?"

I did get him out, got him back to his room at the Marlton — the very same hotel he'd been staying in the first night I met him. This time he'd ended up there because of a quarrel with his old friend Henri Cru. Henri Cru, a three-hundred-pound moving man Jack had known since Horace Mann prep school, was a celebrated gourmet cook. In Jack's honor, Henri had prepared one of his most elaborate feasts, and

Jack had offended him deeply by being too drunk to eat it.

The Marlton, with its clientele of junkies and aged alcoholic Bohemians living on welfare, was probably the last place any of the people who'd paid to see Jack Kerouac perform at the Vanguard would have thought of looking for him. The Yorkshire Hotel seemed luxurious in comparison. The elevator was broken, and as we were climbing the dirty stairs Jack ran into a couple of musicians he knew and hailed them like long-lost brothers. They said they had some grass, and suddenly they were coming with us, and they too crowded into Jack's tiny room with its iron bed and torn shade and rickety flophouse chest.

There was no way to escape the endlessness of this night except by going home. I lay shivering on Jack's bed wrapped in my coat, watching Christmas lights blink on and off in the windows of the house across the street.

Jack's engagement at the Vanguard ended a couple of days later — a week before it was supposed to. He moved in with me. Like a fugitive he hid out in the apartment, double-locking the door behind me when I went to work, keeping the phone off the hook. He'd slip out only for cigarettes during the day, quick runs to the corner. When I'd come home in the evening with my bag of groceries, I'd find him lying in the darkness staring at nothing. I could feel the silence of the Void pressing in on us, seeping in with the grey dust through the air-shaft window. I'd rush around turning on lights, rattling dishes, asking what he wanted for dinner. Potatoes? A salad? Sometimes I'd lie down next to him. Pressing my face into his back, I'd drift into sleep, and wake up at midnight remembering what I'd dreamed. Once a crowd tore Jack limb from limb before my eyes. "Put no stock in dreams, Joycey," he said. "They only prophesy on a subconscious level."

We lived those weeks by a clock that seemed to tick four seconds to every one. Time was like familiar music slowed down so much it could hardly be recognized, each note dropping off into a deep well, a vibrating stillness. We could have been together on Desolation Peak rather than East Thirteenth Street.

One morning I woke up and heard the typewriter. Jack was working on my old Royal portable. I stayed in bed, afraid to walk in and disturb him. Then the typewriter stopped and the front door opened and closed. In a few minutes he was back with bacon and oranges, announcing that this time *he* was going to make breakfast, and then he was going to write all day, and furthermore he was going to take me to the movies when I came home from work. He'd realized we'd never gone to the movies together, like normal American young couples were supposed to.

That night he took me to the old Varieties Theatre on the Bowery, where *The Sweet Smell of Success* was playing. He bought us two tickets for twenty-five cents apiece and squeezed my hand. "You'll never see a place like this again. Don't be afraid — I won't go to the men's room and leave you." This was one of the places bums came to stay warm, he explained. They'd sit all day and night on the broken seats, dozing and coughing and watching whatever movie it was over and over — they weren't particular. There'd been times in his life when he'd done that, too. I knew he was thinking how strange it was that those times were over for good.

In those days I believed, much more than I do now, in the therapeutic properties of art. I thought that if you could only write with perfect honesty about the very thing that was troubling you, you could transcend it, lay it to rest. I kept urging Jack to write a book about fame. He promised me he would, and that I'd be in it, too. It would start with his coming down from the mountains, and he'd write it the way he was writing *The Dharma Bums*, keeping the prose simple so the most ordinary people could read it. Shorter sentences, which would please Viking. The thought of pleasing anyone except himself was new to him — but he could see the practical wisdom of it. He'd go back to *Memory Babe*, which he was having trouble with, and write it that way, too, why not? Meanwhile *The Dharma Bums* would probably become the giant best seller that *On the Road* wasn't, enabling him to buy his house and hide away from everyone forever, if he wanted.

"From me, too?" I asked him.

"Oh, I'll be sneaking into New York and I'll always come and see you and take you to Bobo's in Chinatown. But I'm too old for you, you know. I'm only an old Zen lunatic."

"That's what you always say."

"Ah, you never believe what I tell you."

*H*E GAVE ME one of his first bound copies of *The Subterraneans* from the box Grove Press sent over. There was a picture of Golden Gate Bridge on the cover, although everything that happened in the book had actually happened in New York. The subterraneans were those same twilight hipsters Allen had pointed out to Elise in the San Remo, and Heavenly Lane — where Mardou Fox was loved and mistakenly, pointlessly lost by Leo Percepied — was a tenement yard called Paradise Alley, two blocks away from me on East Eleventh Street.

In retreat in his mother's house in Ozone Park for three days in 1953, Jack had written himself out of the pain he felt at the end of his brief affair with Irene May, a young black woman whose *fellaheen* beauty was so compelling to him that he once told Lucien Carr she was Indian. But there had been terror for Jack in the power of such beauty. Irene had understood him with alarming, tough intelligence, and she embodied his sexual fantasies all too well. He did whatever he could to drive her away, never staying with her for more than a day or two, wearing her down with his marathon drunken wanderings through the night streets of the Village. She'd given up on Jack and taken up with Gregory Corso. Jack had been relieved and heartbroken.

I sat in a strange state of pain and excitement, reading

every word. From the first sentence, Jack took me by surprise with what he was willing to reveal about the man he called Leo: "This is the story of an unselfconfident man, at the same time of an egomaniac..."

Most of all, this book seemed a confession of Jack's desolate need to deprive himself of sexual love. There were truths in it I had not known Jack knew about himself, truths harder and more implacable than I was willing to accept even as I read them. "Now do you believe me?" his voice kept whispering in my ear with infinite sadness.

"Leo," Jack permitted Mardou Fox to say, "I don't think it's good for you to live with your mother always." Her words could have been my own.

There was really no hope in what Mardou said, it was only an opinion. It made no difference that Leo even knew she was right — "The weight of my need to go home, my neurotic fears, hangovers, horrors." Memere was omnipotent, Leo was helpless. Memere was eternity, the great immutable Always, her son's only home, his terrifying, isolating safety. Like a deity, Memere engulfed Leo, possessed his soul. All other women — blondes and dark ladies alike — flittered across his consciousness like shadows. In this book about a lost love, Jack had even given himself the name of his mother's husband.

> I saw bending over me the visage of my mother, with impenetrable eyes and moveless lips and round cheekbones and glasses that glinted and hid the major part of her expression, which at first I thought was a vision of horror...

"I would very much like to take care of you all your days," she murmurs through those frozen lips. "Pauvre ti Leo."

In the room where another child has died, a small boy, Jean Louis Kerouac, lies waiting for his Memere. She will kiss him and turn out the light, abandoning him to the dark that has taken his brother. One day he will go to sleep and never wake up, for all the prayers of the nuns at the school and the priests in their black suits and his mother's weeping.

She comes into his room and bends over him, and for a moment he does not know her. Her face has lost all its youth, has been transformed by grief into a stone. Perhaps she is thinking, Will life deprive me of this child too? She's thinking, I'll never let this one go. I'll protect him from everything bad.

The stone comes down upon him, turns into flesh.

There is no one to blame here.

The Subterraneans taught me that Jack and I had gone as far together as we could, that there was nothing further to hope for. But I wasn't quite ready to accept what it said about Jack and Memere.

Instead, it was thoughts of Irene May that I found wounding. If Jack ever ended up with anyone, it would be someone like this Irene, I'd think, not someone like me. Hadn't he warned me from the start that I was not his type? Never would he write of me

> And I also see the earth in your eyes that's what
> I think of you, you have a kind of beauty, not that
> I'm hung-up on the earth and Indians and all that
> and wanta harp all the time about you and us, but
> I see in your eyes such warm — but when you
> make the madwoman I don't see madness but glee
> glee glee — it's like the ragamuffin dusts in the
> little kid's corner and he's asleep in his crib now
> and I love you, rain'll fall on our eaves someday
> sweetheart.

In Irene's kind of beauty, Jack found a magic fatality. Perhaps Irene really could have won him from Memere, if she'd only been more patient, less restless herself. In the intense fictionalizing light of Jack's memory, Leo and Mardou belonged together. Even reading The Subterraneans jealously, I wept with Jack over their parting. Was I to take their story as real? "I don't write novels," Jack once said to me. "I only write books. BOOOGS," he said. "That's what I call 'em."

He'd shown the manuscript to Irene May four or five days after he finished it, and said he'd throw it in the fire if she asked him to. "I have to laugh," she told an interviewer years later. "Jack would never have brought his only original manuscript to throw in the fire. I just don't believe it, but I did then, though." The rawness of the writing had shocked her, but it must have seemed a safe bet then that *The Subterraneans* would never be published, that it would be added to the file of all the other "impossible" manuscripts at the MCA Literary Agency. She wasn't happy in 1958 that it was coming out.

Jack went to make peace with her one night, and brought me along. So strongly had the book laid its spell on me that I was afraid to see them together — and afraid not to. If Leo Percepied and Mardou Fox embraced before my eyes, I knew that my sympathies — despite my anguish — would almost have been with them.

Irene May lived several flights up in a dark West Village tenement. Standing outside her door with Jack, I could hear a baby whimpering. The baby was hers, and she lived alone with it in a cold-water flat that smelled of milk and diapers and Johnson's oil; she supported the two of them with odd typing jobs. Sometimes she sat up all night typing, and when the baby was sick she couldn't even get out to the store. She didn't seem angry or excited to see Jack — she only seemed weary. *The Subterraneans* was just another immense hassle in addition to all the other present difficulties of her life.

Paying no attention to me, she addressed herself to Jack with the caustic affection of someone whom hard times had made bitterly wise, while others, such as he, were running in circles making idiots of themselves. Well, you and I know you're doomed, she seemed to be saying. *The Subterraneans* wasn't a real picture of her or of anything, just a lot of distorted impressions for the media to feed upon. She seemed to have taken no notice of the tenderness expressed in it.

His head hanging lower and lower, Jack drank steadily and gloomily from the wine he'd brought with him. The baby kept waking and crying, and she'd get up to go and tend it. "We should go, Jack," I kept telling him, but he shrugged me off blindly. "Want to stay."

Irene laughed. "Yes . . . well . . . not this time, baby."

"Come on, Jack. Don't do this to me!" I felt humiliated, and determined all the more to end this evening.

I looked up and saw Mardou Fox watching with the dark glittering eyes Jack had written about, wearily amused to see someone else still struggling to get Leo Percepied home.

ONCE HE DID tell me he loved me. That was in January, right after he'd taken the train back to Memere.

> Anyway, may I say I enjoyed our last hours (and weeks) together more than ever, I find you to be the sweetest girl in the world and I want you to know that I respect you for that and even love you (as a woman, as a friend, as a anything.)

Somehow these words didn't make me happy. The thought kept coming to me that Jack was getting himself ready to say good-by. If you were planning to disappear, you'd want to put everything in order.

In the spring he'd be bringing Memere back up north with him to the house he was going to buy her. Somewhere out on Long Island, he thought. He'd live with her in that house.

Memere had already laid down her conditions — no visits from Allen or Burroughs. "Which sounds strange," Jack admitted wonderingly one day on the phone, "since I'm buying the house and I'm thirty-six years old."

At last he'd have his quiet hideout in the nightwoods, from which he could pass freely to New York, the Nation of People. Sitting at his typewriter in Florida, where he was still working on the manuscript of *The Dharma Bums*, he longed to enter into a period of "mingling with human beings again."

It was rainy, gloomy, vibrationless, where he was. "I told my nephew not to bring friends around," Jack complained, "so now the house is full of his friends. It's a mockery of me in my own house. My mother probably whispers to them that I'm crazy, pay no attention. So I have to sit locked in my room."

"Buy yourself some Petri Port and sit on the rug and play Sid and light candles," he advised me wistfully. "Do you know New York is full of electrical vibrations? That black sweater of mine I sleep in always crackles and bristles in New York."

In the dullness of Florida, he expressed some doubts in one of his letters about *The Dharma Bums*. It seemed to have a flaw toward the end, it lacked a mad climactic moment like *On the Road*, but he thought Viking would like it anyway. Yes, he was sure the whole thing was enormously readable, which was after all what they wanted — and in some parts, "sublime."

"Any more yawks about my Vanguard reading, or anything, let me hear of it, Miss Grapevine."

He asked me to send him the real-estate section from the Sunday *Times*, which I did for several weeks. Remembering my description of Northport, he was looking for a house out there.

"Found a nice prospect," he announced in February. Soon he'd be back to speak to realtors in person. Once he settled in Long Island, though, he expected me to keep his address a secret from the general public, including "Edward R. Murrow." He had a fear of various mad types bursting in on him and disturbing his carefully planned solitude. Maybe he'd give his address to Lucien. "Lucien is mad but I wouldn't mind Lucien my best friend bursting in, but but . . . there are too many hipsters looking for me."

One day when I went into the bathroom of my apartment on East Thirteenth Street and locked the door, the doorknob — shaft and all — dropped off on the other side. I panicked, not knowing how I would ever get out. There was no window where I could yell for help. Perhaps after a few weeks people I knew at the Cedar would notice my absence. "Anyone seen Joyce around lately?... Oh yeah, she must have gone to California." Hettie would begin to worry, I could count on Hettie. And Jack would wonder why my letters had stopped coming. But by the time they broke in and found the body curled on the red bathmat, it would be too late.

With the aid of a toothbrush handle, I managed to escape this ignominious fate. Afterward I lay on my bed and wept, astonished that I felt such terror.

Life was becoming arduous. The super and his wife had their suspicions about me even before Jack's visit in December. Now they knew the worst. The crazy girl in Apartment 3 was one of those beatniks, she lived with men. They were authorities on beatniks, even if they didn't know a thing about Jack Kerouac or *On the Road.* Beatniks meant sex and filth and communism right in their neighborhood, and all respectability robbed from them forever, if they weren't careful. It became hazardous to put out the garbage or collect the mail. They'd appear on the landing to vent their passionate rage, their faces red and contorted, their voices hoarse as they screamed their hatred. "Filthy beatnik, you you you! You, Miss, sleeping with the bums, we know! Don't fool nobody! You hear?"

"Keep it up!" I'd shout back, trembling. "I'll tell the landlord!" But I knew I wouldn't and so did they. Sometimes coming home from work I'd see the super standing outside the building. I'd walk around the block a few times until he was gone, or give up altogether and head for Rappaport's or Hettie's house or any place I could think of, hating myself for being so scared. Whenever I went out and locked the door behind me, I'd think how wonderful it would be, how peaceful, never to come back.

One night my disembodied feet carried me through the snow to the Cedar, where I sat for hours at a table of people

I hardly knew, speechless and shaking. I was terribly cold, but couldn't tell whether the cold was inside me or coming in with the drafts from the street. It occurred to me that I might be officially sick. I walked back cross-town, crept up the stairs to my apartment, and took my temperature — as a matter of academic interest. It was 105. I lay down on my bed with the sense that I was finally rising very, very high above my general despair, floating in an atmosphere where nothing mattered.

It took me a day to call 116th Street. Like many prodigals, what I feared more than death was going home.

My father came to get me. In his overcoat and the large-brimmed hat he always wore in the winter over his carefully combed, thinning hair, he stood in the room with the air-shaft window, glancing around only when he had to at the place where his daughter lived.

I hadn't seen him for a couple of months. His face had always been as round as mine, but I thought I could almost see the bones of it underneath the skin, the teeth of an aging man.

He wrapped a blanket around me even though I was in my coat, and took me uptown in the cab that waited downstairs. My mother put me to bed in the room I'd left nearly three years ago, the pink container of my childhood. There was my abandoned globe of the world, all polished, the drawer of my musical compositions, dustless copies of *Ivanhoe*, *Black Beauty*, *The Last of the Mohicans*. Snow fell softly into the courtyard as I went to sleep. When I woke in the morning, I could hear my mother vacuuming the rug under my old enemy the piano.

I stayed there for three weeks. It was strange how well we all got along, how polite we were to each other — as in the old days before I began to grow away from them, when we'd never raised our voices. Ever since I'd left, I'd been afraid that if I ever weakened, my childhood world so fiercely preserved by my mother would recapture me. I'd dreaded the questions they might ask about my life.

Once during those weeks I alarmed them by telling them

I knew Jack Kerouac. But doesn't he take stimulants? my mother fearfully asked. No, I said, that was only fiction. They didn't ask about him again.

My real life was something they would never know, as I would never quite know theirs, yet they continued to love the child I'd been. For that child, they'd always be there. It seemed we were bound to each other for good — incompletely, imperfectly, our painful love as unspoken as all the other truths we'd never bring into the light.

One day I got well and it was time to go downtown. They didn't try to talk me into staying.

14

N JANUARY, Leo Skir had heard from Elise. She wrote him from the Cedars of Lebanon Hospital in San Francisco, where she had just had a psychiatric abortion. In March, she called him and asked for a loan. She wanted to come back. She turned up in New York in the middle of the month, just around the time Jack came back to find his house.

Elise was thinner than I'd ever seen her. Oh yes, she'd achieved her lifelong ambition to be slender. Didn't I notice, she hoped, a striking resemblance to Katharine Hepburn? Her hair had grown down below her shoulders — also an improvement, she admitted. She was altogether the new, improved Elise. She was going to get herself a job right away, find an apartment down near me, report to Washington Heights for Friday-night dinners. Maybe by fall she'd borrow money from her father to go to graduate school. Maybe. Meanwhile she moved in with Leo Skir, who had a big new apartment on the Upper West Side, in a brownstone that belonged to the sculptor Chaim Gross.

She said very little about what had happened in California — a quick account with few details. There'd been "this cat" she lived with for a while who was an Irish painter but mostly an alcoholic; he was the one who'd knocked her up. He remained "this cat" — she never spoke his name. Slowly, in little pieces, the story of the abortion came out. It was really very difficult to get a psychiatric abortion in California, but she'd had no choice, no money to do it any other way. She couldn't exactly have called her parents, could she? She'd done about enough to them. So she'd just kept going around. From doctor to doctor. Sat on benches in a lot of different waiting rooms. Finally she'd convinced the psychiatric staff of the Cedars of Lebanon Hospital that she was on the brink of suicide. "Maybe it wasn't such an act. Maybe I was over the edge by then."

All this had taken four months. And four months, of course, was much too long. Besides, it was Christmas and the doctors were all away on skiing trips. "So it had to be more than a simple D and C," she said quietly. "But it was cool. It just took longer to get well."

She didn't tell me the worst of it. To Elise, I was still the little sister who couldn't quite be given all the facts of life. She'd had a hysterotomy, she told Leo.

The books she carried on the subway when she came downtown to visit me were by Apollinaire and Ezra Pound. She'd stolen the New Directions edition of the *Cantos* from the Columbia University bookstore. In the mornings at Leo's she slept late and got up long after he'd gone to work. He'd often find her still in pajamas, reading, when he came home. She was embarrassed about this, but she couldn't quite rouse herself to do everything she'd planned. She'd read the want ads in the *Times*, circle a few of them, and throw the paper in the garbage. "Leo noodjes me like my mother," she'd say with a rueful laugh.

Once I asked her if she'd known the girl who'd been killed in North Beach. I'd been uncannily right. Elise and Connie had been neighbors in the same hotel. Connie had knocked on Elise's door to bum cigarettes the day of her death. "You know what she talked about? How much she wanted one of those new shift dresses. She'd just seen one in a window that she was going to get for eight dollars. That was all she wanted. It was her idea of beauty — I mean, it'd come down to just that. She had the eight dollars with her when she died."

*

237

Jack had reentered New York in March with a gleeful, insatiable energy. Now that he was back in the Nation of People, he couldn't seem to get enough of it. Not even his fights with Viking over revisions on *The Dharma Bums* pulled him down into gloom. Long nights at the Cedar made him heavy-headed and sweet as a little child as I, the sober one, led him home to bacon and eggs, shushing him as he sang on the landing outside the door, swaying against the bannisters. He seemed to have forgotten all about his intention to go out to Long Island to meet realtors. There were too many other things to do. He thought he was finally learning to be famous.

On the phone he made excuses to Memere in French. Steve Allen, the famous star Memere always watched on TV, who'd once sat in with the musicians when Jack was at the Vanguard, wanted him to do a record album. Offers from all the magazines were pouring in to Sterling Lord. He could whip off pieces on the Beat Generation for the rest of his life, making thousands of dollars on that alone. In the fall, he was definitely going to Hollywood to meet Marlon Brando, whom he thought would be the perfect Dean Moriarty in *On the Road*. Fame had become a ticket that could take him anywhere he wanted to go.

As Jack filled up my life again, I saw that before I hadn't been scared so much as lonely. Even Mike the super no longer seemed terrifying. "How you doing?" Jack would hail him as we ran up the stairs together linked in sin. I'd think about following this example of bold politeness, but a quick nod now and then was about all I could manage.

In someone's car one night, we sped out toward Brooklyn where Jack was to give a talk to a group of students at Brooklyn College. The car was absurdly packed with people. Even my ballet-dancer neighbor was in it with her husband, and a couple of poets and musicians we'd just met, and Elise, and two or three others I can't remember. I was sitting on Jack's knees up in front. We were passing around a joint of marijuana and laughing. Our grassy breath clouded the closed windows. On Second Avenue and Houston Street we stopped for a red light. A patrol car drew up beside us and a cop got

out and approached. Everyone froze. Was this the end? JACK
KEROUAC ARRESTED WITH BEATNIK PALS.

Jack had the presence of mind to stub out the joint and
swallow it. A window was opened cautiously, just a crack.
We were all afraid a burst of marijuana smoke would en-
velop the policeman. "You're driving without lights," he said
sternly. "Thank you, officer." We rolled up the window and
drove on. To recapture the composure necessary for his talk,
Jack dosed himself heavily with Thunderbird.

The "lecture" was sponsored by the English Department,
and a mob of English majors with notebooks turned out for
it, prepared — although they should have known better —
to hear a discussion of style, symbols, influences, delivered
of course in a relatively flamboyant manner. I'd been to such
things at Barnard, sedate occasions in a large parlor with tea
doled out at the end by a student stationed at a brass urn. An
author was a visiting dignitary from the Mount Olympus of
literature, not a disheveled Zen lunatic whose answers to
questions were so direct and uncomplicated they seemed
obliquely insulting. *Why do you write, Mr. Kerouac?* "Because I'm bored." This did not seem an adequate response
from a "real" writer, who also made the outrageous claim
that he was like Dostoevski. Had Dostoevski been bored?
How about Proust? Was this man conning them? *Why do
you publish what you write?* "For money," Jack answered
with some honesty.

Whispers ran through the room that Kerouac was making
a fortune. The audience split quickly into opposing camps —
those who decided their personal dignity was threatened by
the man on the platform and those who realized with excitement that Kerouac *was* his book, the living embodiment of
On the Road. David Amram, a young musician and composer
who had recently become Jack's friend, recalls one curly-
headed student asking whether Jack's mother ever worried
about him — what with his trips to the desert and Mexico
and all. From both camps — most of whom were after all
still living with their mothers — there was an explosion of
laughter.

A group of Kerouac enthusiasts kidnapped Jack and the rest of us and carried us off to a party deeper into Brooklyn. There a boy got up the courage to ask Jack what it was like to smoke marijuana. Jack found him a joint and took great pains in instructing him how to inhale it. Overwhelmed by this intensive lesson, the boy staggered into the bathroom and vomited.

Despite Jack's hopes that spring, I had the feeling he never would learn how to be a public figure. He was still an awful failure as an egomaniac — much too innocent and without the will to manipulate others. Those who loved Jack somehow instinctively knew this about him from the start.

David Amram understood Jack better than most of the other new people he'd met — the hundreds of admirers, supporters, and flatterers who scribbled their phone numbers on the scraps of paper that were always falling out of Jack's pockets. Everyone called Amram "Sunny Dave," because of his truly radiant disposition. He was a nervous, good-hearted Greenwich Village angel of the French horn and piano, with a mile-a-minute jazzman's way of talking that often left his listeners dizzy. Amram's rapid-fire delivery astounded Jack, and reminded him of Neal Cassady. How does he do it? he'd wonder, shaking his head in admiration under the shower of words. Whenever Jack decided he liked someone, that person instantly became "remarkable."

Sunny Dave talked Jack into doing two midnight poetry-and-jazz readings with Philip Lamantia, a San Francisco poet, and Howard Hart, a local one, at a small theater on Bleecker Street. They'd tried this once before in December, and Jack had felt so at ease with Amram's piano filling up the chinks of silence that he'd even spun off into a little scat-singing. Even so, he was nervous about these new appearances.

The first one went smoothly, but on March 22, the afternoon before the second one, he went for a long walk by himself in the Village. Every now and then he'd call me from a

240

phone booth to say he'd decided to back out. Or that he'd do it — but only if all his friends could get in free. He'd ask to speak to Peter Orlovsky, who was just back from Paris and was visiting me that day. What if he just read Peter's poems?

Peter was using my Royal portable to type Allen a long tender chronicle of everything that was happening in downtown New York. He'd been working with one finger for hours. Elise had dropped over, too. She'd made the three of us onion sandwiches for lunch. She shook her head when Peter asked her if she had a message for Allen. "Just hello." But I'd typed in: "Allen — New York is full of snow and poets, dancing girls, Elise, etc. Come back to New York soon. Everybody misses you."

By the time Jack returned from his walk with a gallon of wine, he'd made up his mind that whatever happened, he couldn't disappoint Dave Amram. For a while he took over the typing of the letter to Allen, as Peter dictated enthusiastically: "Jack is gonna read tonight with Lamantia & Hart with good spirits giving pigeons off his breast & hes gonna tell every body to hold hands instead of clap . . ."

I liked Sunny Dave so much myself that I was delighted to observe Elise slipping away with him after that reading. If only they would fall in love. She went home with him several nights in a row, but within a week or so it was over — with no hard feelings on either side.

Another person Jack found remarkable that spring was a Swiss photographer named Robert Frank. I'd met Robert one day when I'd accompanied Jack to Viking Press. As I sat in the waiting room while Jack was inside talking to Keith Jennison and Malcolm Cowley, Robert Frank walked in with a couple of boxes of his work. For several years he'd been going around the country taking photos for a book he planned to call *The Americans*. He was hoping to convince Jack to write an introduction. He asked me if I'd like to look at the pictures. The first one I saw was of a road somewhere out west

—blacktop gleaming under headlights with a white stripe down the middle that went on and on toward an outlying darkness. Jack's road! I thought immediately.

Frank had a European dourness and pessimistic wit that delighted Jack. He asked him many questions about how he worked, and wondered at his ability to merge with his surroundings, becoming almost invisible as he awaited the image he would capture with his Leica. Robert was a great photographer because he knew how to become a shadow, Jack told me.

We became frequent visitors at the loft on Ninth Street and the Bowery where Robert lived with his wife Mary and their small son and daughter. Mary was only a little older than I was. She'd married Robert shortly after she'd graduated from the High School of Music and Art. She was a sculptor, working on an enormous piece of wood in a little corner of the studio. There was something heroic about Mary, I thought. She reminded me of one of the Greek women of Picasso's white period. Sometimes when Robert invited us over for dinner, she seemed distracted, almost sullen. She'd been working on the piece, but then the children had gotten mischievous and impossible, and then it had been time to slice the vegetables. Oh how she despaired of producing anything under these conditions! A place of her own was what she needed. She wound her long brown hair up into a knot and carried huge platters of delicious food to the round oak table where Jack and Robert sat talking about future collaborations. Perhaps when Allen came back from Europe, Robert would do a movie with Jack, Peter, Gregory Corso, and Allen. "What do you think, Mary?" Jack would ask. "Sure. Do it." She'd march back to the stove, looking flushed and stormy, casting a glance at the half-chiseled block of oak in the corner by the window.

More people would show up and sit at the round table, some previously invited, some not. One or two of the Franks' friends seemed to come over every night. Wine would flow, records would be put on the phonograph, and the evening

242

would blossom into an impromptu party. To inspire everyone to dance, Mary would disappear into her bedroom and return in one of the extraordinary twenties gowns she collected, transformed from sculptor, mother, and housewife into a sequined night creature. Her anger forgotten, she'd be the liveliest one of all, luring Jack into a tango, which he'd dance as if he were carrying a football, while her two children raced around them madly, eyes gleaming with exhaustion, enchanting little gypsies up hours after their bedtime. If I ever had kids, I'd think, I'd want them to be wild just like that. And I'd sometimes wish I could be a little more flamboyant myself. But the most unusual thing about Mary Frank, I decided, was that she was as fierce about her work as a man. In her mind, at least, it somehow always came first—even though all the other parts of her life were always pulling her away from it.

I remember having the feeling that spring that I've always had in periods when I've been happiest — a sense of being part of an endless family whose individual members only needed to be discovered one by one. For a while Jack seemed to have that feeling too about people — very strongly. He was no longer hiding out the way he had in January. I allowed myself to hope that even if he found his house and moved into it with Memere, he really wouldn't be staying there very much. When he was absent, I'd use the time to work hard on my novel. Somehow I could never manage to write anything when Jack was with me. I always wanted to be with him more than I wanted to be at the typewriter. I wondered if this would change if we spent more time living together. Was Jack someone you could ever get used to?

Recently, in a copy of *Zen Flesh, Zen Bones* that hadn't been opened in years, my son found a scrap of green paper. It had been part of a wrapper for Eagle-A Onionskin. On the blank side Jack had jotted part of a conversation we must have had one of those early spring days of 1958.

*

Somebody told me that W. C. Handy had just died
— I said "He was never even born" — "Oh you,"
she said.

"Essence went thru as something called W. C.
Handy," I thought, "but since essence is never
coming or going, W. C. Handy must have been
there already." This is a pretty heavy stone to have
in my mind.

"I dont believe it. I dont see no Dharma," she said.

"Who wrote that?" my son asked.
"Jack Kerouac," I said.
"It must be very valuable, Mom."
"Probably," I said, staring at this scrap of the past that had
been retrieved so unexpectedly. I had the feeling that the
conversation had just taken place. There it was, that old
fundamental tug of war between me and Jack — but written
down with such affectionate humor, like a chord that re-
solves all dissonances by gathering them in together. I felt
again that odd peacefulness that I've always called "family."

*O*NE NIGHT THAT April, Jack went out drinking with Gregory Corso. The two former subterraneans made a circuit of the Village, visiting the drinking places of their more anonymous years. Everyone seemed to know Jack Kerouac — from high-school kids to sunken-cheeked hipsters, strung out since the old days, who'd materialize out of doorways in shabby coats to ask for loans. Around 1 A.M. they ended up across the street from the San Remo in the Kettle of Fish, popular at the time with a crowd of hard, belligerent drinkers who made their living moving furniture. At the bar a quarrel started. A stranger claimed Jack Kerouac had insulted him. Neither Jack nor Gregory could remember afterward what it was all about.

When they left the place, they found themselves surrounded outside by the stranger and his friends. The man threw Jack to the sidewalk and began pounding his head against the curb, while Gregory looked on befuddled and appalled, yelling "Stop! Stop!"

My doorbell rang and woke me. When I opened the door, I found Jack clutching Gregory's shoulder, hardly able to stand. Blood was running down his face.

Gregory was ranting on about whatever had just happened being the worst thing he'd ever seen. Jack seemed so

245

stunned I was afraid he'd had a concussion. "We have to take him to a hospital," I told Gregory, running to get my coat. Jack kept protesting he didn't want to go. "Leave me alone," he moaned. He wasn't giving anyone in any hospital his name. No one was to know who he was, he kept insisting. I wet a towel and tried to wash the blood off his face.

"No hospital!"

"You *have* to!" I pleaded, pulling at his arms, nearly weeping myself. I made Gregory help me, and we got him down to the street and walked him the four blocks to Beth Israel Hospital.

"Cauterize my wounds!" he cried out wildly in the empty marble lobby. "Cauterize my wounds!"

At the emergency ward I signed Jack in as Jack Glassman. According to the doctors there, Jack had no concussion — only cuts and bruises. No permanent damage. Hours later, with white gauze taped to his forehead, he walked out unsteadily into the cold dawn light.

The next day he told me he had to get out of New York as soon as possible. He'd never meant to stay so long.

He remembered even less about what had actually happened than Gregory did. Even going to the hospital seemed a dream. Had he really asked to be cauterized? Where would that idea have come from? With horror he looked at his bruised, swollen face in the mirror. Perhaps he was thinking of the nightmare he'd had before *On the Road* was published, when bandaged he'd run from the dark forces that were trying to capture him inside the Victory Theatre. They seemed to have caught up with him at last.

For days he spoke of a wound inside his head that the doctors had carelessly failed to detect, and a pain in his right wrist that made it difficult for him to use his hand. And somehow I too had failed him. As Memere had predicted, he'd come to harm.

Just before Jack went back to Florida, he asked Robert Frank to drive him out to Northport. He'd made up his mind to buy a house in one day. This was a rash plan, Robert thought. He looked at me skeptically. But neither of us could have talked Jack out of it. He could only feel safe again in a house ruled by his mother. Every mile that slipped away under the wheels of Robert's car told me Jack would be farther away from me in Northport than I'd ever imagined.

I sat alone in the back seat. Up front Jack and Robert were talking about the movie they were going to make together that fall — at least Jack would have to be coming into the city for that. Robert was also going to take him to a place on Delancey Street where Jack could buy a huge roll-top desk like the one Robert had. His house was going to be filled with everything he'd always wanted — massive old easy chairs and oak furniture, maybe even an upright piano on which he'd teach himself to play jazz. It would be so comfortable out there with Memere in the kitchen making roast-beef dinners, there'd be little reason to ever go anywhere else.

It was a blindingly bright spring day. Trees seemed to have budded overnight. Northport lay in a haze of green. Out in the bay clammers were at work, standing up in their flat-bottomed boats in the blue rippling water. Robert drove slowly down Main Street until we spotted a real-estate office. Before we went in, Jack put on a baseball cap he'd bought that morning and pulled the brim down over his forehead.

There was a woman behind a desk with strawberry-blonde-tinted hair and a lot of costume jewelry. She stared at Jack's cap, my black stockings, Robert's sandals and unruly halo of wiry brown hair, then introduced herself to us as Mona. Her eyebrows rose to her scalp when Jack told her his name, and she became extremely animated. She'd heard so much about him, of course. She hadn't read his books, but now she'd certainly make it her business to get them from the library. Soon she was calling him Jack and describing Northport as if it were the Paris of the North Shore. Why, a famous retired actor lived there, and someone who wrote for the *Reader's Digest*. There was even a sculptor— a very *unusual* man who worked in welded metal. She'd love to introduce them.

Jack said he intended to live very quietly.

This disappointed Mona, but in the next breath Northport had become the quietest place in the world, a crypt where a writer seeking solitude could bury himself. Wait! Now that she knew his needs, she even had the perfect house for him, an "older" house with an attic that would make a delightful study. Triumphantly she held up a photo of a shingled house with a small porch and a steep roof.

Jack became excited and called out to Robert. It looked like the houses he'd known in Lowell. Mona locked up the office and drove us over there right away.

Northport High School was just around the corner from this house, and its playing fields extended right up to what would be Jack's back yard. By September he could sit up in his attic study and watch the Northport football team working out.

With a sinking of the heart, I knew that it was, as Mona said, perfect.

The house was still occupied by the family that was moving out of it — some corporate transfer to the Midwest. Already deep in his fantasy of how it was going to be to live there, Jack hardly seemed interested in looking around as Mona led us up and down stairs, chattered about how the kitchen could be modernized, and tried to determine whether or not I was Jack's fiancée. "And it's ideal for children," she finally added, turning her sharp, mistaken smile on me.

"I'll take it," Jack told her in the car. He refused to look at anything else.

She said it was the fastest sale she'd ever made.

Jack took a plane back to Memere the next morning so they could immediately start packing. Trains, he'd decided, were much too slow — and too many people talked to you. From now on when he went anywhere he would fly.

ELISE BROUGHT HER two suitcases down from Leo Skir's that summer and moved in with me. At last we were roommates. And weren't we like *New Yorker* girls now that we'd achieved such propriety, scrubbing our worn-out underwear in the kitchen sink while Lady Day sang "I Cover the Waterfront" to us from the phonograph.

My roommate did life modeling at the Art Students League; strangers with charcoal pencils regarded her round breasts, the scar on her belly. I was typing letters for a boss with a married, desperate mistress who called him up using different names, Mrs. Brown or Mrs. Green; he sent monthly payments to an underground colony in Bolivia to which he planned to retire in the event of an atomic holocaust. My roommate and I fantasized him and Mrs. Brown finally united there in a novel by William Burroughs.

By night we bloomed and ran around. Or entertained Leo Skir, Howard Shulman the Mad, Peter Orlovsky, and assorted Cedarites who walked us home. I discovered 2 A.M. was the finest time to write my novel, if I took one of Elise's dexamils. Everyone on the East Side was taking dexies. One prescription serviced half a dozen people.

We gave some to Jack when he came into the city from his new house, but nothing seemed to speed the flow of *Memory Babe*. He said that now he had the form, he felt

249

uninterested. Christmas in Lowell, 1933. The events were too
far back, he couldn't remember the details of Ti-Jean's
Golden Vision of the Manger.

But there'd never been anything Jack couldn't remember.

I went out to Northport once to see him, but took the
wrong bus at the station and ended up on the grounds of a
mental institution, where limp men in shoes without laces
shuffled aimlessly on a lawn. I was shaken by the time I got
to Jack's house and was met at the door by Memere in her
flowered apron, who asked me what time I was going back
on the train. I couldn't sleep over, Jack had again explained,
because only married people could sleep together under his
mother's roof, and we weren't married. I saw his writing
room, his old office desk, the notebooks of all his dreams,
the scroll of *Memory Babe*, which I'd interrupted by my
visit, in his typewriter. A gang of teen-agers showed up and
took us off in their convertible to someone's beach house,
where Jack got very drunk while a seventeen-year-old girl
who was in love with him told me he was the saddest person
she'd ever met in her life. By the time we were delivered
back to Memere, it was all over for Jack, who fell asleep at
the table, his head beside his plate of roast beef, mashed potatoes, creamed onions, and biscuits. "Too much drinking,
too much drinking. I keep telling him all the time. I don't
know what I'm gonna do," Memere lamented angrily. She
surprised me by giving me a sort of compliment. "Jackie
says you took pretty good care of him."

"Joyce, please don't come out here anymore," Jack had
written a few days later. He didn't want to disturb the "tender routines" of an old lady. What Memere had really
thought of me I never found out — except that I'd used far
too much hot water when I'd helped her do the dishes. Such
prodigality had scandalized her — that and my being Jewish.

Elise said I might have to touch bottom before I could let
go, but that even if I didn't get back together with Jack, years
later I'd look back and be very glad I'd known him, and anyway I'd always make something else happen — "So try not
to be too sad, Glassmangirl." Sometimes, regretfully, she'd

speak of herself as "cured," not of love for Allen but of all desire for him. Staring at herself in the mirror on her twenty-fifth birthday, she said, "I wonder how I'll wear my hair when I'm thirty."

Around Columbia, Howard Shulman met a student of Lionel Trilling's whom he insisted we had to dig, and showed up one night with a blond, thin, eager kid with the wisp of a little mustache. Keith Gibbs was from Berkeley, California; that lovely mellow sound of the West was in his voice. He was struggling with poetry, intent on unlearning Columbia the way Jack and Allen had had to. At the end of the summer he and Howard Shulman would be driving to California in Howard's wreck of a car. He'd heard a lot about Elise and seemed awed by her, laughed at himself for being tongue-tied when she spoke to him. He wanted so much to win her with all the stories of his hitchhiking adventures and such, which were only the stories of a boy.

The four of us wandered all over the Lower East Side, showing Keith parts of the city he'd never seen. Coming down East Thirteenth Street toward dawn, we heard singing from a Puerto Rican Pentecostal church that had moved into an abandoned synagogue. Keith said we had to go in. Three women in black and an old man were singing, weeping, exhorting God in Spanish, to the rattle of a tambourine. Sadness overwhelmed us as we sat listening on broken chairs, embarrassed unbelievers every one of us. Keith held on to Elise's hand. When we came out, the sky had turned a mottled grey and silver. "It's a mackerel sky," he said. I loved the name he'd given it. I drew Elise aside and whispered, "Make something happen." It was time for one of us to be happy.

He came upstairs with her that night. He hitchhiked to North Carolina and wrote her four long letters, but sent only one. "How to open, open" — the trouble with words came over him again — "I wonder what my love means to you — not CAN mean to you . . ." When he returned, he moved in with us for a while. At the end of August he and Howard left for California. Overnight Elise decided to go with them. A week later, Allen Ginsberg came back from Paris.

Picture post cards kept coming to me from the road. In Rutherford, Pennsylvania, there were "pastel oil trucks, green sunsets," and a "Pennsylvania Dutch pay toilet." They reached Sandusky, Ohio, having passed over the Allegheny Mountains, where someone had said, "They were made over a million years ago but I can feel them pushing up," and in Cleveland found a "great Negro bar where Howard danced with balling cat who held crotch" and where they drank wine that tasted "like Yiddish Thunderbird . . . Feel so fine & like yes! yes! yes! The houses of Cleveland are youth traps and fattening pens. Full moon turned my tide. Almost sorry."

"Barreling thru Colorado," said the last one, a picture of Rabbit Ears Pass, U.S. 40, altitude 9680 feet.

*J*ACK AND I never got back together. We split up on a street corner that fall.

There had been too many separations, too many drunken, chaotic nights, and always that confusing distance in him that was both paternal and rejecting — "You do what you wanna do." I needed someone who had desires of his own.

There'd been another woman in the restaurant where we'd sat at a table full of artists — another of Jack's dark women, older than I was — and after much wine, when she and Jack were publicly discovering they were soul mates, I reached that point of "it's never going to change," when what you've been bearing all along suddenly becomes unbearable.

I made Jack come out to the sidewalk. Choked with pain, I searched for the worst words I could think of.

"You're nothing but a big bag of wind!"

"Unrequited love's a bore!" he shouted back.

Enraged, we stared at each other, half weeping, half laughing. I rushed away, hoping he'd follow. But he didn't.

I saw him again one night a few months later when I was on my way home with another man. I looked across Second Avenue and there he was with Allen and Peter and the woman he'd met in the restaurant. It was snowing hard and they'd all joined hands and were weaving and staggering

253

against the wind like a frieze of shamanistic dancers. And I glimpsed his face in the red neon from Rappaport's window — so far away forever now with the snow falling between us and the traffic grinding its way downtown.

The old year had just ended. It was New Year's of 1959.

15

April 10, 1959

Dear Joyce,

First days of Berkeley spring and we are going subtly mad with it. Early fogs thicker than smoke and then blue green and petal colors all day. There's a park near where I work and I spend lunch hours goofing with the ants, flat on my back.

Howard is staying with us. The day he wrote a long poem on civilizations falling apart there were two earthquakes. Keith has become a Webster-wolf staying up for days on end and attacking everyone with theories, phrases, finally subsiding into sleep with a sly smile. Sam space cat has been laid, we think, for the first time. Who says the Mediterranean climate and colors weren't responsible for their civilization?

What are you doing around now?

Keith has come into part of his inheritance, so as soon as his paper is finished a hunt for a pickup truck begins. Keith gets a job and come mid-July probably we split for Mexico. Can't wait for Summer — Mexicali Rose I Love You, If the Weather Be Fair I'll Comb My Hair and Walk the Road

Again — or Little Girl, Little Girl, Tell Me Where'd You Sleep Last Night. God, I can't wait to be moving again.

Any special summer plans? Want to go to Mexico on a pickup truck? The boss is coming up the steps so will filch a stamp and close.

> Love to you and all N.Y.
> Elise

* * *

ONE FEBRUARY NIGHT in 1962, my mother called. "Your friend killed herself," she said. "It's in the paper."

I ran out and got the *New York World-Telegram*. It was a very small item — WOMAN 28 FOUND DEAD.

Elise had jumped from the window of her parents' living room in Washington Heights. She'd just been released from Hillside Mental Hospital in the Cowens' care, and they'd planned to take her with them to Miami.

For a long time I sat staring at the word WOMAN. Had we both grown up, then, become women?

She'd never made that journey to Mexico with Keith three years earlier. Allen had passed through Berkeley in the spring and had visited her. Soon after, she'd returned to New York. Allen was living with Peter Orlovsky in an apartment on East Second Street, many tiny rooms where there were always different strangers sleeping and the phone rang all the time. He got Elise a place in the same building.

When Allen finished *Kaddish*, his long poem about his mother Naomi, Elise typed the manuscript. "You haven't done with her, yet?" she asked. A question Allen recorded in his journal.

In another entry (Dec. 6, 1960) he wrote:

> Woke up this moment and more
> beautiful than poem is Elise standing
> in dawn in middle of room in
> black high on Mescaline —

256

Three and a half months later (March 23, 1961), he and
Peter embarked for Europe on the S.S. *America*:

> At the dock, Elise peering over her eyeglasses,
> Janine whitefaced blond in black jacket waving
> scarf, & Lafcadio with half smile, fluttering
> a straw hat ambiguously — Peter above deck cupping
> his hand to heart in a Russian cap — and when I
> called their names I saw them, drifting away
> with their skulls.

"Me? Reproduce myself? Never," Allen wrote in his hotel
room in Paris. "The trial of existence is a complete failure."

I began to lose track of Elise after Allen left. She was spinning downward very fast, caught up in the dark whirling
currents of the East Village, experiments with drugs that
stretched the mind until it came apart. Disappearing from
170 East Second Street, she drifted from one sunless pad to
another, her possessions in shopping bags.

Methedrine withered her. One midnight she came to my
door to borrow a typewriter; there were three long death
hairs growing out of her chin. A few weeks later she was
taken to Bellevue from a tenement on Avenue D.

On the floor of a closet there, notebooks were found. Leo
Skir rescued them. They contained the poems Elise had never
shown to anyone.

> Alone
> Weeping
> I woke weeping
> Alone
> In black park of bed.

There was one that may have been her last, that had messages to me and all the rest of us confused bystanders who
only thought we knew her.

> No love
> No compassion
> No intelligence

No beauty
No humility
Twenty-seven years is enough

Mother — too late — years of meanness — I'm sorry
Daddy — what happened?
Allen — I'm sorry
Peter — Holy rose youth
Betty — such womanly bravery
Keith — Thank you
Joyce — so girl beautiful
Howard — Baby take care
Leo — Open the windows and shalom
Carol — let it happen

Let me out now please —
— Please let me in

People passed her poems around for a while. Suicide made
Elise mythic briefly. Traveling with Peter in Nairobi, Allen
added her to the list of his dead:

Bounced out of Mboyas Wedding feast for not wearing ties
& Jackets
in the marvelous Nairobi heat — cool nights near the movies
turning a corner from the Indian restaurant —
a big square we walked, saw doctor for germs —
or the study of logistics, or Cosmic Paranoia
the inhumans talking over Microphone Consciousness —
They got Elise? — She's where the dead are that went to the
burning ghats
or suffered "Chinese brutality" in the Himalayas

Two years later Allen used his influence to get a few of
the poems published in *City Lights Journal*. The small photo
that accompanied them was from the passport Elise had never
used. He wrote a note about her, too, in collaboration with
Lucien Carr. Their voices alternate — unidentified — from
line to line:

258

How old was dear old Elipse when she went her merry way? I wish people I didn't like did that instead of her. I feel more loyalty than love for Elipse.

The poems, they're awkward. But it's a special kind of awkward that comes when someone is direct and (if there is an honest) honest. And the beauty of the written lines that she could see and I could see but neither of us could see in her ...

Either Lucien or Allen said, "She has that quality of alert solitude." I want to think it was Allen Ginsberg.

* * *

Some of us defied death and reproduced. Never mind the mushroom clouds of doom! Rashly, perhaps, we peopled the uncertain future with our babies.

Kellie Elizabeth Jones was born one May morning in 1959. When Hettie went into labor, LeRoi was out of town doing a poetry reading, and no one knew whether he'd get back in time. A bunch of Black Mountain poets and I took Hettie to the hospital. Orderlies put her on a metal cart and wheeled her away as we all stood anxiously chain-smoking in the green linoleum corridor.

"Good-by!" she waved to us, smiling with amazing serenity. "See you later ..." She blew us a kiss as she went off alone to have Roi's child.

* * *

My father died when I was twenty-four — of complications following an operation for ulcers — before he could take the grand vacation he and my mother had been talking about for several years.

As I sat by his bed stroking his hand, he told me I was beautiful. He whispered something else, and I had to bend down to hear him —

"We should have gone to Europe."

* * *

My novel was published when I was twenty-six.

I saw Paris when I was twenty-eight — after the death of

James Johnson, my first husband, in a motorcycle accident on Grand Street.

He'd always had wheels. Together we'd ridden that second-hand red Harley all the way up to Cape Cod, and along the highways out to Montauk. My arms were around his waist and my knees dug into his hips and he taught me to lean in and out with him, swerving as the roads curved, and not to be afraid going down "death alley" between cars that moved slower than we did, watching out for patches of sand or slick that could kill you if you came up on them too fast. Riding with each other we had the illusion we were safe. It was the happiest summer of my life.

Sometimes the Harley would take us out to Northport. Jack and Memere had moved away by then to a house in Hyannisport, but there were people around who remembered them. My new husband wanted to know everything that had happened to me, even the most painful things I had to tell him. He seemed to understand, better than I did, why I'd loved Jack, what I'd been looking for — which I had now, didn't I? And I'd say yes, I had it now, finally.

My husband had been on a mine sweeper at Anzio that had been shelled continuously for two and a half months. Between life and death, he said, there was a hair of difference. I hated to hear him talk about such things.

After his death, I believed him.

* * *

A museum of the cinema revives *Pull My Daisy*, the film Jack made with Robert Frank. With trepidation, I go to see it for the first time in twenty years. Its images are like solidified memory. There are Allen, Peter, and Gregory, benign pranksters — all beautiful young men. A familiar sooty light comes in through the loft windows. Dave Amram plays his horn. And Jack, the unseen narrator, is everybody all at once, making perfect, tender, absurd sense. But it's too bad the women are all portrayed as spoilsports.

Could I have remembered Jack's voice? I keep trying to match it to the one I last heard on the phone in 1964, when he called me up out of the blue in terrible drunken loneliness somewhere out there in America — "You never wanted anything but a little ol' pea soup." Which wasn't really true, of course, but I cried after he hung up.

"So what was it all about?" my companion asks as the final credits flash on the screen.

"I think it was about the right to remain children."

* * *

The sixties were never quite my time. They seemed anticlimactic, for all their fireworks. Some culmination had been short-circuited. I saw hippies replace beatniks, sociologists replace poets, the empty canvas replace the Kline. Unenthusiastically, I observed the emergence of "lifestyle." The old intensities were blanding out into "Do your own thing" — the commandment of a freedom excised of struggle. Ecstasy had become chemical, forgetfulness could be had by prescription. Revolution was in the wind, but it never came — and if it had, there would have been no room in its orthodoxies for a Kerouac —

Who retreated farther and farther from the center of the stage into the dusty wings, out to the back alley, tunneling backward through decades toward the Lowell of his earliest vision, and — finding it a narrow place, the wonder gone from it — making the desolate effort to assume its prejudices, its bitter suspicions. "The pure products of America go crazy," Dr. William Carlos Williams had written.

But has it become my own madness not to have outgrown those years when the door first swung open on a world I never managed to explore as completely as I longed to?

I see the girl Joyce Glassman, twenty-two, with her hair hanging down below her shoulders, all in black like Masha in *The Seagull* — black stockings, black skirt, black sweater — but, unlike Masha, she's not in mourning for her life. How could she have been, with her seat at the table in the exact center of the universe, that midnight place where so much is converging, the only place in America that's alive? As a female, she's not quite part of this convergence. A fact she

261

ignores, sitting by in her excitement as the voices of the men, always the men, passionately rise and fall and their beer glasses collect and the smoke of their cigarettes rises toward the ceiling and the dead culture is surely being wakened. Merely being here, she tells herself, is enough.

What I refuse to relinquish is her expectancy.

It's only her silence that I wish finally to give up — and Elise's silence

> Under the dismal onion
> Blind dreams in a green room

posthumously attesting to the lessons of Pound in stolen books, and the poems Hettie kept mute in boxes for too many years . . .

* * *

I'm a forty-seven-year-old woman with a permanent sense of impermanence. If time were like a passage of music, you could keep going back to it till you got it right.

About the Author

JOYCE JOHNSON is the author of two novels, *Come and Join the Dance* and *Bad Connections*. The latter was hailed by E. L. Doctorow as a "sad, beautiful casebook of unrequited love, unrequited humanity." She lives in New York City with her son and works as an editor at The Dial Press.